SILENCING THE DRUM

SILENCING THE *DRUM*

RELIGIOUS RACISM AND AFRO-BRAZILIAN SACRED MUSIC

DANIELLE N. BOAZ & UMI VAUGHAN

Amherst College Press

The complete manuscript of this work was subjected to a partly closed ("single-anonymous") review process. For more information, visit https://acpress.amherst.edu/peerreview/.

Published in the United States of America by
Amherst College Press
Manufactured in the United States of America

Library of Congress Control Number: 2023951772

DOI: https://doi.org/10.3998/mpub.14419786

ISBN 978-1-943208-75-3 (paper)
ISBN 978-1-943208-76-0 (OA)
ISBN 978-1-943208-90-6 (hardcover)

For Luca. You are my favorite research assistant.

For all the devotees, activists, and scholars who are fighting religious racism in Brazil and other parts of the world.

D.N.B.

For my son Rumi and my daughter Luanda.

Your laughter is music to my soul.

For all the sacred drummers, singers, and dancers of Brazil.

Defend your magic, keep the fire blazing…

Nguzu/Axé!!!

U.V.

Contents

Tracklist

To access all audio examples referenced in this book, please visit the open access version on Fulcrum at https://doi.org/10.3998/mpub.14419786.

Sacred Rhythms

Sambas da Bahia

Glossary

Atabaque	general name for the sacred drums used in most Afro-Brazilian religions
Babalorixá	head priest, leader of a terreiro
Batuque	an Afro-Brazilian religion; also a broad term that was used to refer to African drumming and dancing in the nineteenth century and earlier
Ekedi	special role for female initiates of the terreiro. They do not become possessed by orixá
Favela	informal settlements, usually located on the outskirts of a city
Filha/o de Santo	protege, initiate, mentee within Candomblé
Ilekes (also Elekes)	sacred beaded necklaces
Iyalorixá	head priestess, leader of a terreiro
Macumba	similar to the English term "voodoo." Often used by outsiders as a derogatory term for Afro-Brazilian religions and implies "black magic" or "sorcery." Originally macumba referred to a percussion instrument made of a serrated gourd, scraped or tapped with a stick
Macumbeira/o	a person who practices *macumba*
Ogan	special role for male initiates of the terreiro; they do not become possessed by orixá

Quilombos	independent communities built by enslaved people who ran away/escaped
Terreiro	the physical temple and grounds of a Candomblé community. There are shrines to various spirits and divinities. Many kinds of ceremonies take place at the terreiro. In some cases, food is grown and animals are raised at the terreiro, and some members, including the head priest or priestess, might reside there

List of Figures

Chapter 3

Chapter 4

Percussion, the Ancestral Mother Tongue

By Carlinhos Brown

In the vibrant heart of Brazil and its diasporas, percussion echoes like an ancestral call, a universal language that transcends borders and generations. It is in this same vibrant, universal spirit and with the deepest pride and admiration that I welcome the masterful work *Silencing the Drum: Religious Racism and Afro-Brazilian Sacred Music*, a landmark creation forged by the brilliant minds of Danielle Boaz and Umi Vaughan. This book, unparalleled in English or Portuguese, illuminates the shadows of religious racism and celebrates the sacredness of Afro-Brazilian music with a depth and precision rarely seen.

Danielle, a renowned historian and lawyer, and Umi, an anthropologist and musician with a heart that beats to the rhythm of the sacred, join me and so many others in the ancestral battle against intolerance and religious racism. Our weapons are words, music and, above all, the love and axé that we share in this fight.

This work is not just a book; it is an act of resistance and a celebration. The inclusion of an exceptional recording of sacred rhythms, made with master drummer Totô Cruz, under the musical direction of Mario Pam (from Ilê Aiyê), harmonizes the voice of the drum with the voices of the people within Afro-Brazilian religiosity. By doing so, *Silencing the Drum* transcends "reading material" or "research" and becomes a sonic manifesto that breathes, vibrates and pulsates with the life of our communities.

The art that adorns the cover, courtesy of the talented artist and activist Junior Pakapym, encapsulates the essence of this project: a testament to our collective resilience and resistance and a community creation imbued with abundant love and axé. This book not only illuminates the nuances of our cultural heritage, but also serves as a beacon of hope, guiding us towards a future where music and faith are celebrated in all their forms, free from prejudice and intolerance. Long live Afro-Brazilian sacred music, long live our incessant fight for justice and equality. Axé.

Preface

On August 17, 2023, as we were completing this manuscript, Maria Bernadete Pacífico, better known as Mãe Bernadete, was assassinated. In addition to being an iyalorixá (Afro-Brazilian religious leader), Mãe Bernadete was the leader of the Pitanga dos Palmares quilombo (a community founded by runaway slaves) and the former Secretary for Racial Equality in Simões Filho, in Bahia state. The assassins reportedly invaded the quilombo and shot Mãe Bernadete more than ten times. Her grandchildren and community members were present at the quilombo during the attack.[1]

As if this crime were not terrible enough, Mãe Bernadete is the mother of Flávio Gabriel Pacífico dos Santos, better known as Binho do Quilombo, who was murdered almost six years prior in a similar act of violence. Shortly after the assassination of Mãe Bernadete, Denildo Rodrigues, from the National Coordination of Articulation of Black Rural Quilombola Communities (CONAC), opined that she was killed by the same group responsible for Binho's execution. Rodrigues stated that quilombo and Afro-Brazilian community leaders in Simões Filho are constantly threatened by groups linked to real estate speculation who seek ways to occupy these territories.[2]

Members of Candomblé communities reacted immediately to express their indignation over the murder of Mãe Bernadete and demand redress. Among them, a few of our interlocutors made their voices heard. Sandro Teles, a leader and musician for afro bloco Ilê Aiyê wrote: "We are living in a moment of extreme terror[ism] against the Black community [in Brazil]. This crime cannot go unpunished.

We demand that the Secretary of Public Safety respond and address this hate crime."[3] Reflecting on the effect of this crime in the context of the new, liberal Lula government, which inspired hope of a decrease in violence against Black people, artist, activist, and Candomblé Angola priest Junior Pakapym wrote: "What pain. The dog [Bolsonaro] left the presidency but Bahia never escaped chaos. The political right on one side, the political left on the other, and the Black community continues to die. How sad!"[4]

The brazen nature of the murder of Mãe Bernadete demonstrates the flagrant and cruel acts of violence that disproportionately target "traditional" communities in Brazil, including quilombos and terreiro communities. Like the murder of Binho do Quilombo, this violence often goes unpunished, with the state assigning insufficient resources to the investigation. In other cases, like that of Mãe Bernadete, authorities dismiss the motives of the perpetrators as robbery or drug-related disputes, ignoring significant evidence of religious racism, land grabbing, and other discriminatory purposes. Although our book is not directly about the assassination of Mãe Bernadete or other recent murders of Afro-Brazilian religious leaders, one can understand this heinous act as the most severe end of the spectrum of discrimination and violence that Afro-Brazilian religious and traditional communities experience every day.

Acknowledgments

We owe a debt of gratitude to numerous individuals without whom this book would not be possible. First and foremost, we would like to thank all of the devotees, religious leaders, activists, scholars, and government officials who shared their stories and perspectives on religious racism. Those who are directly referenced in the book include: Ana Paula Mendes de Miranda, Baba Alan Crave, Baba Alexandre Savi, Baba Pecê, Babazinho de Oxalá, Desirée Tozi, Doté Amilton, Ilzver Matos, Iyá Rosiane Rodrigues de Almeida, Jandira Mawusi, Maria Alice Pereira da Silva, Mãe Baiana, Mãe Dora, Mãe Jaciara de Oxum (Jaciara Ribeiro), Mãe Pauli de Oxumarê, Neto Azile, Pai Anderson de Oxalá, Pai Carlos Brottas, Pai Diego, Pai Duda, Pai Gilmar de Yansan (Gilmar Hughes), Pai Eusébio, Pai Joselino, Pai Rychelmy, Patricia Zappone, Ricardo Costa, Rose Mary Jesus (Ekedi Rose de Ogum), Túlio Aguiar, and Pai Vilson Caetano de Sousa Jr. However, there are also countless others with whom we had formal and informal conversations that helped shape our understanding of the situation in Brazil, including but not limited to: Igbonan Rocha, Wagner Lima, Berg Silva, Sonia Souza, Conceição Carlos, Bira Santos, Edson Bezerra, Pai Aurelio, Ana Flávia Magalhães Pinto, and Marcos Resende.

We would also like to thank our Brazilian colleagues and research associates: Rosiane Rodrigues de Almeida, Ana Paula Mendes de Miranda, Sueli Conceição, Rosana Chagas, Iyaromi Ahualli, Aisha Diéne, Moisés Lino e Silva, and José Mário Bezerra da Silva (Mario Pam). They helped us reach out to informants and access spaces that would have been much more difficult or impossible without their assistance. On a few occasions, some of them used our questions and conducted interviews on our behalf. They also shared their own insights with us about religious racism and discrimination against sacred music.

Adupe Olorum to the drummers who played and sang so beautifully on the audio recording: Luís Fábio da Silva Batista, Mário Sérgio da Silva Bomfim (Sergio Pam), Rudenilson Santos Paixão, Ueslei dos Santos Cruz (Totó), and José Mário Bezerra da Silva (Mario Pam), our musical director. Thanks also to Pracatum Studio in Candeal (Salvador) and our recording engineer Paulo César.

Matondo to Junior Pakapym for his powerful cover art, "Tamborzão da Resistência."

We would like to thank the Global Religion Research Institute for the funding to conduct the research for this project. Thanks to all the staff at California State University Monterey Bay who helped us route and distribute the funds: especially Cindy Lopez, Clarisa Avila, and Christine Limesand. Dr. Boaz would also like to thank the University of North Carolina at Charlotte for a Faculty Research Grant that provided additional support for her travel. We thank our editor Beth Bouloukos at ACP for immediately recognizing the valuable contribution this book could make. Thanks to the anonymous reviewers who provided us with detailed feedback that encouraged and challenged us to make the book better.

We thank our ancestors and all the orixás, voduns, nkisis, and other spirits and entities that guide us for the opportunity to serve them by telling this story.

INTRODUCTION

Entering Intolerance

In September of 2018, Ilê Asé Omo Odé Egbe Logun Edé, a Candomblé community in Iturama, Minas Gerais, was hosting an initiation ceremony.[1] Neighbors of the *terreiro* (temple) called the authorities to complain about "noise pollution," due to the playing of *atabaques* (sacred drums). Several cars full of police officers arrived at the terreiro, seized the atabaques, and issued a citation to the religious leader, Pai Diego. The devotees were unable to complete the initiation ceremony, costing them R$90,000 (~ $18,000 USD) in wasted food, ceremonial clothing, and fees for ritual officiants. The atabaques, which are not supposed to be touched by persons who are not initiated to the drums, were held in an evidence locker at the police station for 15 days before authorities finally returned them. Pai Diego was never compensated for the costs of the aborted ceremony or the emotional distress of the invasion. This is just one example of a common problem in Brazil – prejudiced persons are characterizing Afro-Brazilian sacred music as a form of moral and/or environmental pollution and committing acts of physical and institutionalized violence in an effort to silence Afro-Brazilian religious communities.

Silencing the Drum explores the role of sacred music in Afro-Brazilian religions and provides detailed accounts of religious racism connected to music, particularly in relation to the drum. The book situates these attacks within a long history of state repression and persecution of Afro-Brazilian religions – particularly between the late nineteenth and mid-twentieth centuries. Although official policies and outsider perceptions have varied over time and in different regions, drums have been targeted intermittently for hundreds of years as a "primitive" element of religious worship that disrupts society and promotes "superstition." As we explore in Chapter 1, since the earliest arrival of enslaved Africans in the Americas until the mid-twentieth century, colonial authorities periodically prohibited drumming as well as African-derived religions through policies limiting the gathering of enslaved persons and the use of "loud instruments" as well as legislation supposedly protecting public health and morality.

Over time, the specific state authorities, laws, and mechanisms have shifted, but the energy and end goals of oppressing Black people and eradicating their music and religions have remained eerily consistent. We argue that the process of neighbors initiating "noise" complaints against Afro-Brazilian religious communities; police and other authorities investigating and adjudicating those complaints; and vigilante violence against leaders and devotees all serve as modern mechanisms of silencing what many still view as "primitive" practices. We also contend that unless Afro-Brazilian sacred music is protected from a rising wave of attacks, such as the one against Pai Diego and his terreiro, the effects on these important practices could be (and perhaps already have been) devastating and permanent.

RELIGIOUS RACISM IN THE TWENTY-FIRST CENTURY

This examination of efforts to suppress Afro-Brazilian sacred music is a case study exploring one aspect of a rapidly growing problem in the twenty-first century. Some readers might be familiar with the extensive history of discrimination against African-derived religions in the Americas (part of which is explored in Chapter 1); however, prejudice and violence against these religious communities (whether carried out by the state or private citizens) are definitely not a thing of the past. As discussed in detail in Dr. Boaz's recent book, *Banning Black Gods: Law and Religions of the African Diaspora*, devotees of these religions face numerous challenges. For instance, more than a dozen countries in the Anglophone Caribbean continue to bar the practice of Obeah more than 260 years after colonial legislators first enacted such proscriptions in Jamaica, fearing the use of spiritual rituals in rebellions.[2] Moreover, appellate courts in Canada have ruled that police officers may pose as Obeah practitioners and conduct fake spiritual rituals to trick Jamaican Canadians into confessing to crimes.[3]

In nearly every way, courts have eroded any pretense that devotees of African diaspora religions have the same rights as adepts of other religions. Devotees have been barred from courtrooms – as observers, litigants, and even lawyers – for simply wearing necklaces, head coverings, or other attire that express their beliefs.[4] Child services agencies and courts have ripped custody from devotees who are parents of minor children, in some cases, solely because of the parent's religious affiliation.[5] In other cases, adepts of African diaspora religions have faced inconceivable violence, often with little or no protection from the state.[6] For instance, in 2010, lynch mobs murdered at least 45 Vodou priests in Haiti who they blamed for the cholera outbreak that was sweeping the country.

Some forms of discrimination and violence against African diaspora religions in Brazil echo the challenges that other African diaspora religious communities are facing. For instance, several Candomblé devotees have been prohibited from entering legal forums while wearing religious hats meant to protect the head.[7] Similar to appellate court rulings about Obeah in Canada, judges in Brazil have debated whether Candomblé and Umbanda are legally recognized "religions" and whether they deserve the same protections granted to other belief systems.[8] Furthermore, especially during the Covid-19 pandemic, family members and state agencies are removing children from the custody of adherents of Candomblé at alarming rates and questioning whether exposure to Afro-Brazilian religions constitutes child abuse.

While some of the discrimination against Afro-Brazilian religions resembles that against other African-derived religious communities in the Americas, there are also forms of discrimination and violence in Brazil that differ from and exceed what is occurring in most other places. For instance, Brazil has monuments or statues to the orixás in many cities throughout the nation. These statues, which have often been erected in highly visible public spaces, are typically government-funded acknowledgments of African cultural heritage in Brazil. Although similar, if not greater, public investments have been made in Christian statues and parks, Evangelicals have mounted significant opposition to state funding of Afro-Brazilian religious sites. Moreover, existing monuments have suffered nearly constant vandalism – graffiti, stoning, decapitation, and even arson (see Chapter 3).

Afro-Brazilian religious communities have also suffered through a disturbing wave of violence against both devotees and their places of worship. For example, Evangelical groups have resurrected an antiquated method of violence and begun stoning Afro-Brazilian temples. The perpetrators often wait until the community is mid-ceremony and then hurl large rocks at the most fragile parts of the structure (usually the roof) in hopes that they will intimidate or injure devotees. Furthermore, arsonists have burned dozens of Candomblé terreiros and Umbanda centers in the past few years. In many cases, the perpetrators leave no clues as to their identity or the motive for the attack.

Perhaps most troublingly, drug trafficking gangs in the state of Rio de Janeiro have been carrying out violent assaults against adherents of Afro-Brazilian religions and their temples (see Chapter 5). After converting to Evangelical Christianity, several of these gangs have prohibited the practice of Afro-Brazilian religions in the territories they control. They have prevented adepts from wearing religious symbols or holding ceremonies. When religious leaders have refused to heed their prohibitions, gang members have invaded terreiros, beaten religious leaders, destroyed sacred objects, and set fire to the temples.

Our goal in writing this book and publishing it open access is to draw attention to a humanitarian crisis of epic proportions. Although the rampant discrimination and violence against African-derived religions is well known by society and scholars in Brazil, this issue is largely unrecognized outside of Brazil and inadequately addressed by the Brazilian government. Therefore, this book shines light on religious discrimination and racism in Brazil and is a bridge to Brazilian scholarship on the subject. In particular, it highlights how "noise pollution" complaints serve as a pretext to persecute Afro-Brazilian religious communities.

CONCEPTUAL BACKGROUND

To our knowledge, this will be the first book, in English or Portuguese, to examine "noise pollution" and related complaints as a form of modern-day discrimination and violence against Afro-Brazilian religions. This is largely because, while historians have studied well the persecution of Afro-Brazilian religions in the nineteenth and twentieth centuries, scholarship in English addressing any form of present-day discrimination against Afro-Brazilian religions is still nascent. Nevertheless, our book would not be possible without the rich body of Brazilian scholarship on this problem, including a few notable journal articles and dissertations centered on specific noise pollution cases.[9]

As the reader has probably already noticed, our discussion of the persecution and prosecution of African-derived sacred music employs the framework of "religious racism," a phrase used by devotees and activists in Brazil. The terminology of "religious racism" is an evolution of legal and political phrases used to identify discrimination and violence against Afro-Brazilian religions. For decades, Pentecostals – the main group carrying out attacks against Afro-Brazilian religious communities – have described their actions as a "spiritual" or "holy" war. According to their ideology, these assaults are attacks against the devil or other evil forces.

Milton Bortoleto explains that, as scholarship analyzing Pentecostal attacks against Afro-Brazilian religions increased from 1997 to 2007, researchers began using the term "religious intolerance" to describe them.[10] This shift pushed back against the "holy war" language promoted by Pentecostals and thus against the notion that the attacks were somehow justified, and that Afro-Brazilian religions represented "evil" forces. It also incorporated terminology deployed by devotees of Afro-Brazilian religions.

However, in recent years, scholars and devotees have given a multitude of reasons for rethinking the term "religious intolerance." Some researchers suggest that we can trace the rejection of "religious intolerance" back to a 2009 meeting of leaders of Afro-Brazilian religions in which two of them, Mãe Beata de Yemonjá and Makota Valdina, argued "it is not enough just to be tolerated, we want to be respected."[11] Over time, this language has often been repeated by prominent religious leaders. For instance, Makota Celinha, national president of CENARAB, has been quoted as saying the following at a public hearing at the Legislative Assembly of Minas Gerais in 2017: "I tolerate headaches, menstrual cramps and annoying boy[s], I tolerate that! Now, I respect the rest. We don't want to be tolerated, we want to be respected!"[12] We heard numerous devotees express these same sentiments, almost verbatim, in our interviews for this project.

What exactly do devotees mean when they demand "respect," not "toleration," in a conversation about the use of the phrase "religious intolerance"? Scholars who have analyzed this shifting terminology have explained that the opposite of "religious intolerance" (and thus the apparent answer/response to it) is "religious tolerance."[13] The notion of tolerance, they argue, is problematic because it originates in a time when officially established religions were the norm in Europe and toleration signified that an unofficial religion was permitted to exist.[14] As such, it automatically implies a situation where there is an unequal power dynamic, with one dominant religious community choosing to "tolerate" the other(s).[15] If that is the case, the dominant religion can choose to take away that tolerance and threaten the other's rights. Moreover, the concept of "tolerance" suggests that the "tolerated" group is not really accepted; rather, they are just allowed to exist.[16] This makes it apparent why devotees are demanding "respect" instead of mere "tolerance."

Furthermore, scholars point out that there have been other cases in which societies have recognized that "religious intolerance" is an insufficient concept to encompass the discrimination that is occurring.[17] In particular, the term "anti-Semitism" developed to describe the various aspects (i.e., ethnic, racial, cultural, social) of discrimination against

Jewish communities.[18] Although we haven't observed this example being used in the Brazilian scholarship on religious racism, we would note that, similarly, "Islamophobia" has evolved to refer to the multifaceted nature of discrimination against Muslims. "Religious racism" reflects the need for new terminology that underscores the fact that discrimination and violence against Afro-Brazilian religions are much more than mere religious intolerance.

Nevertheless, the development of the term "religious racism" is not just a rejection of "religious intolerance"; it is an attempt to find a term that better describes the situation in Brazil. For one thing, it clarifies that Afro-Brazilian religions are not merely "religions."[19] As Wanderson Flor do Nascimento eloquently explains, these communities

> also conserved values of social organization, ancestral knowledge, ways of caring for life, health, other people, and economic processes that were inherited from the African continent. Therefore, we can say that these religions are much more than religions, in the way the West understands: they are ways of life that contain a spirituality within them. If they are religions, they are much more so in a political connotation, in terms of rebuilding bonds broken by racism and colonization between African people and their histories prior to the enslaving process that happened in our country: they had – and have – the function of reconnecting communities broken by the violent process that dehumanized and enslaved millions of people who were forced to leave their families, their traditions, their territories.[20]

This is particularly important because these African aspects of Afro-Brazilian religions – practices such as animal sacrifice, ancestor reverence, and their politics, family structure, etc. – are often the reasons that people discriminate against them.[21]

As we will discuss further in Chapter 1, after emancipation, Brazil implemented various strategies to "whiten" their population and eradicate non-European practices, including the criminalization of Afro-Brazilian religions. Scholars who advocate for the use of "religious racism" emphasize that, despite the repeal of such laws, Brazilian society remains grounded in discrimination against non-Eurocentric practices.[22] Additionally, this terminology recognizes that other non-Christian religions that do not share the same history of racialized repression do not experience the same frequency and severity of discrimination and violence in Brazil.[23]

Another reason to use the term "religious racism" is because it points out that the discrimination and violence these communities experience is a widespread and systemic problem, as "racism" is known to be.[24] This contrasts with religious intolerance (and even some ways of framing race-motivated crimes), because intolerance is understood as an individual offense carried out by an intolerant person. In cases of "intolerance," the focus is often placed on the perpetrator (in this case, usually Evangelical Christians) and not on the victims of discrimination and violence.[25] "Religious racism" shifts the focus to the victims and denotes a larger problem that requires effort to eradicate beyond merely punishing a bigoted individual. In particular, it indicates that the problem is something that "permeates the entire society and, in particular, the State."[26]

This ability to encompass the State as an actor that contributes to the problem of "religious racism" is critical. As we will explore in further detail in Chapters 2 and 3, local, state, and federal governments in Brazil have all been known to capitalize on public representations and celebrations of Afro-Brazilian religions. The government has also developed laws and programs to help improve the lives of these communities, including establishing offices to hear reports of crimes against them and a National Day to Combat Religious Intolerance. Nevertheless, the government is also creating laws and policies that infringe on the rights of these communities, such as those that restrict sacred music. This paradox, scholars have argued, is a reflection of how systemic racism works.[27]

The term "religious racism" also demonstrates that the movement to combat discrimination against Afro-Brazilians religions is deeply connected to the broader fight for racial equality in Brazil.[28] This is something that is undeniably true. Anyone with even superficial familiarity with the organizations that are fighting for the rights of people of African descent in Brazil will have observed the prevalence of devotees of Afro-Brazilian religions in these organizations. One can also observe that government organizations designed to combat racism, such as SEPROMI (Secretariat for the Promotion of Racial Equality and Traditional Peoples and Communities) in Bahia, are also sometimes critical resources in the fight against religious racism. Since discrimination against Afro-Brazilian religions is rooted in a history of racial discrimination and permeates society, including the State, this association with the struggle for racial equality not only makes sense, it is essential. As Nascimento reminds us, "to combat violent practices against 'religions' of [African] matrices is, also and above all, to combat the colonial heritage of racism that, although it has many ways of expressing itself, remains masked in our country."[29]

The terminology of "religious racism" is not without its critics. Some people have pointed out that the shifting religious landscape in Brazil over the past few decades has brought substantially more white devotees to Afro-Brazilian religions and more Black Brazilians to Evangelical churches, thus changing how we understand what represents the religion of Black people.[30] This has been precisely a position held by Black Pentecostals, some of whom argue that Afro-Brazilian terreiros have become white spaces and that "the 'true' spaces of struggle and political resistance of black people would take place in Pentecostal *holdings*, due, also, to the assistance provided to prison populations, favelas and peripheral areas."[31] However, the race of the devotees does not negate most of the foregoing reasons that people use "religion racism" (i.e., the history of discrimination that is/was part of anti-Black racism, the incorporation of African worldviews and social structures in these religions, etc.). Moreover, some of our interlocutors stressed that, although the government doesn't release data about the race of the victims in cases of discrimination and violence against devotees of Afro-Brazilian religions, they strongly suspect that Black devotees are being targeted at much higher rates.

In this book, we employ the term "religious racism" because these rationales that some scholars and devotees have provided for adopting the phrase to speak about discrimination and violence against Afro-Brazilian religions hold true when we assess the specific problem of discrimination against sacred music. It is rooted in a history of racial discrimination that, as we will discuss in Chapter 1, saw African religions, drumming, and dancing targeted by authorities in various regions and time periods. Attempts to silence sacred music remain grounded in prejudice against the non-European cultural practices in Brazil. And, without question, the problem is widespread and systemic, with the State playing a central role in denying devotees' rights. Finally, and most importantly, the resolution to the problems discussed in this book requires more than tolerance alone (which can be taken away on a whim); it requires deep, meaningful changes to public perceptions and official policies. These changes must be grounded in profound respect for Afro-Brazilian religions (and not simply when it is convenient or profitable) and commitment to an equitable society that is free from racial prejudice.

Although we choose to use "religious racism," one will note as we quote our interlocutors that they varied in their choice of terminology. Some emphatically and exclusively use "religious racism," others preferred "religious intolerance," and some varied between the two. In most interviews, we asked about the person's preference in terminology, and we provide some quotes at the end of the book that allow the reader to hear our interlocutors explain in their own voices why they describe the situation in the way that they do. However, no one openly disagreed that "religious racism" is applicable and, interestingly, some people switched to this phrase after the question about which term they prefer.

It may be possible that "religious racism" is such a new phrase that it has not fully replaced "religious intolerance" in everyday speech, particularly among people who are old enough to have been part of the movement to force public discourse to use "intolerance" in place of Evangelicals' "spiritual warfare" terminology. However, one factor that we observed, although by no means universally applicable, was that devotees who self-identity as "white" were more likely to use "religious intolerance."[32] Black Brazilians, especially those who are deeply involved in the broader fight for racial equality, might have made this transition from "intolerance" to "racism" more smoothly, as they are accustomed to thinking and speaking about how racism impacts their lives.

Regardless of the reasoning, it is important to note that neither terminology should be viewed as wrong and that both have developed as part of the struggle to call attention to the widespread discrimination and violence against these communities. Additionally, while scholars draw these distinctions over semantics, no one, regardless of terminology, seemed to believe that the problem was not widespread and systemic, that the solution didn't require a reversal of long-standing racial prejudice against these religions, or that "tolerance" (as described earlier) would be a sufficient response.

METHODOLOGY

This work is based on a variety of sources and resources, including: interpretations of interviews that we conducted with religious leaders, musicians, and activists in Brazil, as well as legal texts, news reports, and even social media posts. To make sense of these materials, the book draws from multiple disciplines. As an attorney and legal studies scholar, Dr. Boaz provides a close reading of police reports, legislation, court cases, and other legal documents. As a musician and anthropologist of music, Dr. Vaughan explores the importance of sacred drumming and the impact of restrictions on musical practice. In addition to traditional prose, samples of music as well as images and maps help tell the story. For example, as part of our research we brought together a group of musicians under the direction of master drummer José Mário Bezerra da Silva (Mario Pam) at Pracatum studio in Salvador to record various tracks of the Afro-Brazilian sacred rhythms that are being endangered by religious racism.

Although this work is based on a variety of sources, we consider our fieldwork (conducted from 2020 to 2022) to be the backbone of this study. During this time, we traveled to the Federal District, Rio de Janeiro, Bahia, Alagoas, and Maranhão. In each location, we were

Figure 1: Drummers at Pracatum Studio

welcomed by Afro-Brazilian religious communities, activists, police officials, and politicians, among others. Each encounter and conversation held pieces of the complex story that we weave together in this book.

The primary focus of our field research was on the experiences of people who had suffered religious racism. As such, the majority of our interviews took place in terreiros. We visited renowned terreiros as well as lesser-known ones to achieve diversity and understand differences in the experiences of terreiros with these divergent profiles. We talked to devotees and communities who were harassed constantly as well as those who had never directly experienced religious racism but were well aware of and able to reflect on it as a dire problem in Brazilian society.

In addition to formal interviews, we had informal conversations with knowledgeable Brazilian scholars like Dr. Rosiane Rodrigues, Dr. Ana Paula Miranda, and Dr. Ilzver Matos. We attended ceremonies and participated in community rituals, such as the cleansing that happens annually for orixá Obaluayê syncretized as Saint Lazarus. We visited orixá monuments, paid homage, and made offerings there. We (re)visited historic sites such as Little Africa and Valongo Wharf in Rio de Janeiro, Pelourinho in Salvador, and the Parque Memorial Quilombo dos Palmares in Alagoas. As a historian, Dr. Boaz observed the public narrative that these important sites weave about the history of Black people in Brazil and the often-deafening silence about Afro-Brazilian religions and the persecution of these faiths. Additionally, during these and prior trips to Brazil, Dr. Boaz visited government offices such as the SEPROMI in Bahia and specialized police stations designed to investigate crimes of bias such as racism and religious intolerance. In addition to meeting with representatives from these offices, Dr. Boaz took the opportunity to observe the physical locations and the resources available to victims of religious racism. As an anthropologist, Dr. Vaughan tuned in to stories and wordplay, interpreting language and reading between the lines to better understand what people were saying about religious racism. As a musician, Dr. Vaughan learned from accomplished drummers about their experiences and perspectives about the role and meaning of the drum in Afro-Brazilian religions.

The fieldwork conducted for this project was extremely fruitful and we are grateful to our friends and colleagues, as well as to the orixás, who opened the road for us. Nevertheless, this journey was not without its challenges. The chief obstacle to our work was that the entirety of our travel took place during the height of the Covid-19 pandemic. We endeavored to conduct as many in-person interviews as possible, but we were, understandably, limited by access to safe, outdoor locations to conduct interviews and by personal concerns about safety (both our own and that of our interlocutors). On some occasions, we even found ourselves stuck under strict lockdowns, conducting virtual interviews from our accommodations in Brazil. However, it turned out to be a blessing in disguise that the pandemic forced so many people throughout the world to become more familiar with technologies like Zoom and Google Meet (in addition to the already popular WhatsApp platform). These virtual meeting spaces allowed us to reach people in areas of Brazil that we could not have physically traveled to due to limitations of time and financial resources.

In addition to the unique challenges brought by the Covid-19 pandemic, there were other barriers to completing this project. Even under normal circumstances, some Afro-Brazilian religious communities are not very accessible. We often traveled long distances to the outskirts of cities, at times down dirt roads to places with no cell phone reception, to conduct interviews. Additionally, some communities were difficult to locate or contact; in particular, some victims of violence had relocated following an attack. Thankfully, we had the benefit of connecting and reconnecting with generous people who helped expand our networks in each of the places we visited. Despite the challenges of the pandemic and other factors, we found that most devotees of Afro-Brazilian religions recognized the increasingly grave nature of the situation and were anxious to help shine a light on what has been happening. We appreciate the profound ancestral traditions and bountiful love that live in these communities. We wrote this book to raise awareness about religious racism in Brazil and to motivate readers to take action to protect them.

OUTLINE OF CHAPTERS

The book is composed of seven chapters. Chapter 1 introduces the reader to the importance of drums in African diaspora religions, especially those in Brazil. It also provides examples of some of the historical persecution of African-derived religions in the Americas, with an emphasis on the policing of sacred music. Chapter 2 describes our fieldwork in greater detail, with the intention of providing more foundational information to readers who are unfamiliar with Brazil. In the third chapter, we examine the recognition of Afro-Brazilian religions as part of the cultural heritage of Brazil and the tensions between this official recognition and religious racism.

Chapters 4, 5, and 6 explore different forms of discrimination and their relationship to sacred music. Chapter 4 introduces how neighbors harass Afro-Brazilian religious temples through targeted, discriminatory noise complaints, mobilizing the police to try to silence and displace these communities. Chapter 5 examines vigilante violence against Afro-Brazilian religious communities in relation to their musical practices. Most significantly, it explores the Evangelical drug traffickers in Rio de Janeiro who have systematically tried to expel Afro-Brazilian religions from the territory that they control. The traffickers have prohibited devotees from playing drums or hosting public ceremonies; devotees have also altered their own religious practices, sometimes silencing the drums, to avoid being detected by the traffickers. Chapter 6 centers on the broader climate of police violence in Brazil and how incidents of police brutality intersect with noise complaints against Afro-Brazilian religious communities. The final chapter/conclusion considers the possible effects of this religious discrimination. It features quotes from religious leaders about the potential impact of restrictions on sacred music, discussing why these incidents occur, how they might change religious practice, and whether the situation in Brazil might improve in the future.

CHAPTER 1

The Roots of Racism Against Africana Sacred Music

Afro-Brazilian religions such as Candomblé and Umbanda are part of a spectrum of religions that developed in the Americas based upon beliefs and rituals imported from Africa and blended to varying degrees with Indigenous and European spiritualities. These religions, collectively referred to as African diaspora religions, African-derived religions, and Africana religions, incorporate worldviews and ceremonies from many of the African ethnic groups who were trafficked in the Atlantic trade. Some of the most recognized groups are the Kongo (modern-day Angola, Gabon, Republic of Congo, and Democratic Republic of Congo), Yoruba (modern-day Nigeria, Benin, and Togo), Dahomey/Fon (modern-day Benin and Togo), and Akan (modern-day Ghana). There are dozens, perhaps hundreds, of Africana religions in the Americas. Some of the most studied religions or belief systems include: Lucumí/Regla de Ocha/Santería and Palo Monte/Palo Mayombe/ Regla de Kongo from Cuba; Vodou from Haiti; Obeah from the British Caribbean; and Candomblé and Umbanda from Brazil. In Brazil, there exists a wealth of other, less studied African-derived or influenced religions such as Batuque, Xangô, Tambor de Mina, Quimbanda, Candomblé de Caboclo, Jurema, Encantaria, Pajelança, Jarê, and Catimbó.

Most of the cases and controversies about sacred drumming that we discuss in this book are connected to two Afro-Brazilian religions: Candomblé and Umbanda. Candomblé is an umbrella term that encompasses different branches or "nations" that each have distinct but related beliefs and practices. The most widely recognized nations were heavily influenced by a few ethnic groups: the Yoruba, the West Central African Bantu-speaking people, and the Gbe-speaking peoples.

Enslaved people from the Bantu region of West Central Africa (Kongo/Angola) arrived in Brazil as early as the start of the sixteenth century. These people would form the Candomblé Angola nation. The eighteenth century saw Gbe-speaking people from the empire of Dahomey arrive and form the Candomblé Jeje/Gege nation. In the early nineteenth century, with the effects of civil war, people from the Oyo Empire and surrounding territories were trafficked in higher numbers to the Americas, where they became known collectively as Yoruba peoples, forming the Ketu/Nagô nation within Candomblé. Each group maintained connections to languages, musical practices, and rituals brought from Africa and adapted for use in Brazil.[1] In some cases, African divinities and ideas were disguised under and influenced by Catholic ideology and symbols, as well as blended with Indigenous ones.

Gary Edwards and John Mason list several basic beliefs of the Yoruba people. Despite the diversity of Africana religious beliefs, these fundamental principles (with a few slight modifications) also apply generally to many Africana religions, including the Ketu/Nagô, Angola, and Jeje nations of Brazilian Candomblé. These communities believe:

1. There is one God who created and controls the universe and all that is contained therein
2. There are selected forces of nature called òrìsà (orixá)[2] (or nkisi or voduns)[3] that deal with the affairs of humankind on Earth and govern the universe
3. A person's spirit lives on after death and can reincarnate back into the world

4. Ancestor spirits have power over those who remain on Earth, and so must be remembered, appeased, honored, and consulted by the living
5. In divination (communicating with ancestors, spirits, divinities, or other sacred entities using mediumship and/or rituals employing tools such as seeds, nuts, or shells)
6. In the use of offerings (*adimú*) and animal sacrifice[4] (*ebbó ejé*) to elevate their prayers to the divinities, spirits, and ancestors
7. In the ability of rituals, practices, and unseen forces to impact the natural world[5]
8. In the spiritual and medicinal use of herbs
9. Ritual song and dance are a mandatory component of certain ceremonies
10. Humans can commune with ancestors, orixá, God, and/or other higher beings through the vehicle of trance possession

The term "Candomblé" can be traced back to at least 1826, when it was used in reference to "a house where a group of rebellious slaves had taken refuge."[6] Scholars believe that the term "Candomblé" is likely of Bantu-Kongo origin.[7] Candomblé is a decentralized faith, with the previously mentioned "nations" dividing further into spiritual houses or *terreiros* that are under the direction of high priests who are known as *iyalorixá* (*mãe de santo*, mother of the saint) or *babalorixá* (*pai de santo*, father of the saint) in Ketu/Nagô communities.[8] As these titles suggest, terreiros foster a strong sense of communal lineage and spiritual kinship. Mães and pais de santo initiate and teach new devotees who become their spiritual offspring. These individuals sometimes depart from established terreiros and create new ones that carry on a specific lineage. The physical structure of the terreiros may be an entire compound with meeting spaces, shrines, reception areas, and other indoor spaces surrounded by gardens and other natural habitats.[9] It is a sacred space, where an initiate's spiritual life and lineage are anchored.[10]

While most Candomblé communities trace a large portion of their beliefs and practices directly to Africans, Umbanda developed as a combination of religious traditions from Africans, Europeans, and Indigenous ("Amerindian") Brazilians. As it is such a conglomeration,

Umbanda is sometimes viewed as a truly Brazilian religion. However, as one will see throughout this book, Umbanda communities suffer similar forms of intolerance as other African matrix religions, likely due to its incorporation of some visibly African elements such as the wearing of white, the veneration of the orixás, and the use of certain drums.

Umbanda was founded in the Brazilian state of Rio de Janeiro in 1908, drawing from multiple African religious traditions as well as Kardec Spiritism. Adherents believe that each person has a spirit or soul that exists independently of the physical body and moves to another plane of existence after a person dies.[11] Many of the rituals and ceremonies in Umbanda center on the communication with and veneration of several types of spirits. These include *pretos velhos*, who are spirits of enslaved Africans who lived until old age; *crianças*, who are spirits of children; and *caboclos*, who are spirits of Indigenous Brazilians.[12] Umbanda devotees also believe in the orixás; however, the orixás are more remote divinities than those honored in certain lineages of Candomblé. They do not directly possess followers. Instead, pretos velhos, crianças, and caboclos serve as intermediaries between human beings and the orixás.

Umbanda rituals or ceremonies concentrate on the invocation of the spirits through singing and drumming. The spirits possess certain adepts who serve as mediums and communicate with devotees. They offer advice on how to solve various problems – economic, social, physical, etc.[13] Although it can be found in all parts of Brazil, Umbanda is often considered to be an "urban" religion. In contrast to Candomblé, which might have entire religious compounds set aside for worship, Umbanda ceremonies more often take place in private homes or in buildings designated as religious centers.

GENERAL HISTORY OF AFRO-DIASPORIC AND AFRO-BRAZILIAN DRUMMING

The roots of African diaspora sacred music lie in West and West Central Africa. Africans who were transported to the Americas as enslaved laborers brought with them profound musical legacies with a heavy emphasis on polyrhythm[14] and the drum in combination with dance and call and response singing. Between the early sixteenth and late nineteenth centuries, more than 10 million Africans landed in the Americas – predominantly from the region stretching south from the Senegal River through the vicinity of present-day nations such as Sierra Leone, Liberia, Ghana, Togo, Benin, Nigeria, and down through modern-day Angola. The majority of them arrived in the Caribbean and Latin America, especially Brazil. In most, if not all, of their homelands, music was organized and performed as an important part of everyday life. As such, the Black music traditions that they initiated in the Americas typically incorporate drumming and other performance practices such as call and response singing, circle and semicircular formations, counter-clockwise circular motion, heavy emphasis on improvisation, multi- or intergenerational participation, "conversation" between musicians and dancers, musical or dance challenges or "duels," and so on.

Africans and their descendants have sparked sacred music traditions throughout the Americas. In Cuba, batá drums recreate tonal language to praise or "call down" the spirits, known as *oricha* or *santos* in the Yoruba-derived Afro-Cuban religion called Lucumí, Regla de Ocha, or Santería. In Haiti, various drum batteries dialogue with spirits known as *lwa* within Haitian Vodou families. In the Dominican Republic, palo drums salute deities known as *misterios* (mysteries) within a spiritual system called the 21 Divisions. Each of these styles features "hot" (intense, at times fiery) drumming, call and response singing, and spirit possession. They have often been regarded as backward and illegitimate by local elites and mainstream society.[15]

In Brazil, many musical genres have African roots. Some of them, particularly sacred music in Afro-Brazilian religions, have very clear roots in Africa. For example, Brazilian Candomblé comprises a vast yet discrete liturgy of rhythms and songs that competent singers and percussionists must know. Such musical traditions evolved in the Western Hemisphere, including shifts in the instruments used and the language of singing (sometimes incorporating European languages or creole mixtures of European, West African, and Indigenous), but they maintain a clear relationship to specific, earlier drum traditions in West and Central Africa.

There are other styles that are more homegrown in the Americas. Even as these styles or genres continue to employ African performance principles, they express a sense of place, a certain rootedness, in the new diasporic location. Brazilian *tambor de crioula*[16] and *samba de roda* are great examples. Here, song lyrics in Portuguese with a very strong call and response feel accompany intense dialogue between solo dancer and lead drummer. Specific phrases punctuate (react) or dictate (initiate) dance gestures, in accordance with West African performance norms. The chief singer, head drummer, solo dancers, and a chorus of singers and observers jointly manipulate communal energy.

There are contemporary styles that go even further, combining elements from the former two categories. In these genres, African and European rhythms, instruments, and approaches jointly form the foundation for several developments within Afro-Brazilian dance music from the first half of the twentieth century, on to the present day and into the future. For example, various styles of Brazilian samba incorporate guitar and other harmonic instruments. Samba reggae incorporates electronic instruments such as synthesizers and fuses influences from the Caribbean and the United States. *Baile funk* is a hardcore, urban music from Rio de Janeiro that borrows some of its projection and feeling from hip hop, while reinterpreting Afro-Brazilian rhythmic patterns on drum machines.

Drums have come to symbolize African-descended sacred music in Brazil, the Caribbean, and throughout Latin America. Drummers play a key role by supporting ceremonial events with music, synchronizing their art with singers and dancers to make these spiritual events *happen*. Therefore, it is not surprising that oftentimes when colonies or states have attempted to eradicate African religion in the Americas, they have begun by forbidding the use of the drum.[17] Harassed by colonial authorities, people of African descent maintained evolving music traditions that combine drum, dance, and song in ways that fomented wellbeing in the community. The maintenance of these traditions, against all odds, is a testament to the resilience of African peoples in the Americas. Afro-Brazilian Candomblé drumming is an example par excellence.

The drums of Candomblé are called *atabaques*. They are single headed, barrel-shaped drums, originally developed to emulate drum styles from among the Yoruba people of modern-day Nigeria, Dahomeyan traditions from modern-day Benin and Togo, and Kongo drum styles from modern-day nations such as Democratic Republic of Congo, Republic of Congo, Gabon, and Angola. As such, the same three-drum ensemble is used in most Candomblé terreiros, including Angola, Ketu/Nagô, and Jeje/Gege nations.[18] In addition to the atabaques, many terreiros use an iron bell, known as *agogô* or *gã*, which plays rhythmic patterns that undergird and provide a central focus or feeling for each rhythm. New players begin their learning on the bell.

The generic term for the sacred drum used in Candomblé terreiros is *atabaque*. Three atabaques are played together. Each atabaque in the trio has a distinct size and pitch, function within the group, and an

FIGURE 1: Atabaques at Terreiro Incimimó. Cachoeira, Bahia

FIGURE 2: Atabaques at Terreiro Vodun Zo. Salvador, Bahia

identifying name that can vary according to which nation the terreiro and their drummers belong. The most generalized names for each atabaque seem to derive from the Jeje nation. The smallest, highest pitch drum is known as *le* (pronounced LEH) – it is the time keeper of the group and generally plays the simplest part. The middle drum is *runpí* (pronounced hoon-PEE); it either doubles the pattern of the small drum or plays a contrasting part. The lead drum with the lowest pitch is called *run* (pronounced HOON). The lead drum initiates new rhythms and special patterns within rhythms and improvises in dialogue with dancers. Within Jeje houses, lead drummers are known as *Runtó* (hoon-TOH). Alternatively, and in addition to the basic names, in some Ketu houses the smallest drum is called *ilu osi* or the drum that sits to the left (the junior drum); the middle drum is called *ilu otun* – the drum that sits to the right. The lead and largest drum is simply called *ilu* (Yoruba for drum).[19] Within Ketu and Jeje terreiros, accompanist drummers perform on the runpí and le with slender wooden sticks called *agidaví*, while the lead drummer performs on the *run* using one agidaví and one open hand. In Ketu houses master drummers are given the title *Alabé*.

In Candomblé Angola terreiros, the atabaque is also called *ngoma*, which simply means drum in Bantu languages to this day. The specific terms for each of the three atabaque-ngoma are *munjola* (lead drum), *mungongo* (middle drum), and *mungonguinho*.[20] Master drummers are called *Xikarangoma* (shee-ka-ra-en-GO-ma). In Angola terreiros and in Umbanda, all three atabaques are played with open hands.

In Candomblé, music accompanies many moments in the life of the terreiro. "Tudo tem uma melodia, tudo tem um batuque."[21] "Everything has a melody and a rhythm."[22] Drums accompany songs and prayers. Sometimes drums alone praise the deities. Drums accompany ritual animal sacrifices as a way to honor the lives of the animals and make their passage more pleasant.[23] Drums are used along with song and dance to make spirit manifest in the bodies of devotees in the terreiro during celebrations called *xiré*. Each terreiro owns its own set of atabaques and drummers are members of the terreiro with special charges to play for the spirits. As such, drummers in Candomblé are not commonly paid to play for ceremonies. In some cases, new terreiros that do not yet have drums or drummers will hire people to play.

Gregorio Jose Pereira de Queiroz describes Umbanda as "a musical religion in its essence," explaining "the music is crucial to the religious ritual: it works to the rapprochement (or reconnection) between human and the divine, especially by the incorporation of guides and deities."[24] *Ponto cantado* (sung point) is the name given to "a devotional song, musical prayer, chant, hymn, or sung verse" in Umbanda. The songs are "points" of contact with spirits, bridges to strengthen the mediumship connection once it is established. In some cases, "Umbandists compose *pontos* before rituals, while others believe that spirits compose them during rituals."[25]

Similar to Candomblé, atabaques are a crucial component of Umbanda; however, the music played in the two religions can be very distinct.[26] Music making in Umbanda is more open to innovation in terms of practitioners creating new songs, particularly ones sung in Portuguese and with influence from Brazilian folk, samba, or other popular music.[27] Additionally, Umbanda does not require three drums at all times; in different centers and situations, Dr. Vaughan observed one or several drums being played to support the ceremony.

Throughout this book, we mostly use the term atabaque because it can apply to the drum in Candomblé *across* terreiros regardless of nation, as well as within Umbanda centers. Although atabaques do not exist as such in Africa, they represent an evolution of African sacred drumming in Brazil. The atabaque drum traditions within the three main Candomblé nations and Umbanda centers represent a musical fusion sparked by Black people in Brazil.[28] Atabaques exemplify the kind of history shared by many Afro-descendant music styles from the colonial era. As a basis for understanding the music under discussion in this book, we urge you to listen to the recordings we made of Candomblé music. Tracks 1–3 are rhythms used within Candomblé Angola terreiros. Track 1 (Cabula) is a prototype of what would become the world-famous Brazilian samba beat and features call and response singing in honor of the trickster/messenger spirit Pomba Gira (Mpombo Nzila).

Tracks 4–6 are from Candomblé Ketu/Nagô. Track 4 (Vassi) features a song honoring Ogum, the spirit of iron, technology, and war. Track 5 (Ijexá) is an iconic Candomblé rhythm used often in Brazilian commercial music and pop culture. In traditional settings, it is played

Please visit Fulcrum to hear this audio file.

Track 1: Cabula. This rhythm comes from the Candomblé Angola nation.

Please visit Fulcrum to hear this audio file.

Track 2: Barra Vento. This rhythm comes from the Candomblé Angola nation.

Please visit Fulcrum to hear this audio file.

Track 3: Congo. This rhythm comes from the Candomblé Angola nation.

TRACK 4: Vassi. This rhythm comes from the Candomblé Ketu nation.

TRACK 5: Ijexá. This rhythm is one of the best known beyond the terreiros. It has heavily influenced Brazilian popular music.

TRACK 6: Avamunha. This rhythm comes from the Candomblé Ketu nation.

to honor Oxum, spirit of the river, sensuality, and commerce. Track 6 (Avamunha) is a Ketu nation rhythm played to call the priests of the terreiro into the dancing space for ceremony and to signal their time to retire.

Track 7 (Sato) comes from Candomblé Jeje and features a song for Omolú, vodun of sickness and healing. Tracks 8 and 9 feature the Ijexá rhythm again, but now with just solo drumming on the lead atabaque (*run*). This is meant to give the reader an idea of the artistry plied by master drummers and emphasize the fact each drummer's voice or style can be vastly different.

Tracks 10–16 represent a spectrum of Afro-Brazilian rhythms starting with Cabula as played in Candomblé terreiros and ending with samba reggae as performed by renowned groups like Olodum and Ilê Aiyê.

Many Brazilian musicians have been trained in and/or deeply influenced by participating in Candomblé terreiros.[29] The idea we wish to convey is that the music of Candomblé reaches far beyond the walls of the terreiro to enrich Brazil and the world culturally and even financially.

Please visit Fulcrum to hear this audio file.

TRACK 7: Sato. This rhythm comes from the Candomblé Jeje nation.

Please visit Fulcrum to hear this audio file.

TRACK 8: Ijexá (run solo Totó). This solo on the ijexá rhythm shows the unique style and virtuosity of lead drummers in Candomblé.

Please visit Fulcrum to hear this audio file.

TRACK 9: Ijexá (run solo Rudenilson). This solo by a different drummer on the ijexá rhythm shows more of the unique style and virtuosity of lead drummers in Candomblé.

Please visit Fulcrum to hear this audio file.

TRACK 10: Samba de Caboclo (Cabula). The sacred rhythm Samba de Caboclo contains the original groove that underlies all forms of samba.

Please visit Fulcrum to hear this audio file.

TRACK 11: Samba de Rodar. Afro-Brazilians used marching band instruments to create myriad styles of samba such as Samba de Rodar (different from samba de roda).

Please visit Fulcrum to hear this audio file.

TRACK 12: Samba Duro. Samba Duro (hard samba) is a staple for street parties and processions in Salvador, Bahia.

Please visit Fulcrum to hear this audio file.

TRACK 13: Marcha Rancho. Afro-Brazilians used marching band instruments to create myriad styles of samba such as Marcha Rancho.

TRACK 14: Batucada. This may be the most famous Brazilian samba rhythm, performed at Carnival by samba schools like Mangueira, Salgueiro, Vila Isabel, and so on.

TRACK 15: Samba Afro. This style was created by the afro bloco Ilê Aiyê, incorporating elements from ijexá, batucada, and other rhythms.

TRACK 16: Samba Reggae. This style was created by Neguinho do Samba from the afro bloco Olodum, blending elements from samba afro with reggae and other rhythms.

TRACK 17: Sambas da Bahia. This is a potpourri of tracks 10–16, connecting the sacred rhythm Samba de Caboclo with other secular forms of samba that developed after.

OUTLAWING DRUMS DURING SLAVERY IN THE AMERICAS

At different points in time and under different circumstances, European colonists from every empire – England, Spain, Portugal, France, etc. – observed, judged, and often regulated African musical practices. Colonial policies toward these practices varied over time and region, ranging from strict prohibition to toleration to selective encouragement.

Speaking of Brazil, Rachel Harding explains:

> [It is] important to recognize that even within the dominant society there was seldom a consensus about how to respond to the ubiquitous presence of batuques, atabaques, Candomblés, calundus, sambas and other forms of black drummed and danced expression. Throughout the history of slavery in Brazil, slave owners and civil and religious authorities had deeply ambivalent responses to the tendency of African slaves and their descendants to gather together in the practice of songs and dances "in the style of their land." There were two major schools of thought among elites about this widespread custom. One side feared that such gatherings were socially disruptive and potentially dangerous to the established order. Not uncommonly several hundred blacks congregated to dance in a single, unsupervised setting and authorities feared such gatherings as opportunities when plots and rebellions could be planned. Certainly the

> prevalence of African rhythms unfamiliar (and perhaps disquieting) to Portuguese tastes, prolonged and energetic collective dancing, and songs and conversations in African languages, could be conceived as threatening to a population of whites, who, in the plantation regions and major port cities, found themselves vastly outnumbered by Africans and their Brazilian descendants... The other side of the debate was articulated by those who believed that allowing slaves to maintain African cultural traditions would enhance ethnic divisions and release some of the tensions and frustrations of a life of enslavement.[30]

Despite these varied approaches in different areas and time periods, we will focus on discrimination and prosecution. This is not intended to skew the reader's perception of how these practices were treated historically; we simply believe that identifying some of the rationales for and methods of restricting African music helps lay the groundwork for understanding discrimination against them today.

The prohibition of African music making, including drumming, dates back to around the same time as documentation of their arrival in the Americas. There were at least two primary reasons behind the legal restrictions on African musical practices, including drumming. Daniel Johnson explains "'[n]oise' was in fact a major contributor to social disorder in the early modern world, signaling disruption of the public peace and, if uncontrolled, the upending of established authority."[31] In some parts of the Americas, colonists believed that people could be "lured" or "seduced" by "vulgar" sounds into engaging in disorderly or irrational behavior.[32] At times, we can see colonial preoccupations with public order and morality in laws restricting Black cultural practices.

For example, in the North American colonies, "New York City's first race-based ordinance concerned not crime, flight from bondage or rebellion, but rather" a 1681 statute that prohibited Africans and Native Americans from engaging in Sunday gatherings or pastimes that disturbed the peace.[33] Similarly, in the early eighteenth century, Philadelphia courts regularly heard complaints against servants and free Black people about cases of "rhythmic disorders."[34] Neighbors complained that festivals, dances, and other assemblies generated noise that disturbed them and that in some gatherings, participants swore and engaged in other behavior that authorities or the public considered vulgar. Officials worried that at major festivals, free Black people might drink alcohol to excess, which interfered with their work over subsequent days.[35] Similarly, in Barbados, white colonists disdainfully observed that Black gatherings involved "drumming, dancing and riot practising frenzied incantations over the graves of their deceased relatives and friends."[36] Thus, a law governing the lives of enslaved persons in the early nineteenth century barred "any heathenish or idolatrous music, singing, or ceremonies."[37]

Scholars have made similar observations about Brazil. They have noted that, in some circumstances, batuques could be viewed as "immoral, barbarous, [and] bad for labour productivity."[38] For example, Mattijs van de Port asserts that "Nineteenth-century reports speak about noisy gatherings situated in the filthy and repugnant life world of the black Bahian masses, and many observers were unable to discern whether these blacks were merely entertaining themselves or involved in religious practices."[39] Rachel Harding adds "Although many visitors to Brazil talked about the metamorphosis which occurred in black dancers as they danced, most failed to see the development in terms of anything other than a 'wildness', something uncontrollable or even demonic that both fascinated and evoked a certain wariness."[40] João Reis cites the words of politician and police officer Antonio Luiz Affonso de Carvalho, who spoke in favor of a law against batuques in the town of Maragogipe in 1855. Attempting to define *batuque*, Carvalho described them as "the most barbarian [sic] and immoral dances, with non-rhythmic and loud voices ... the most complete orgy.' "[41]

In some regions, authorities restricted these "repugnant" and "demonic" African forms of music and dancing. In parts of Pernambuco, batuques and other forms of dancing and drumming were prohibited in the early nineteenth century as acts that endangered "public morality." Two laws implemented in 1836 provide examples. In Itamaracá, batuques were penalized in the same article that barred screaming in the streets, using obscenities and other "boisterous diversions."[42] Violators could be fined R$4,000 (~ $800 USD) or jailed for eight days. Enslaved violators would be whipped 36 times; 72 times for repeat offenses. Similarly, in the town of Cabo, a clause governing "tranquility and public morality" dictated that shop owners who allowed enslaved people to meet, dance, or beat drums would be fined 4,000 reais.[43]

Similar to the ordinance in Cabo that restricted dancing or playing drums as a violation of "tranquility," some other Brazilian cities or provinces barred sacred or secular drumming as a form of noise pollution. For instance, in 1846, a law implemented in the City of Diamantina, Minas Gerais, prohibited "batuques com algasarra [sic]" (noisy drumming) that disturbed the neighborhood. Violators would be sentenced to one day in jail.[44] The town of Itajubá, also in Minas Gerais, imposed a similar ban in 1853 – punishing participants in batuques accompanied by loud noise with imprisonment for one day.[45]

The other reason that some colonial governments prohibited African drumming was fear of their use in rebellions. In particular, they "banned slave drumming out of fear of the instrument's military association in Africa."[46] It is important to recall that many Europeans, particularly Iberians, were first introduced to African drums in the context of war. The Muslim Almoravid army that invaded the Iberian Peninsula in the eleventh century included soldiers from Africa, primarily from the region stretching between Senegambia in the West to Sudan in the East, who incorporated drums as part of their arsenal.[47] These drums "intimidated the defending soldiers and terrorized the population when besieging the city."[48] As a means to amplify speech, the drums also allowed communication and provided directions that all soldiers could hear. Stories about the utility of African drumming in warfare in the Almoravid armies, combined with observations during more recent encounters between Africans and Europeans, laid the groundwork for well-justified concerns about the organizing power of music in enslaved communities in the Americas.

Scholars also point out that Europeans were intimidated by African musical performances because they were unable to decipher their meaning. They were unfamiliar with the significance of the performance and the rhythms, and the songs that accompanied drumming were typically in African languages. Africans could have been performing a call to arms, a display of mourning, a musical prayer, or any other expression; Europeans had little grounds to differentiate between them.[49]

Indeed, music played a key role in some of the most well-known rebellions in the Americas. Perhaps most notably, enslaved people played drums and sang, using music to "call others to join the rising," in the Stono Rebellion in Charleston, South Carolina.[50] This rebellion, which occurred on September 9, 1739, has been identified as "the largest slave uprising in colonial America."[51] Although white South Carolinians were able to quickly band together and put down the rebellion, the loss of life and property destruction demonstrated the precarious hold that the colonists had over enslaved Africans and how quickly things could go awry in a society where Black people greatly outnumbered whites peoples.

As was often the case following a major slave rebellion in the Americas, the colonists immediately implemented new legislation after the Stono uprising in an effort to prevent future insurrections. Part of the Code prohibited "using or keeping of drums, horns, or other loud instruments, which may call together or give sign or notice to one another of their wicked designs and purposes."[52] Moreover, any master or overseer who permitted enslaved persons to "beat drums, blow horns, or use any other loud instruments" would be fined 10 pounds for each offense.[53]

Although we are not aware of any single rebellion in Brazil where the use of drums was so central and the uprising so impactful that it led directly to laws like those in South Carolina, there was a close relationship between slave rebellions and the bans that were passed against Black musical practices. João Reis explains that from 1807 onward, "Nagôs and Hausas [two African ethnic groups], together or separately, would organise over twenty conspiracies and revolts, some of them fought to the sound of war drums."[54] A few examples help illustrate how such associations sometimes led to arguments for suppression of African drumming.

In 1814, merchants and citizens of Bahia sent a petition to the prince regent, Dom João. Concerned about the unusually high number of slave rebellions in Salvador and surrounding regions, they called upon the government to control Africans through "fear and rigorous punishment." The petitioners lamented that the batuques had been permitted to take place (even though they were prohibited by law), and that Africans had been allowed to play musical instruments and gather together for public ceremonies and "pageantry." They averred "it is since all this has been permitted that we have witnessed most of the acts of violence and disobedience."[55] The petitioners theorized that "failure to establish firm principles spoils these people."[56]

Several years later, in 1822, the city of Cachoeira (located in a famous and historically significant area in the interior of Bahia state) issued emergency provisions to prevent slave rebellions. Among these, they dispatched "escorts of armed militiamen" to regions with large populations of enslaved people to prohibit Africans from meeting under the "pretext" of playing atabaques (here spelled "autabaquis").[57] Like those implemented in South Carolina after the Stono Rebellion, Rachel Harding explains that such prohibitions on "batuques and other dance-drum gatherings" were part

> of a larger corpus of legislation and custom which limited the mobility of slaves and freed people, restricted their residential options, delimited hours of appropriate presence in commercial establishments, constrained employment and political participation for libertos, and otherwise sought to contain black movement within acceptable physical, cultural, political and psychic boundaries.[58]

João Reis agrees, explaining that, following Brazil's independence from Portugal (1822–1823), "local authorities tried to improve control over the slave population through provincial laws and municipal ordinances including the prohibition of batuques and other forms of black revelry 'everywhere and at any time.'"[59] A major slave uprising in Bahia in 1835 solidified these fears, and Reis contends that at the time of that rebellion "any batuque was largely interpreted as an attempt against slavery."[60]

In some cases, additional laws against African music and dance were passed after emancipation in Brazil. For instance, in 1889, just one year after the abolition of slavery, Rio imposed a law banning batuques. Five years later, in 1904, Salvador passed a similar statute.[61] Historian Marc Hertzman explains that there were a "handful" of prohibitions on instruments, styles/genres of music, or the hours that music could be played; however, African music and dance were not broadly prohibited by the Brazilian penal code.[62] Furthermore, at least in Rio de Janeiro, where Hertzman conducted archival research, Black musicians were not prosecuted using vagrancy laws (which were a popular post-emancipation legal tool in many parts of the Americas to arrest Black people for engaging in activities or professions that were regarded as illegitimate and/or immoral).[63] Nevertheless, he argues, laws and legal records don't capture lived experiences, and Black musicians may have been informally targeted and harassed by the authorities in the late nineteenth and early twentieth centuries despite a lack of documentation.

PROHIBITIONS OF AFRICAN-DERIVED RELIGIONS DURING SLAVERY

In the history of the Americas, African-derived religions were also often restricted or outright prohibited. Similar to the limitations on drumming, these regulations were typically connected to fears about slave rebellions. At times, colonists broadly prohibited spiritual gatherings or the practice of an entire religion; in other cases, they barred certain practices that religious leaders performed during rebellions such as the use of poisons, oaths, and charms. In Catholic colonies, unorthodox religious practices – including African ones – could be handled as cases of "witchcraft" by the tribunals of the Inquisition. In other colonies, they were often prosecuted by slave courts or other tribunals.

To a certain extent, one can see these concerns and restrictions in Brazil. According to Dain Borges, non-Catholic spiritual practices (which could be categorized as "superstitions" or "witchcraft") were criminalized in the Portuguese Philippine Code (which applied to Brazil) from 1603 to 1830. Before the Portuguese Inquisition was abolished in 1821, it could (and did) hear cases of "witchcraft."[64] However, in 1824, Brazil's new constitution "proclaimed toleration of discreetly practiced non-Catholic religions; and the articles criminalizing witchcraft were omitted from Brazil's Criminal Code of 1830. Thus, during most of the Brazilian empire (1824–1889), there was no national criminal law against 'witchcraft.' "[65] Nevertheless, Afro-Brazilian religions were sometimes restricted using laws governing enslaved persons.

In the most basic sense, attendance at Candomblé rituals and ceremonies was sometimes regarded as disruptive to slave owners because time spent in religious spaces was time that enslaved people were not working.[66] Some of these enslaved persons left without permission of their masters and, for those undergoing initiation or other significant rituals, could be at the terreiro for months at a time.[67] Moreover, terreiros "became a major haven for runaway slaves, who sought them for religious obligations and other kinds of assistance, spiritual and secular."[68] Although Candomblé was rarely involved in actual uprisings,[69] slave owners also feared that religious gatherings could be "precursors to insurrection."[70]

Additionally, like other places in the Americas, enslaved persons in Brazil "frequently looked for religious specialists to obtain herbs and concoctions to pacify their masters and to enlist the services of gods in obtaining the slaves' freedom."[71] For example, Paul Johnson reports that a 1862 police report indicated that "Candomblé devotees often left their meetings with 'drinks and mixtures' to mollify their masters upon their return."[72] Therefore, some restrictions on African religions in Brazil resulted from slave owners' concerns about being poisoned.[73]

Despite various concerns about African religions, historians explain that one cannot speak of a blanket prohibition of them in Brazil. Johnson argues that in Brazil, African diaspora religions were "neither always nor absolutely prohibited by state authorities."[74]

Instead, each region of Brazil had its own local legislation governing enslaved peoples, and such legislation varied widely in the text and interpretation. None of these laws, according to Johnson, directly focused on enslaved peoples' religions; rather, they governed other activities that authorities believed could lead to rebellion. Perhaps the best example of this comes from the state of Bahia.

Rachel Harding identified 25 municipal and provincial laws in Salvador and the Recôncavo region from the period of 1807 to 1885 that barred Afro-Brazilians from gathering together.[75] Some of these would have been the laws prohibiting "batuques," like those described in the previous section. Others "created specific penalties for African funeral gatherings, quilombos, Candomblés, and 'disturbances'" by Black people.[76] Harding explains that these were the types of laws that were deployed when police raided terreiros.[77]

Similar regulations were implemented in other parts of Brazil. In the State (then Province) of Rio de Janeiro, a decree was issued in 1836 that, according to its title, placed restrictions on enslaved people, free Black people, and "other foreigners" for the purpose of avoiding slave rebellions.[78] One of the ordinances in this decree criminalized holding gatherings for dances or Candomblé in one's home or "in some other adjacent house" that included enslaved participants. Any person who held such a gathering would be sentenced to eight days in jail and fined R$30,000 (~ $6,000 USD) for the first offense; they would be sentenced to 30 days in jail and fined R$60,000 (~ $12,000 USD) for any subsequent violations. Enslaved people who were arrested at dances or Candomblé gatherings could be sentenced to up to 100 lashes.[79]

Even where a plethora of laws against Afro-Brazilian religion existed, they were not consistently enforced, and there were "simultaneous and alternative tendencies of repression and tolerance" of these religions.[80] Johnson argues that some of the leniency came from slave owners who, at the time, viewed their religious gatherings "as a useful technique for blurring sentiments of slave unity and focused efforts at rebellion."[81] Moreover, some local newspapers criticized police "suggest[ing] a lack of initiative or even complicity with the candomblés," asserting that there would be no ceremonies if the police did not allow them.[82] However, it is important to describe the impact of the policing of terreiros when it did take place.

Johnson describes the police invasion of a Jeje Candomblé terreiro in 1829 after a judge issued a mandate to interrupt a ceremony that had lasted for almost three days. He explains

> Sacred objects and money were confiscated, and 36 persons were taken prisoner. Eleven of the women were quickly released, as they were needed to do the laundry for their masters. The rest stood trial, during which a drum and the "vile instruments of their diabolical toys" (citation omitted) were destroyed in the presence of all in a demonstration of civic power.[83]

This was not an isolated occurrence. Harding reports that persons arrested in raids of Candomblé gatherings, especially religious leaders and enslaved people, were punished harshly, including lengthy terms of imprisonment and whipping.[84] Particularly in the case of African-born persons, some accused individuals were deported. Oddly, some persons would be conscripted to serve in the military or police. If forced to labor with the police for participating in Candomblé ceremonies, this might help explain the ambivalent response of police to terreiro communities.

In addition to the punishment of religious leaders and participants, "[a] variety of kinds of material objects related to Candomblé were identified in raids on Candomblé gatherings and in the homes of Africans. Many of the items were destroyed by police – some were broken, others burned."[85] Of particular importance for this study, "[d]rums and rattles (chocalhos) were among the items most commonly associated with raided Candomblé and the searched homes of Africans throughout the nineteenth century."[86]

HISTORY OF RELIGIOUS RACISM POST-EMANCIPATION

After emancipation, the proscription of African-derived religions continued – and indeed some might argue expanded – but the purported basis for these prohibitions shifted. Colonial authorities contended that African-derived religions posed a threat to the safety and morality of the population. In some cases, they argued that adepts of these religions were charlatans who preyed upon gullible people and promoted "superstitions." In other circumstances, colonial authorities in the Americas falsely claimed that devotees of African-derived religions engaged in barbarous rituals such as cannibalism and human sacrifice. Such denunciations of Black religious practices reflected Europeans' anxieties about the status of newly freed populations. Depictions of African-derived religions as harmful superstitions created a justification to keep Black people subjugated under white rule, to restrict their rights to vote and participate in government, and to limit further immigration of non-white people.

Throughout the Americas, police forces often raided Africana religious temples, arrested priests and other devotees, and seized sacred and musical instruments. Such raids reached their height between the last two decades of the nineteenth century and the middle of the twentieth century. They had a significant negative impact on Africana religious communities – reducing public ceremonies, promoting secrecy, and, sometimes, destroying entire communities.

Brazil was no exception to the hemisphere-wide concerns. At this time, when "progress and modernization were tied to 'whiteness'; backwardness and indolence to 'blackness,'"[87] Brazil, the recipient of 4.8 million (44%) of the 10.7 million enslaved Africans who landed in the Americas during the Atlantic slave trade,[88] had an uphill battle on its hands. Bahia in particular was seen as the epitome of barbarism with its large Black population. It was known to the rest of the nation as "a decaying provincial backwater."[89]

Countless examples show the relationship between this deeply negative perception of Bahia and prejudices against Afro-Brazilian religions and their sacred music. Mattijs van de Port describes that "a well-to-do citizen of Salvador wrote a letter to the editor of a local newspaper, urging the city authorities to tighten their grip on the organization of the city's carnival."[90] In this letter, the author cautioned that, with the approach of carnival, "the African drums are already preparing to tell the world once more about our low level of civilization, turning celebrations such as this one, so pleasant in other cities, into true candombles"[91] Similarly, an employee at the U.S. consulate told scholar Ruth Landes in the 1930s that "The blacks are always holding secret meetings, killing animals, dancing and beating drums in the jungle in the dead of night ... We'll never get anywhere as a nation until the temples are gone!"[92]

Brazil had to take drastic measures in the post-emancipation period to combat assumptions that its large Black population doomed the nation to barbarism. One method was that the government encouraged European immigration to Brazil, hoping that they would whiten the population.[93] Scholars have argued that this immigration plan was unsuccessful because those Europeans who arrived in Brazil did not settle in the predominantly Black areas in the northeast and shift the racial dynamics of the populations there.[94] Instead, they settled in the south and formed communities far from the areas where Afro-Brazilians were/are concentrated.

In addition to trying to physically whiten the population, the government also engaged in cultural whitening efforts. The latter process involved discouraging, restricting, or outright prohibiting African cultural practices such as capoeira, samba, and African clothing styles and street food vendors.[95] Among the prohibited practices, "the emerging tradition of black drum bands called afoxes, who during carnival would take their drums to the streets, and sing the chants of their terreiros, was to be prohibited (which in fact it was, from 1905 well into the 1930s...)."[96]

Perhaps most significantly, in 1890, the federal government introduced three new articles to the penal code that created a basis for persecuting African diaspora religions.[97] The first of these, Article 156, limited the practice of medicine (including dentistry, pharmacy, homeopathy, dosimetry, hypnotism or "animal magnetism") to individuals licensed by the government.[98] The second of these, Article 157, barred any person from using talismans, or practicing spiritism, "magic," or fortune telling.[99] The code specifically proscribed these practices when used to cure disease, induce feelings of hate or love, or "fascinate and subjugate public" belief or credulity.[100] The third article,

158, barred any person from working as a faith healer or *curandeiro*, including administering or prescribing any cures.[101] The penalties for these offenses ranged from one to six months' imprisonment and could also include a fine of up to 500,000 reais (~$100,000 USD). If any person died after receiving treatment by a faith healer, the term of imprisonment increased dramatically to six to 24 years. These new provisions of the penal code subjected Afro-Brazilian religious communities "to a continuous process of regulation through police investigations and criminal proceedings."[102]

Thirty years later, Decree 3987 of January 2, 1920, wreaked further havoc on these communities by creating "a health or sanitary police force" that had the right to invade any private or public building to address matters of public health. This police force regularly raided Afro-Brazilian terreiros in the 1920s to investigate purported threats to public health.[103] Such twentieth-century policing laid the foundations for recent harassment of these same communities and the depiction of drumming, singing, and other sounds emanating from religious temples as a form of pollution or contamination that threatens public health. Describing the climate in Salvador in the 1920s, Miguel Alonso and Norman Smith explain:

> authorities waged a merciless and brutal campaign of repression against certain segments of Salvador's Candomblé practitioners. Temples were raided, religious altars and icons destroyed or confiscated, and many spiritual leaders became more and more accustomed to the inside of a jail cell. All the while the police continued to be guided to their targets by a seemingly endless flow of newspaper accounts; letters to the editor; and citizen complaints giving names, addresses, and the specific violations of law allegedly committed by the temples.[104]

Scholars have argued that Afro-Brazilian religious communities engaged in a variety of techniques to avoid persecution in the early twentieth century. Those terreiros located in Salvador moved to other areas of the state, such as Cachoeira, or to other states, such as Alagoas, Rio de Janeiro, or Recife.[105] Particularly in Salvador, persecution by the police also led Candomblé communities to flee to the peripheral areas of the city where they could avoid constant harassment and also "take advantage of the abundant natural resources that play important roles in the religion."[106] This tactic seems to have been effective. Angela Lühning cites newspapers from the 1920s that discuss patrols "in which the mounted police passed through different neighborhoods, looking for candomblés, letting themselves be guided by the sound of the atabaques, often getting lost in the bush for hours, due to the difficult access of many candomblés."[107]

Although movement to peripheral areas made Candomblé communities more difficult to locate, scholars have contended that urban flight was exactly what the government wanted Afro-Brazilian religious communities to do. If they could not completely eradicate these religions, they could at least try to "sanitize" urban areas by using policing to move these religious communities (and other Black organizations or businesses) to the outskirts of the cities.[108]

Scholars also contend that bestowing a now-common religious title, "Ogan," emerged as a strategy to combat persecution.[109] Alonso and Smith explain that especially the most influential Candomblé leaders (many of whom were women)

> began the process of employing and redefining a multilayered auxiliary religious role known as the Ogan. The Ogan is a religious position allowing men to perform vital ritualistic functions. But there existed at the time a second class of Ogans whose title was more honorific than spiritual, and signaled their commitment toward the physical protection and financial support of the temple to which they were attached.[110]

Religious leaders would strategically incorporate powerful persons into their temple as Ogans to discourage government harassment. These might include politically influential persons such as senators, federal ministers, and police chiefs or even prominent scholarly researchers.[111]

After the first three decades of the twentieth century, things began to change. In the 1930s and 1940s, more researchers began to study

Afro-Brazilian religions.[112] Additionally, although the state governments varied in their approached to Afro-Brazilian religions, during the dictatorship of Getúlio Vargas (1930–1945), the federal government began to soften its position against them and recognize the potential economic and social benefits of embracing Brazil's African heritage and encouraging miscegenation (racial mixing).[113] These shifts corresponded with movements throughout the Americas to celebrate (and in some cases appropriate) African culture and religions as part of a nation's folklore.[114]

In 1940, Brazil implemented a new penal code that contained sections that were reminiscent of those in the penal code of 50 years prior but had some significant differences. This penal code, which went into effect in 1942 and remains in effect today, maintains three articles that could apply to the practice of Afro-Brazilian religions. The illegal practice of medicine remains proscribed, but it no longer lists homeopathy, dosimetry, hypnotism, or "animal magnetism" as types of legally regulated "medicine." Former Article 157, now numbered 283, prohibits "charlatanism," which is defined as "Inculcat[ing] or announc[ing] healing by secret or infallible means." The third continues to proscribe "curandeirismo," which is vaguely defined as "prescribing, ministering or habitually applying any substance," "using gestures, words or any other means," or "making diagnoses." The penalty for "charlatanism" is imprisonment for up to one year and for "curandeirismo" is imprisonment for up to two years.[115]

Scholars have argued that these changes to the 1940 penal code were the result of different Afro-Brazilian religious communities lobbying and strategizing to obtain official recognition and to demonstrate that their beliefs and practices did not fall within the vague proscriptions in the 1890 penal code. One of the main disputes in this process was over the prohibition of "spiritism" in Article 157 of the 1890 code. Umbanda communities argued that there were distinct forms of spiritism in Brazil – the "high spiritism" practiced in Umbanda terreiros and "low spiritism" practiced by Candomblé and Macumba[116] communities. As this terminology suggests, Umbanda adepts argued that there was a hierarchy between these forms of spiritism. They contended that high spiritism should be recognized as a religion because it focused on "the cultivation of 'higher' spirits through techniques of "concentration" rather than African rituals."[117] They argued that low spiritism involved the veneration of "baser" spirits and more "primitive" African practices such as "drumming and animal sacrifice."[118] Low spiritism, Umbanda adepts asserted, should be surveilled by the authorities.[119] For this reason, the atabaques were excised from official Umbanda practice in the 1920s.[120]

Here we also see the origins of a controversy about animal sacrifice that has continued until the present day. Numerous religions (Islam, Judaism, Hinduism, etc.) include some form of the ritual slaughter of animals (whether for food preparation or ceremonial purposes). Yet, authorities throughout the Americas have long differentiated "animal sacrifice" as performed by devotees of Africana religions from the ritual slaughter of animals as performed by Abrahamic religions. In Afro-Brazilian religious ceremonies, the meat is typically consumed following a sacrifice. However, unlike Abrahamic religions that perform ritual slaughter to cleanse the meat to make it pure or safe for human consumption, the primary purpose of this ceremony in Africana religions is the *sacrifice* – to offer the blood and energy of the animal to ancestors, spirits, or divinities. In certain circumstances, such as sacrifices to cleanse a person, the meat may not be consumed. Although this distinction means little in practical terms regarding concerns about the regulation of health, safety, and animal welfare that are often raised by opponents, this difference has frequently been used to vilify and persecute Africana religions. This will be discussed in greater detail in Chapter 2.

Candomblé devotees did not merely accept these distinctions passively. While Umbanda adepts tried to protect their faith by claiming proximity to European religions and proclaiming their practices more "evolved," Candomblé communities sought legitimacy by arguing the opposite. Scholars explain that "An emerging nationalist imaginary – developed by Brazil's intellectual and artistic vanguard in the 1920s, and institutionalized under the populist Vargas regime in the 1930s – had sought to redefine Brazil as the nation of the white, Indian, and black races."[121] During this time period, Candomblé was still depicted as barbaric and primitive, but it also began to be described as mystical and magical – a symbol of Brazil's unique African heritage.[122] As J. Lorand Matory extensively documents, this corresponded with a movement in which some Candomblé communities engaged in campaigns to "purify" their religion by ridding them of non-African components.[123] This movement involved trans-Atlantic commerce and travel between Brazil and the African continent, with certain Candomblé communities claiming legitimacy based on their "purely African" goods and rituals. Matory describes a variety of factors that drove the movement to "purify" Candomblé; however, scholars have noted that one significant result was their ability to capitalize on this movement to recognize Afro-Brazilian culture and declare that they should be protected because of their "pure" African heritage.[124] Beginning in the mid-1930s, Candomblé leaders "negotiated with governors and police chiefs to form boards of cult leaders and doctors that would certify traditional centers as authentic folkloric religions, exempting them from the persecution."[125] Ultimately, some scholars would join in these debates, arguing in favor of the recognition of Nagô Candomblé and Afro-Brazilian religions that incorporated beliefs and practices from European, Indigenous, or other influences.[126]

Two important trends arose from Umbanda and Candomblé devotees' competing claims for legal recognition. The first was the vilification of certain African-derived practices – such as drumming and animal sacrifice – as more "primitive," and thus prosecutable. This argument gained more traction in Rio de Janeiro and in Southern Brazil, where Umbanda flourished and their arguments about low versus high spiritism were more accepted. One can see from the recent efforts to criminalize these practices in southern states like Rio Grande do Sul and Santa Catarina that these debates continue to have an impact on religious freedom. This is discussed further in Chapter 2.

The second significant trend that resulted from these disputes is the evolution of the word *macumba*. The origins of the term are somewhat obscure. One of the early uses of *macumba* in Brazil is that it was the name given to a Brazilian percussion instrument of African origin. The instrument known as *macumba* is a hollow gourd with a serrated body that is struck or pulled against to produce a rhythmic scratching sound, similar to the guiro from salsa music and the guira from merengue. It is similar to a more commonly known Brazilian instrument called reco reco.[127] Macumba is also said to be the name of a drum. Over time, *macumba* and *macumbeiro* (players of the instrument or people associated with its music) came to be used in reference to Afro-Brazilian religious practices, especially music and offerings. Historically, Macumba was most frequently used to describe Afro-Brazilian religions of Bantu (West Central African) origin.[128]

As noted previously, in the early twentieth century, both Umbanda and Candomblé adepts used Macumba as an example of the antithesis of legitimate religion – Umbanda adherents denigrated Macumba as a form of "low spiritism" and Candomblé devotees dismissed Macumba as syncretic or "impure." Therefore, in common parlance, Macumba came to represent unlawful and illegitimate beliefs and practices. Particularly after spiritism was removed from the 1940 penal code, persons prosecuted for "charlatanism" were designated as *macumbeiros* or *macumbeiras* – practitioners of Macumba.[129]

Today, Macumba shares many similarities to the term "Voodoo" in North America.[130] It is employed by non-devotees to denigrate, harass, and stereotype Afro-Brazilian religions. In popular usage, it represents assumptions about black magic, superstition, and the worship of "primitive" or evil spirits.[131] It carries the stigma of the decades of persecution of Afro-Brazilian religions and often indicates that the person using the term is referring to something that they regard as the opposite of "religion." When people commit acts of discrimination and violence against Afro-Brazilian religions, they frequently utter the word *macumba* or *macumbeiro/a* in the process.

However, like Voodoo, Macumba is still the name for a religion of African origin. Additionally, devotees of other Afro-Brazilian religions, including Candomblé, sometimes informally refer to themselves as *macumbeiros* and to their religion as "Macumba."[132] For example, some adepts of Candomblé will say, "Vou pra macumba" (I'm going to a macumba) when they are on their way to a ceremony. This is a common trend in African diaspora religious communities – adepts will internally use and reclaim terms that were once used to denigrate them.

CONCLUSION

By the 1950s, Candomblé had become a staple of Bahian tourism. Still depicted as barbaric, guidebooks encouraged visitors to come witness its supposedly primitive beauty.[133] As we discuss further in Chapter 3, the African roots that the government once sought to eradicate became a vital part of the tourism industry. Paradoxically, during this same time, the actual practice of Afro-Brazilian religions remained restricted in Bahia and other parts of the nation. Until 1976, Candomblé communities in Bahia were required to obtain a "license" to hold religious ceremonies, which was registered with the police station.[134] Many of our interlocutors reflected on this period, mentioning how they or their ancestors had to navigate these discriminatory licensing processes and the harassment that could accompany them. It is clear that this history remains fresh in the minds of Afro-Brazilian religious communities today.

However, the cases and controversies introduced in this chapter are not just designed to explain the impact of memories of historical discrimination. They should be understood to form the foundation for the modern-day discrimination against Afro-Brazilian sacred music and other forms of religious racism that are the focus of this book. The reader should consider how the drums, first feared for their ability to facilitate war and rebellions against Europeans, remain under siege. They should reflect on how narratives about public health and morality, which were used to suppress both African musical practices and African-derived religions, continue to feature in present-day cases and controversies. Perhaps most significantly, one should consider whether recent cases of religious racism against Afro-Brazilian sacred music are having the catastrophic impact of nineteenth- and twentieth-century police raids and repressions.

CHAPTER 2

Moving Through Brazil: From Bahia to Rio Grande do Sul

Brazil is a vast country composed of more than 213 million people who reside in a territory comprising approximately 8.5 million square kilometers, which is divided into 26 states and a federal district. In terms of both population and land mass, it is one of the ten largest countries in the world. Therefore, one cannot talk about the nation as a monolithic place; there are distinct characteristics to each city, state, and region that help to inform some of the problems with religious racism and discrimination against sacred music.

In this chapter, we provide some background information about several different areas in Brazil, primarily through stories about the places where we spent the most time conducting our research. The goal of this chapter is threefold: to provide introductory information about Brazil for readers who might have little familiarity with the country, to describe our research methods in greater detail, and to discuss some aspects of Brazilian society that we believe are critical to understanding discrimination and violence against Afro-Brazilian religious communities. We will begin with the parts of Brazil where we spent the most time and end with some background information about one of the states where we had hoped to conduct research but time constraints and pandemic-era travel limitations prevented us from going.

BAHIA

Of all the states in Brazil, we have spent the most time in the state of Bahia – both for the purposes of this project and in our other research trips to Brazil. Bahia is composed of more than 564 million square kilometers of land in the northeast region of Brazil, along the Atlantic ocean. As of the 2010 census, the State of Bahia was home to slightly more than 14 million people; it is the fourth most populous state in Brazil.[1] Of these 14 million habitants, 10.7 million (76%) self-identified as Afro-Brazilian (brown or Black).[2]

The Portuguese first arrived in Brazil on April 22, 1500, in an area that would become known as Porto Seguro in the southern region of what is now Bahia state. The following year, in 1501, the Portuguese arrived in an area that they baptized the Bay of All Saints, at the heart of what would later become the city of Salvador.[3] This region was inhabited by the Tupinambá people; however, over the following decades, more Portuguese arrived and began to colonize the area. As part of the process of colonizing the land and establishing agricultural enterprises, enslaved Africans were brought to Bahia as well. By the end of the sixteenth century, Salvador became one of the principal cities of the Americas and the capital of Brazil. It would remain so until the mid-eighteenth century, when the capital was transferred to Rio de Janeiro. Salvador was the wealthiest and largest city in Brazil until the early nineteenth century.

Of the 10.7 million enslaved Africans who disembarked in the Americas during the Atlantic slave trade, more than 1.5 million arrived in Bahia.[4] Today, Salvador is often referred to as an "African city in the Americas" and has the second largest population of people of African descent in the world (after Lagos, Nigeria). In 2010, the official population of Salvador was 2,675,656 people.[5] It is the third most populous city in Brazil after São Paulo and Rio de Janeiro. In the 2010 census, 2,120,095 people (79.2%) self-identified as Afro-Brazilian (brown or Black).[6]

Although the state of Bahia is often celebrated for its African roots, merely 94,129 people (0.6% of the population) self-identified as adherents of Candomblé, Umbanda, or other Afro-Brazilian religions in the 2010 census.[7] The majority of these, 55,318 people, reside in the city of Salvador (2% of the city's population; 58.7% of devotees of Afro-Brazilian religions in Bahia state).[8] Adherents of Afro-Brazilian religions often say these statistics likely underestimate the actual figures because many people don't want to disclose their religious affiliation on the census or because they participate in Afro-Brazilian religious ceremonies but are not official, initiated members. Even accounting for these factors, it seems fair to estimate that less than 10% of the population of Salvador and 5% of the population of Bahia are affiliated with Afro-Brazilian religions. Some adepts of these religions are white, but census data suggests that nearly 90% are brown or Black.[9]

Although the people who openly claim to be adherents of Afro-Brazilian religions represent a small portion of the population of Bahia, these religions (especially Candomblé) form a significant part of public representations and the imagined culture of the state. Visitors to the most famous parts of the state encounter countless images of Candomblé. These symbols and other icons of Afro-Brazilian culture are perhaps most prevalent in Pelourinho (Figure 1) and Mercado Modelo (Figure 4), in the historic center of Salvador. There, in the precise areas where enslaved persons once disembarked from the Middle Passage as chattel, were quarantined and inspected, sold, and publicly whipped, today tourists purchase t-shirts, paintings, and statues of Candomblé orixás. Some shops even sell unconsecrated versions of the sacred necklaces (*ilekes*) worn by devotees, marketing these representations of the power and protection of the orixás as some kind of costume jewelry (Figure 5). In plazas and on many street corners, women dressed in traditional Candomblé attire cook and sell a popular street food called *acarajé*.[10] These spaces, including the images of African-derived religions, are marketed to Brazilian and foreign tourists as representative of the city of Salvador and the state of Bahia.

As we will discuss in greater detail in Chapter 3, throughout the city of Salvador, there are various busts, statues, and parks that feature representations of Afro-Brazilian religions. Although similar public representations exist in various parts of the country, they appear to be

Figure 1: Pelourinho

Figure 2: Women dressed in Candomblé attire interacting with tourists in Pelourinho

more common in Salvador than any other city. As we will also discuss further in Chapter 3, the state of Bahia also has the greatest concentration of Candomblé terreiros that have been declared part of the cultural patrimony of the nation. Additionally, there is an annual festival in Salvador in the neighborhood of Rio Vermelho, honoring Iemanjá

FIGURE 3: Statue of Zumbi and vendor stalls in Pelourinho

(an orixá). This festival is one of the largest celebrations in the city and draws thousands of locals and tourists.

Based on this background information, it should not be difficult to imagine why we chose to devote much of our time to conducting research in Bahia, especially in the city of Salvador. After witnessing all these public celebrations of Afro-Brazilian religiosity and reading

FIGURE 4: Aerial view of Mercado Modelo

FIGURE 5: Shops selling ilekes, drums, and other goods in Mercado Modelo

FIGURE 6: Rio Vermelho, site of the annual Iemanjá festival

scholarship about the centrality of African heritage, including religions, to the tourist representations of this part of Brazil, we wanted to understand how noise complaints could be part of a society that is so reliant upon the visibility of these religions.

We were also drawn to this state by the data on religious racism in Brazil. A study carried out by the International Commission to Combat Religious Racism, first released in 2019 and updated in 2022, reveals that Bahia is one of the most common sites of reports of religious racism in the country, second only to Rio de Janeiro.[11] Combined, the states of Bahia and Rio de Janeiro represent nearly half of all the cases documented in the ICCRR's study.

RIO DE JANEIRO

We also spent a significant amount of time in Rio de Janeiro (which is the name of both a city and a state in southeastern Brazil). There are several factors that influenced this decision to conduct research in Rio. First of all, as the most visited tourist area and the most internationally famous part of the country, it is an obvious choice. Brazil is known for the beaches of Copacabana and Ipanema, which are located in the south zone of the city of Rio de Janeiro, and the enormous Christ-the-Redeemer statue that towers over the city. Carnaval in Rio is arguably the most famous of such celebrations in the world. Rio de Janeiro has hosted some of the world's largest sporting events, including the Pan American Games in 2007, the FIFA World Cup in 2014, and the Olympics in 2016. Especially with African cultural heritage like samba and capoeira playing such an important role in public images of Brazil, we wanted to explore the paradoxical role of noise complaints in the "marvelous city" (as Rio is known) and surrounding areas.

We also chose Rio as a research site because of the historical significance of the city and state. The Portuguese arrived in Rio in 1502, just two years after they landed in the area that is now the state of Bahia. In the mid-eighteenth century, after gold and diamonds were discovered to the north of Rio de Janeiro in the area that is now the state of Minas Gerais, Rio's Guanabara Bay became an important port. In 1763, the Portuguese transferred the administrative capital from Salvador to Rio de Janeiro. It would remain there until 1960 when a new city, Brasília, was built to serve as the capital.

Rio is also significant because of its involvement in the Atlantic slave trade. Valongo Wharf is located in the port region of Rio de Janeiro (Figure 7). Construction started in 1811 and before the Atlantic slave trade ended later that century, an estimated 900,000 enslaved Africans disembarked at Valongo.[12] To put this in perspective, this accounts for 18.5% of all enslaved Africans who landed in Brazil and 8.4% of all enslaved people who landed in the Americas.[13] The wharf was later covered over by other structures but was excavated in 2011. Valongo Wharf was recognized by the federal government as a cultural heritage site in 2012 and protected by UNESCO in 2017. The latter lauds the site as "the globally most significant remains of a landing point of enslaved Africans in the Americas."[14]

FIGURE 7: Valongo Wharf

Despite Valongo wharf's undeniable historical significance and its excavation more than a decade ago, this site remains in relative obscurity in Rio. Located only one kilometer from Rio's acclaimed Museu do Amanhã (Museum of Tomorrow), Valongo was inexplicably left out of the development of the port area in preparation for the Olympic games in 2016. In a 2017 episode of NPR's All Things Considered, Giovanni Harvey, who helped apply for UNESCO recognition of the site, explained that the recognition was important for racial justice in Brazil because it encourages the difficult process of "remembering something many people want to forget."[15] NPR reporter Catherine Osborn emphasized that the government of Rio had provided $55 million to fund the new Museum of Tomorrow but did not lead tourists to the neighboring Valongo Wharf or a nearby cemetery for enslaved Africans who died during the middle passage.

Sandwiched between Valongo Wharf and the Museu do Amanhã lies a historically significant neighborhood known as "Little Africa" (Figure 8). This is the area where some of the region's first Candomblé communities were located in the late nineteenth and early twentieth centuries (Figure 9). It is also where the legendary Tia Ciata resided. Tia Ciata's home is often mentioned as one of the most important locations where samba music evolved into new forms in early twentieth-century Rio.

Like Valongo Wharf, this area lacks the financial support and tourism infrastructure that the government provided for the new museums and marketplaces in the port region. There are a few worn plaques (almost exclusively in Portuguese) that provide some facts about this pivotal area, but one would have to know that this area existed to even attempt a self-guided tour. One should consider this in contrast to Salvador, where Pelourinho, the historic center of the city, is considered a must-see attraction for anyone who visits. Pelourinho houses a residential neighborhood, the Federal University of Bahia's Afro-Brazilian Museum, the Afro-Brazilian Cultural Museum (Museu Cultural Afro Brasileiro), shops, bars, restaurants, performance venues, and so on. In addition to shopping, at some point visitors will usually hear about the area's history as the place where

FIGURE 8: Murals in Little Africa, Rio de Janeiro

enslaved Africans disembarked, were quarantined, often beaten, and eventually sold. Valongo Wharf and Little Africa highlight the paradox of how important the city of Rio de Janeiro is to Afro-Brazilian history and culture but how invisible African presence is in the public sphere.

Rio de Janeiro state, home to nearly 16 million people at the time of the 2010 census, is the third largest state in the country (after São Paulo and Minas Gerais). Of these nearly 16 million people, 7.5 million (47.4%) identify as white and 8.3 million (51.7%) as Afro-Brazilian (brown or Black).[16] These statistics are almost identical to national averages (47.5% white; 50.9% Afro-Brazilian) but are quite distinct from Bahia, where 76% of the population is Afro-Brazilian. At the time of the 2010 census, nearly 4.7 million people self-identified as Evangelical, nearly 7.4 million as Catholic, almost 2.5 million as "without religion," and 283,566 as devotees of Afro-Brazilian religions.[17] There are a few notable things about these statistics that help further illustrate why we selected Rio as a research site.

FIGURE 9: Historic street where early terreiros were reportedly located in Rio de Janeiro

First, unlike Bahia, where Candomblé devotees outnumber Umbanda adepts by more than six to one (nearly ten to one in the city of Salvador), the number of Umbanda devotees in Rio is significantly higher than the number of adherents of Candomblé. Additionally, a larger percentage of the population reports that they belong to both Umbanda and Candomblé than just one or the other.

FIGURE 10: Shrine to Afro-Brazilian religious entity Ze Pilintra, hidden behind the famous Lapa arches in Rio de Janeiro

The relative popularity of Umbanda is likely attributed to the central role that Rio de Janeiro played in the development of this religion. Zélio Fernandino de Moraes is considered to be the founder of Umbanda. He was born in 1891 in São Gonçalo, a city located in the eastern part of the state Rio de Janeiro, across the bay from Ilha do Governador. In 1908, Moraes was in a session with the Spiritist Federation of Rio de Janeiro at his residence in São Gonçalo when he manifested an entity known as Caboclo das Sete Encruzilhadas for the first time.[18] Based on this experience, the next day he founded Tenda Espírita Nossa Senhora da Piedade, the first Umbanda temple. In the mid-1950s, the temple moved to Cachoeiras de Macacu in the peripheral northeastern region of the state. The spiritual descendants of Moraes are still running the temple in this location today.

The second significant aspect of the religious makeup of Rio is the popularity of Evangelical Christianity. Nationwide, approximately 22% percent of the population identifies as Evangelical. In Rio, nearly

30% of the population claims affiliation with this religion. Chapter 5 will explore how Evangelicals, especially drug traffickers who have converted to extremist sects of Neo-Pentecostalism, are systematically carrying out acts of discrimination and violence against Afro-Brazilian religious communities.

Third, in Bahia, considered one of the main birthplaces of Afro-Brazilian culture, only 94,129 people (0.6 % of the state population) self-identified as devotees of Afro-Brazilian religions. Therefore, the state of Rio de Janeiro is home to more than three times the number of devotees of Afro-Brazilian religions than Bahia. This is not only because of Rio's slightly larger population (~16 million) relative to Bahia (~14 million). Devotees of Afro-Brazilian religions also represent a greater percentage of the state population in Rio (1.77%). In fact, it appears that Rio is (officially) home to more adepts of Afro-Brazilian religions than any other state, and it has one of the largest percentages of its population to self-identify as devotees of Afro-Brazilian religions. Yet, unlike Bahia, where statues, monuments, and other sites celebrate this religious heritage, public recognitions of Afro-Brazilian religions are rare and less visible in Rio.

This brings up an interesting and perhaps important contrast between the two states. While it is relatively easy to trace the public presence of Candomblé in Bahia through the histories of its oldest and best known terreiros, the history of Afro-Brazilian religions in Rio follows a different trajectory. Despite the existence of Candomblé terreiros dating back to at least the nineteenth century, these temples do not appear to have become the center of Black communities and are struggling to even be recognized as historic landmarks. This is somewhat curious given the history of public worship in Rio.

The mid-twentieth century is considered a kind of golden age for Candomblé in Rio, characterized by celebrations (including drumming) frequented by working-class Black people as well as middle- and upper-class mixed-race and white people.[19] Scholars have argued that newspapers and other historical sources document devotees of Afro-Brazilian religions making offerings around the state, in areas such as Gloria, Russel, Estacio, Maracaná, Ajuda, Santa Luzia, and Russel.[20]

In the 1940s, there is also the first mention of Afro-Brazilian religious communities holding end of the year celebrations and making offerings to the orixá Iemanjá on the tourist beaches of Copacabana.[21] In the 1950s, the references to Iemanjá festivals and offerings in urban public areas increased.[22] For reasons that go beyond the scope of this book and our scholarly expertise, between the mid-twentieth century and the present, Rio evolved to its present state, where the lack of visibility of Afro-Brazilian religions (historic landmarks, monuments, etc.) starkly contrasts with official census information documenting it as home to the highest percentage of devotees.

All of these factors – the notoriety of Rio de Janeiro; its historical significance as the second capital, the largest slave port, and the founding site of Umbanda; the prevalence of public worship in the twentieth century and the high numbers of devotees today – all contribute to the centrality of this state as a research site. Rio also has the unfortunate distinction of being the state with the largest number of cases of religious racism in the ICCRR 2022 report. Largely because of harassment and violence committed by Evangelical drug traffickers (discussed in Chapter 5), Rio represents nearly one-third of the cases in the report. Furthermore, Rio de Janeiro is also a site of rampant police violence. As we discuss in Chapter 6, such violence is both a form of religious racism and a reason why devotees have difficulty trusting authorities to help combat the discrimination and violence that they experience.

BRASÍLIA

We also conducted field research in the city of Brasília and the surrounding areas of the Federal District. Brasília is a city of around 2.5 million people (at the time of the last census) in the central-west region of the country. It is completely surrounded by the state of Goiás, near the border with Minas Gerais. Since 1960, it has been the capital city of Brazil and the seat of government of the Federal District. Its size and centrality to government alone made Brasília an ideal research site for our project. However, there are other significant distinctions that increased our interest in conducting research there.

In the previously mentioned ICCRR report, Brasília had the fourth highest rates of cases of religious racism, following Rio de Janeiro, Bahia, and São Paulo. Many of these were connected to two recent problems: a string of at least 13 cases of arson of terreiros that took place in between May and November of 2015[23] and attacks against statues of the orixás in Praça dos Orixás on the shore of Lake Paranoá. The arson cases led to the creation of a special police force – DECRIN – that is designed to handle bias-motivated crimes. The attacks against the statues, which have included severing the limbs of the orixás and setting them on fire, among other things, demonstrate the tensions about the visibility of Afro-Brazilian religions in the city. During our visit, we focused our research on trying to learn more about whether noise complaints accompanied these violent challenges to the presence of Afro-Brazilian religions and on understanding the relationship between Afro-Brazilian religions and the police, including DECRIN.

FIGURE 11: Lake Paranoá and Plaza of the Orixás

FIGURE 12: Cachaça, palm oil, and salt for Exu in Plaza of the Orixás

FIGURE 13: Offerings for Iemanjá in Plaza of the Orixás

FIGURE 14: Statue of Iemanjá in Plaza of the Orixás

During our time in Brasília, we were able to visit Lake Paranoá and learn about the attacks against the orixá statues and efforts to repair them.

We also had the opportunity to meet with the staff at DECRIN and interview the leadership at their offices. We were able to speak with several devotees who were central in lobbying for the creation of DECRIN and who continue to communicate with the special police forces about combating religious racism. Our research took us to both the central areas of Brasília and the surrounding Federal District. Like most other places, we were struck by the diversity of circumstances of the communities. Some, especially the older terreiros, were located in urban areas very close to their neighbors. Others were located in the countryside with acres of space to carry out their ceremonies.

ALAGOAS

We also visited Alagoas, a small state in northeastern Brazil that has profound significance in Afro-Brazilian history. Our decision to conduct research in Alagoas was fueled largely by two historical moments. The first historical moment was a story of power and resistance. We visited a small town named União dos Palmares, which takes its name from the great Quilombo dos Palmares, which developed from around the turn of the seventeenth century and thrived until its destruction at the hands of Portuguese forces in 1694. The Quilombo consisted of a series of settlements that may have housed as many as 20,000 people, many of whom were likely Bantu-speaking people from the areas that are now Angola and the Congo.[24] It became famous for being one of the longest lasting and largest quilombos, and for repeatedly defending itself against attempted Portuguese invasions. The quilombo and its last chief/renowned military general, Zumbi, are honored as powerful symbols in Afro-Brazilian history. Today, one of the most important federal holidays for Afro-Brazilians, the National Day of Black Consciousness, is celebrated on November 20, the anniversary of Zumbi's death.

While we were in Alagoas, we had the opportunity to visit the quilombo itself, which lies on a plateau at the top of an incredibly steep incline. Its difficult-to-access location likely contributed to the quilombo's success. There we saw restored versions of grain crushing machinery used to make food. We observed giant trees wrapped with fabric and

FIGURE 15: Statues of Zumbi and other leaders at the entrance of Quilombo dos Palmares

surrounded by calabashes with offerings, fruit, and other things for the ancestors and spirits (Figure 16). We saw the beautiful types of structures where quilombo residents resided and held meetings (Figure 17).

The most powerful moment was when we walked down to the river where the community, including legendary figures like even Zumbi himself, must have bathed. We felt the gazes of ancestors watching us through the thick forest brush. At a certain point down by the riverside, we were overcome by a powerful ancestral energy of resistance that was both somber and joyful. A member of our group, community organizer and sambista Igbonan Rocha, sang a composition for Zumbi that moved us all to tears, his voice cast over the water like a net.

The other reason for visiting Alagoas is as disturbing as the quilombo was powerful. As mentioned in the previous chapter, in the late nineteenth and early twentieth century, attempts to eradicate Afro-Brazilian religions could often be extremely oppressive and violent. One of the most infamous expressions of the power to

Figure 16: Quilombo dos Palmares tree

police Afro-Brazilian religions occurred on February 1–2, 1912, in the northeastern city of Maceió in the state of Alagoas. Typically referred to as "Quebra de Xangô" or the "Breaking of Xangô" (occasionally called "Operation Xangô" or "Xangô War"), this is perhaps the largest single attack on Africana religions in the history of Brazil.

FIGURE 17: Palmares Quilombo structures

FIGURE 18: Down by the lake in Quilombo dos Palmares

Studies have attributed this attack to a broader political controversy with the Malta family, who had widespread political power in the region in the early twentieth century. Euclides Malta was the governor of Alagoas until the end of 1911, when he suffered a massive electoral defeat.[25] Malta's opponents accused him of gaining and retaining power for so many years through affiliation with Afro-Brazilian religions and the use of "sorcery."[26] It is unclear whether or to what extent Malta was a devotee of an Afro-Brazilian religion; however, he is said to have authorized musical processions, celebrations, and festivities that people viewed as affiliated with Afro-Brazilian religious communities, giving the impression that he was lending his political support to these faiths.

The attack that became known as Quebra de Xangô was carried out by a group called the League of Republican[27] Combatants (Liga dos Republicanos Combatentes). The League was composed of Malta's opponents, including "a mix of civil guard and private militia created for the purpose of spreading terror among the supporters of the Republican Party of Alagoas."[28] The assault on Afro-Brazilian religions began at 10:30 pm on February 1, when a group of young men arrived at the home of one of the members of the League, which was also a site where a carnival group held rehearsals. Some of the demonstrators were members of the state police and had not been paid for some time so they took to the streets in protest, chanting "Tear the uniform." Later this became a different chant – "Break!"[29]

The rioters invaded a series of terreiros whose leaders were thought to have supported Malta, beginning with that of Chico Foguinho.[30] At the time that they invaded, the community was in the middle of a religious ceremony. The attackers physically assaulted devotees, some of whom were in the religious state referred to as being "mounted" or "ridden" by the spirits. Attackers seized sacred objects, including musical instruments, and threw them in a pile in the street, which they then set on fire.[31]

The League also assaulted the terreiro led by Tia Marcelina; this Candomblé house was said to have been frequented by Malta.[32] Shortly before midnight, the group of rioters, who at this point were estimated to number around 500 people, invaded the terreiro, which had recently ended its ceremonies. The attackers violently beat the adepts who stayed to defend their community. Tia Marcelina died a few days after the invasion from head injuries sustained during the attack.[33]

As they had done with the terreiro of Chico Foguinho, the mob seized both sacred and secular objects and burned them in a large bonfire in this street. However, they preserved some objects of value (i.e. items made of semi-precious stones or metals) and sold them. They also took other objects to the League's headquarters where they were later placed on display.

As night turned to early morning, the mob proceeded to invade several other well-known terreiros in the same area. Over time, the attacks spread out to other parts of the capital city and then eventually spilled over into other towns "such as Pratagy, Atalaia, Santa Luzia do Norte, Alagoas, former capital of the province, and Tabuleiro do Pinto."[34] As the rioters attacked more and more terreiros over the subsequent days, they paraded through the streets of Maceió with the seized ritual objects and images of Afro-Brazilian religions on display as a public celebration of the atrocities that they had just committed.[35] These items were taken back to the headquarters of the League and kept on display at their headquarters as a mockery of these religions.[36] Ulisses Neves Rafael points out that this exhibit was in itself another violation of Afro-Brazilian religious communities because the League displayed items that were only meant to be seen by certain members within the religious communities.[37]

Scholars have argued that this incident had a profound impact on Afro-Brazilian religions in Alagoas. Writing almost 30 years after the attacks, Gonçalves Fernandes describes the terreiros of Alagoas

> as a closed liturgy, without dances, songs and without the exaltation of the toques of drums. The ceremonies of the time were surrounded by mystery and secrecy, prevailing the whispering and the little extravagant attitudes that contributed to the episode of "Quebra" with one of the particularities surrounding the episode.[38]

Relying in part on the work of Fernandes, Rafael claims that religious services after the Quebra Xangô incident "were held without music, without dances, without toques... without the presence of liturgical objects that have always been the mark of this type of ceremony."[39]

Rafael describes the ceremonies after the Quebra Xangô incident, saying:

> After the incident, the atabaques were silenced. There was no longer any news of its use in any kind of demonstration, in fact, they were also absent in the exhibition held on Rua do Sopapo. Never again was there news of the presence of maracatus in the Carnivals of Maceió; their masters, not without reason confused with the babalorixás of the persecuted terreiros, were no longer in the city. The vast majority sought refuge in neighboring states and even in more distant places, such as Bahia and Rio de Janeiro. The popular demonstrations made up of Black people came to be seen with a certain suspicion, especially the Xangôs, which continued to be developed by the few remnants of those old houses that remained in the state capital, fearing the punishments of the orixás more than those of the police authorities.[40]

Not only did the adepts cease playing drums, they altered nearly all their religious practices to avoid detection. Speaking of 1941, years after the Quebra Xangô incident, Gonçalves Fernandes remarked, "The 'terreiro' of old no longer exists. Today you just have a regular parlor for visitors."[41] In his observations of Candomblé services, Fernandes argued that this new version involved smaller groups of adepts and was more focused on medico-religious healing. Furthermore, he claimed that the religious leader was the only practitioner and the rest of the community were passive participants. For example, he reported that only the religious leader sang in a low voice in veneration of the spirits and orixás. All of the other devotees acted as mere observers who imitated the gestures of the religious leader in silence.[42] He referred to the new sect as an "autistic cult."[43] He contended that this "silent Candomblé" was the only safe mechanism of worship. Those who occasionally engaged in old ways of worship including drumming and singing were harassed by the police and vilified in the media.

This new "sect" of Afro-Alagoan religion also hid the practice of animal sacrifice. Instead of making offerings directly to the orixá Exu, they placed the sacrifice on a white plate that resembled any chicken killed to prepare a soup.[44] Furthermore, Afro-Brazilian religious communities in Alagoas conducted their services or ceremonies without possession or manifestation. Rafael explains, "apparent mediumship was suppressed in favor of a restrained feeling that dispensed with manifestation. There remained whispered prayers, accompanied by discreet claps, as if both believers and orixás were ashamed of still having to cross in such a difficult situation."[45]

Part of our desire to visit Alagoas was to visit this site of extreme historical repression and to understand the long-term consequences of it. Since we are concerned that religious racism today will have a lasting negative impact, we wanted to know whether observable differences had developed in Afro-Brazilian religions in Alagoas as a result of this violent persecution, especially if ceremonies continued to be "whispered prayers" as described in the mid-twentieth century. We also planned to visit the Instituto Geográfico Histórico de Alagoas where the artifacts stolen from communities during the Quebra de Xangô incident (those previously kept in the office of the League of Republican Combatants) are housed.

Unfortunately, the Covid-19 pandemic limited our lofty goals of really immersing ourselves in religious communities in Alagoas. In the time that we spent there, we encountered wonderful people who were very open to speaking to us about their religion and about religious racism. Rather than marred by past persecution, the people we met seemed excited to welcome researchers and noted that it was rare that scholars came to Alagoas to learn about Afro-Brazilian religions. However, prohibitions on gatherings were taken very seriously at the time of our visit, and it was difficult to conduct enough interviews to really gain a deep understanding of the climate in Alagoas today. Furthermore, like many similar institutions, the Instituto Geográfico Histórico de Alagoas remained closed during the duration of our visit, so we were unable to view the collection from Quebra de Xangô. We definitely plan to return to Alagoas in the near future now that the pandemic restrictions have been lifted.

MARANHÃO

Like Bahia and Alagoas, Maranhão is a state in the northeast region of Brazil. As of the 2010 census, it had over 6.57 million people.[46] Of these, over 5 million (76.48 percent) self-identified as brown or Black. We spent most of our time in São Luís, the capital city, which is home to over 1 million people. Of these, slightly more than 706,500 (nearly 70%) self-identified as brown or Black.[47] Part of the reason that we wanted to conduct research in Maranhão is that the area has such a high percentage of people of African descent but receives comparatively little tourism and miniscule scholarly attention.

During the time that we spent in São Luís, our interlocutors repeatedly emphasized the number of people of African descent and the importance of the area's African roots. In fact, many people suggested that researchers were wrong to devote so much time to Salvador while ignoring the rich culture of São Luís. Although the official data disagrees, more than a few people claimed that São Luís, especially the neighborhood of Liberdade, was the "blackest" city in Brazil (referring to the population and the culture). This narrative was important to think about in the context of the tensions between Afro-Brazilian religions as part of the nation's heritage versus racist perceptions of them as pollutants.

In Maranhão, one finds Afro-Brazilian religious traditions that exist nowhere else. In particular, a religion known as Tambor de Mina was founded in São Luís during the nineteenth century. Like some nations of Candomblé, it has strong roots in the Dahomey-Fon and Yoruba peoples from West Africa. It shares some similarities with the Jeje nation of Candomblé, like the importance of drumming and the veneration of voduns; however, devotees and leaders were quick to point out that Tambor de Mina is distinct and in no way derivative of Candomblé or any other Afro-Brazilian religion. Instead, it developed around the same time as but separately from Candomblé.

During our time in São Luís we had the opportunity to visit one of the oldest Tambor de Mina communities, known as Casa das Minas

Jeje, aka Querebentã Toi Zomadonu, and talk at length with its current leader, Pai Eusébio. This is the only terreiro outside the state of Bahia to be recognized by the federal government as Brazilian cultural heritage through a stringent process called *tombamento*, which we discuss further in Chapter 3.[48] Casa das Minas is also the only non-Candomblé terreiro to go through the tombamento process with the federal government.

Located in the historic center of São Luís, Casa das Minas was founded in approximately 1840 by Africans from the Ewe-Fon language group in modern-day Benin.[49] The earliest written record of it is a deed from 1847 for one of its buildings that shows that it was owned by Mãe Maria Jesuína, the founder of Casa das Minas. However, the terreiro may have been in place for a decade or more before this mention.[50] Today, the temple is composed of three buildings – the oldest of which was built in the early twentieth century – located on 1500 square meters of land.

The practices cultivated here diverge from what is common at other Tambor de Mina or Candomblé terreiros we visited. Only people with direct family connection to the original founders can participate. Only women are permitted to *girar* or dance; men are not allowed. Women are commonly accepted as ritual drummers. No tattoos or body markings are allowed, not even ones that refer to or honor one's vodun. Adepts only "receive" or become possessed by one vodun, not multiple voduns or caboclo (as sometimes happens in other Tambor de Mina houses).[51]

Our rich experiences at Casa das Minas and other Afro-Brazilian religious communities in São Luís highlighted what, to us, felt like one of the strongest examples of the flawed nature of census data. At the time of the 2010 census, a mere 8,738 people in Maranhão self-identified as devotees of Afro-Brazilian religions, which equates to 0.13% of the population.[52] About a quarter of these individuals resided in São Luís.[53] Only 64 people self-identified as belonging to "other Afro-Brazilian religions" (not Candomblé or Umbanda). However, in one night, we witnessed dozens of people join Pai Airton at the temple Ilê Ashé Ogum Sogbô for a caboclo celebration.

At this terreiro, we learned about a sacred drum system totally different from the atabaques in Candomblé and Umbanda. Here, drummers played what they called *batá* drums, whose cylindrical shape, double head, horizontal orientation, and rhythmic patterns for the various orixá seemed more similar to Nigeria or Cuba than to anywhere in Brazil. The São Luís batá are played with two

FIGURE 19: Tambor da Mata

FIGURE 20: Beaded gourd shaker instruments

hands on one side of the drum or alternatively with each hand playing one side, as in Nigeria and Cuba. Two batá perform together accompanied by several beaded gourd shaker instruments, a bell, and an upright drum called *tambor da mata* (forest drum), which is inclined on a wooden stand and played with two open hands.[54] This ensemble plays rhythms to support song and dance for various orixás, voduns, and caboclos.

Unlike the city of Salvador, there were few permanent/fixed representations of Afro-Brazilian religions around São Luís. People seemed a bit confused and had to think very carefully about where we might see some statues, for example. But dancing and drumming celebrations flowed out into the streets in several places.

In addition to the celebration at Ilê Ashé Ogum Sogbô, we witnessed a few hundred community members gathered in the streets of Liberdade for a Bomba Meu Boi celebration with its own unique style of carnivalesque, quasi-religious drumming and dancing. Large frame drums up to approximately three feet in diameter and three inches deep were held at shoulder height with one hand and struck with the other open hand. Call and response songs accompanied the multi-part rhythms and stylized dance choreographies in which groups of costumed dancers stepped, skipped, spun, and proceeded back and forth.

In this context, *boi* is a kind of bull that acts as a sacred symbol and representation of numerous neighborhood-based social organizations throughout the city. The boi is constructed like a votive altar

FIGURE 21: Boi from Casa das Minas

piece in the specific colors of the group. On certain occasions like saint days or for competition with other groups, the boi is spruced up and taken out to process through the streets and "dance" with the group. The feeling is similar to *maracatus* in Pernambuco, *escolas de samba* in Rio, *blocos afros* in Salvador, or further off, to *comparsas* and *congas* in Cuba or "social aid and pleasure clubs" with their Second Lines in New Orleans.

São Luís was also an interesting research site because of a non-religious musical genre for which it is famous. Known as the "Brazilian capital of reggae," São Luís boasts its own distinctive style of reggae dancing: a deceivingly simple, very subtle and particular couple dance called *agarradinho* (hugged up). Though people dance mostly to both old and new Jamaican music, we observed Caribbean or other approaches to reggae dancing being often rejected on the dancefloors of the city. This brought home how much of a world apart São Luís is, not beholden to any other place in terms of its culture, particularly music, dance, and religion.

This fierce sense of originality and autonomy expressed itself in the view of some informants that religious racism is rare or nonexistent in São Luís precisely because there are so many Afro-Brazilian practitioners who are too proud of their faith to allow disrespect, defamation, and violence. Neto Azile, director of the Casa do Tambor de Crioula museum and cultural center, told us that the people of São Luís were likely to use force to protect themselves against religious racism, especially physical violence against devotees and their temples.[55]

Our time in São Luís seemed to generally support Azile and the assertions of others about the rarity of overt discrimination and violence against devotees of Afro-Brazilian religions. For instance, our interlocutors at Casa das Minas told us that they had never experienced direct religious racism. This may be due to its high standing in the community. It may also be due to the particular tact and skill of its leadership in building relationships with Evangelical neighbors. However, they have observed and are definitely aware that religious racism is a problem in Brazil.

FIGURE 22: Boi and dancers in Liberdade, São Luis de Maranhão

Although São Luís seems to experience much fewer incidents of discrimination and violence against Afro-Brazilian religious communities than other places, religious racism occasionally rears its ugly head. For instance, on July 23, 2023, a statue of Iemanjá located in the beach district Olho D'Água was vandalized.[56] The perpetrators used an unknown tool to chisel the face off of the statue, which is one of the few public monuments to Afro-Brazilian religion in São Luís.

RIO GRANDE DO SUL

This chapter highlighting our research plan and experiences would be incomplete without noting that there is one major gap in our project. We did not visit any states in the south region of Brazil, which is composed of the states of Paraná, Rio Grande do Sul, and Santa Catarina. This is the region with the highest percentage of people who self-identify as white. Additionally, whereas the northeast is linked to Afro-Brazilian culture, the south has a long history of direct cultural connections to Europe. For instance, Santa Catarina has a large population of Brazilians of German descent, and Oktoberfest in the city of Blumenau is "considered the biggest German festival in the Americas."[57]

The racial and cultural makeup of the south region alone would have made it an important research site. If timing, travel restrictions, and our budget would have permitted, we planned to include a city from this region to allow us to better understand whether religious racism, especially that related to noise complaints, is significantly impacted by a region's racial makeup. We believe it would have been particularly fruitful to visit Rio Grande do Sul, where a recent Supreme Court case about Afro-Brazilian religions originated.

Rio Grande do Sul is the southernmost state in Brazil, sharing borders with Argentina, Uruguay, and the Brazilian state of Santa Catarina. With a population of nearly 10.7 million at the time of the 2010 census, it was the fifth largest state in the nation. Of these, nearly 8.9 million (83%) people self-identified as white. A mere 16% of the population (1.7 million people) of Rio Grande do Sul is Afro-Brazilian.[58] To put this in perspective, one must recall that Afro-Brazilians are slightly more than half the national population.

Because of its racial makeup, it is somewhat surprising that a relatively large portion of the state's population practices Afro-Brazilian religions. On the last census, 315,198 people (2.9%) claimed affiliation with Candomblé, Umbanda, and/or other Afro-Brazilian religions.[59] This is nearly triple the national average. However, they are still dwarfed by adherents of other religions. More than 7.4 million (69%) reported that they were Catholic and nearly 2 million (18%) that they were Evangelical.

The state of Rio Grande do Sul has made national (and occasionally international) headlines in recent years for its legislative assaults on Afro-Brazilian religions through restrictions on the ritual slaughter of animals. Tensions over legal limitations on Afro-Brazilian religions in Rio Grande do Sul date back to 2002, when a state legislator introduced an animal welfare bill that governed a variety of aspects of animal treatment and slaughter. This bill became law in May 2003.[60] From the outset, devotees of Afro-Brazilian religions knew that the 2003 animal protection law aimed to stop their religious practice. In fact, one of the early versions of the bill barred the use of animals in "sorcery" and "religious ceremonies."[61] Although religious communities managed to prevent these sections from appearing in the final version of the law, they worried that remaining clauses that outlawed "physically attack[ing]" animals and required animals to be killed "suddenly and painlessly" would be used to restrict ritual sacrifice.[62] To address this problem, state legislator Edson Portilho introduced a bill clarifying that the animal protection law did not apply to Afro-Brazilian religions. Despite vocal opposition from animal rights activists and the author of the original animal protection law, Portilho's bill passed the Assembly by an enormous margin and was approved by the governor in 2004 as Law No. 12.131.[63]

After the amendment was implemented, the few dissenting legislators remained very vocal in their dismay about its passage. They denounced animal sacrifice as anti-Christian, arguing that it was the duty of Christian people to protect animals and that Jesus had given the ultimate sacrifice so there was no longer a need to offer animals. Echoing descriptions of Afro-Brazilian religions common during the early to mid-twentieth century, these legislators also described animal sacrifice as cruel, absurd, ignorant, and anti-modern.[64] They asked the State Court of Justice to declare Portilho's law unconstitutional.

In April 2005, the Court found that the law was constitutional. However, the justices were far from unanimous in this ruling and it sparked some strong opinions on both sides.[65] For the purposes of this book and our research, one of the most illuminating remarks came from Alfredo Foerster, who quoted a text from 1955 (50 years prior to the court decision) in which the then Secretary of Culture (a white male) describes his alleged experiences attending a Candomblé ceremony with a German visitor. By selecting this material and presenting it in this context, Foerster (one of the few judges to argue against the amendment protecting animal sacrifice) reinscribes a decades-old fear of "demonic" animal sacrifice and "dangerous" African drumming (intermixed with a voyeuristic type of attraction) that torments the soul of mainstream Brazil. Discrimination against animal sacrifice and drumming in the twenty-first century can be read as a reaction to or extension of this primordial trepidation.[66]

In the quoted text, the white Secretary of Culture and German dignitary are hyper-concerned about being surrounded by Black Brazilians. One said to the other: "Don't say anything. We will attract attention because we are white."[67] Additionally, they are made uncomfortable by the sounds of Afro-Brazilian religion: "We heard hens clucking, geese honking, the bleating of sheep, the baaing of goats, and the frightened cries of birds. And, in the background, the constant sound of the drums."[68] When their guide, referred to only as "Black Felipe," warns that these are the animals intended for sacrifice, the white men look at each other as if to say "We have to keep our calm."[69] In accord with a decades-old notion that African drumming was distasteful, the Secretary complains that the "rhythmic sound of the drums [was] so strong that I had to stuff my ears with cotton."[70] When he speaks of the part of the ceremony when the animals were sacrificed, the Secretary emphasizes the relationship between the "magic rhythms" of the atabaques and animal sacrifice, explaining that the devotees brought the animals to the center of the square, "decapitating them with sharp blades. Aside from the rhythmic sound of the drums, the killing [sacrifice] is done in silence."[71] A few lines later, he adds, "Surrounded by the drummers, who beat faster and faster, and excited by the frantic clapping of those present, the Supreme Orixá dances in the center, while the ox's blood runs over him, staining his beautiful garment."[72] Statements from this account clearly express the negative feelings and associations that mainstream Brazilian society often holds toward Afro-Brazilian religions.

In 2008, a few years after the State Court of Justice issued its ruling, the legislature of Rio Grande do Sul passed a law that specifically limited sound emissions in activities in religious temples.[73] During the day (between 6 am and 10 pm), the law limits sound emissions in religious temples to 75 decibels in residential, 80 in commercial, and 85 in industrial zones. At night (10 pm to 6 am), the limits for each kind of area are 10 decibels fewer. The law requires that measurements be taken by environmental authorities while in the presence of a representative of the religious temple. Three separate measurements should be taken at a minimum, at least 15 minutes apart. The average decibel level of the three readings is used to determine violations. Religious temples that are found to be in violation are given 90 to 180 days to remedy the situation before being fined. If subsequent violations occur, fines can be imposed. Like the animal protection laws discussed previously, this law was also introduced by a Neo-Pentecostal pastor.

Unwilling to cease their assaults on Afro-Brazilian religions, the state legislature reopened the issue of animal sacrifice several years later. In 2015, Regina Fortunati introduced a bill that sought to repeal the animal protection code amendment that explicitly protected Afro-Brazilian religious communities.[74] Fortunati claimed the issue should be revisited because animal rights had evolved in the decade since the State Supreme Court decision and the movement against animal sacrifice had gained support. She contended that the ritual slaughter of animals posed a threat to public health and disturbed society. Furthermore, although Fortunati denied allegations that she was prejudiced against Afro-Brazilian religions, she repeatedly defended the bill as part of the "Christian duty" to protect animals.

The bill went through several levels of debate in the state legislature, but the most important part of the process seems to have been the decision of the assembly's Commission of Constitution and Justice (CCJ), which found (in an 11–1 decision) that Fortunati's bill violated the constitution.[75] During a vote on whether the legislature would adopt the CCJ's opinion, some members of the committee described Fortunati's bill as based on prejudice against Afro-Brazilian religions. One member even went so far as to characterize it as "intolerance and fanaticism." The CCJ members explained that they became convinced of the biased framework for the bill after hearing considerable evidence about slaughterhouses, rodeos, cosmetic testing, and even animals killed in roadway accidents that resulted in cruelty and death to many more animals each year than ritual slaughter but were not addressed by activists.[76]

Ultimately, the assembly voted to adopt the CCJ's opinion in June 2015. However, the controversy did not end there. The Public Prosecutor's Office (Ministério Público) of Rio Grande do Sul appealed the decision of the State Supreme Court, asking the Supreme

Federal Tribunal to determine whether the amendment protecting Afro-Brazilian religions was constitutional.[77] After several delays, in March of 2019, the Supreme Federal Tribunal finally reached a decision in this case.[78] Although some justices expressed concerns and reservations about the protection of animal sacrifice in Afro-Brazilian religions, the Court found that the amendment was constitutional. After nearly two decades of controversy, Afro-Brazilian religious communities in Rio Grande do Sul could finally breathe easily for a moment regarding this one issue. However, battles over noise pollution and other issues continue to rage.

CONCLUSION

This background information about the main places where we conducted our research – Bahia, Rio de Janeiro, Brasília, Alagoas, and Maranhão – and the description of the animal sacrifice and other controversies in Rio Grande do Sul should help orient the reader to the complexities of the situation in Brazil. There are many differences between various cities and states. The racial composition of Brazil varies drastically from 16% Afro-Brazilian in Rio Grande do Sul to 76% Afro-Brazilian in Bahia. In the northeastern states like Bahia and Maranhão, Afro-Brazilian culture is proudly on display in public festivals, museums, and the like. By contrast, southern states like Rio Grande do Sul also have festivals honoring their European heritage. While devotees of Afro-Brazilian religions are a small percentage of the census population in every part of the country, their overall numbers vary greatly from state to state, and some Afro-Brazilian religions are more prevalent in certain regions than others. Each state also has its own peculiarities, such as the traumatic history of the Quebra de Xangô incident in Alagoas or the prevalence of Evangelical drug traffickers in Rio, that might inform the nature and frequency of religious racism.

Because of all these distinctions, our initial plan was to divide this book by geographic area and discuss the nuances of religious racism and sacred music in each region. However, we struggled to create sharp distinctions between the types of cases that were happening in each area. When the book underwent peer review, the readers agreed that the regional differences did not seem to be that stark. Therefore, at the end of the day, while all of this background is important to understanding religious racism in Brazil as a varied and nuanced problem, it is striking how much these distinct areas of the nation have in common. From a predominantly white city in the South that has public celebrations of its European heritage to a predominantly Afro-Brazilian city in the northeast that markets Afro-Brazilian religions as its cultural heritage and everything in between, there is no part of Brazil that is free from religious racism and no corner of the country where discrimination against Afro-Brazilian sacred music cannot and does not occur. While some forms of religious racism might be more common in certain areas than others, there is also no part of the country that is immune to any of the different types of discrimination that we discuss in the chapters that follow.

CHAPTER 3

"Pollution" or Public Recognition: Cultural Heritage and Candomblé

When visiting Brazil, it can be difficult to understand how religious racism can occur in a place that, at least on the surface, appears to celebrate Afro-Brazilian religions. As discussed in Chapter 2, one finds numerous public representations and celebrations of Afro-Brazilian religions, including well-known festivals that draw thousands of people from across the nation and abroad, statues of religious leaders and orixás, as well as streets and parks that bear their names. Dozens of terreiros have been recognized by city, state, and federal governments as part of Brazil's protected cultural heritage. Because these public recognitions of Afro-Brazilian religions can, at least superficially, seem to undermine and contradict stories of religious racism, in this chapter we provide some background about how and why this recognition occurs and emphasize how even these sites and symbols become the targets of religious racism.

The government of Brazil plays an important role in determining legitimate markers of Brazilian identity through the declaration of sites and practices as material and intangible heritage. At the federal level, the Instituto do Patrimônio Histórico e Artístico Nacional (IPHAN) decides what is protected as Brazilian heritage. Many cities and states have parallel institutions, such as the Instituto do Patrimônio Artístico e Cultural da Bahia (IPAC) and Fundação Gregório de Mattos (FGM) in Bahia state and Salvador respectively.

One of the oldest and most important forms of protection provided by IPHAN (and parallel institutions) is a process called *tombamento*, which safeguards property and customs considered to be of public interest because of their historic, artistic, or cultural value.[1] Archeological sites, ruins, city centers, colonial buildings; intangible knowledge like agricultural systems, visual art, martial arts, music, and dance; and natural sites such as waterfalls, rock formations, and forest groves can gain protected status. Items and practices that have been protected through tombamento cannot be destroyed, demolished, damaged, or threatened. Anyone who damages protected property can be fined 500% of the repair costs. Additionally, if property protected through tombamento is in need of urgent repair or restoration, the government might pay for such upkeep at no cost to the property owner.

Afro-Brazilian communities have joined with local and state governments to seek the official recognition and "protection" of important natural resources and historic sites and the installation of monuments honoring key activists in the fight against religious racism. While seemingly combating discrimination through heritage protection, the city, state, and federal governments are also able to capitalize on the creation of new iconographies that attract tourists by marketing Black culture and Brazil's African roots. This persistent depiction of Afro-Brazilian religions as the heritage of Brazil has drawn the ire of Evangelicals and resulted in the desecration of these protected sites.

In this chapter, we explore these tensions as context for readers to understand the contemporary attacks against Afro-Brazilian sacred drumming. By further discussing the sites that we visited during our fieldwork and the interviews that we conducted, we will show the constant push and pull between public embrace through representation and religious racism attacks. Before providing these examples, it is useful to discuss some of the scholarship about official policies related to Afro-Brazilian religions to provide some background for understanding how and why these religions are such an integral part of the public sphere in Brazil.

CULTURAL HERITAGE AND AFRO-BRAZILIAN RELIGIONS

In 2001, the State Board of Culture and Tourism of Bahia created a billboard campaign that said "Black City. Salvador. The Most African City of Brazil" (Cidade Negra. Salvador. A cidade mais africana do Brasil).[2] Such campaigns date back to at least the 1960s, when the state of Bahia began promoting tourism by marketing itself as a site of authentic African heritage and culture in the Americas. This involved promoting local Afro-Brazilian practices, including Candomblé.[3] Such cultural tourism picked up in the 1970s and 1980s when "international air travel was becoming less expensive, the black middle class was growing in the United States, and many African Americans were searching for their 'roots,' as Alex Haley's (1976) bestselling novel by the same name illustrates."[4] So-called African heritage tourism took many African Americans to the African continent; however, they also increasingly visited other parts of the Americas with large Black populations and strong African diaspora cultural legacies. The Brazilian government specifically targeted African American university students, especially those enrolled in Black studies courses, hoping to draw Black tourists who were interested in their cultural ancestry.[5] UNESCO's Slave Route Project in 1994 made more people aware of Brazil's role in the Atlantic slave trade and its strong African heritage, increasing its appeal.[6] In fact, Stephen Selka notes that by 2007 demand became so high that "the Secretary of Tourism created the special office for the promotion of 'African Heritage Tourism,' focusing almost exclusively on African American tourism to Bahia."[7]

While such campaigns appear to be most concentrated in the state of Bahia, especially the city of Salvador, other regions and the federal government have also sought to generate tourism by taking formerly banned aspects of Afro-Brazilian heritage, like capoeira and Candomblé, and marketing them as folklore. This approach portrays Brazil as a racial democracy and celebrates Bahia and Afro-Brazilians as contributors to Brazil's national identity.[8] Miguel Alonso and Norman K. Smith assert that "By the 1970s, Afro-Brazilian and

Afro-Bahian culture had come to represent to the world what Brazil was and Candomblé in particular became the nation's second leading tourist attraction, second only to Carnaval."[9] UNESCO and the governments of Brazil, Benin, and Nigeria also coordinated and financed exchanges between Brazil and West Africa that would increase trans-Atlantic connections between these nations, including supporting several Candomblé priests and priestesses to make heritage trips to the African continent.[10] Such voyages enhanced and celebrated Brazilian ties to Africa and helped construct international networks of Black heritage tourism and consciousness.

Scholars have been very critical of these policies and endeavors. Heather Shirey argues that by "taking pride in its African heritage, and calling upon its cultural influence to promote the state's important tourist industry, residents of Bahia and governmental agencies subvert racist attitudes, turning the region's African identity into a lucrative asset."[11] Analyzing how Afro-Brazilian culture and religions can be promoted as "heritage" despite this long history of prejudice, Danielle Hedegard eloquently explains, "In certain contexts, blackness – despite its common stigmatized status – is a valuable cultural resource that people accumulate and convert to social and economic rewards."[12] Rather than a hidden agenda, Victoria Stansky points out that even IPHAN's own website definition of "cultural heritage" connects it to economic gain, describing it as having "significant interfaces with other key economic sectors such as construction and tourism, exponentially increasing the potential for investment."[13]

The cynicism with which many scholars seem to approach the government's promotion of Afro-Brazilian religions is likely rooted in the decades of persecution that these religions suffered before the government's drastic shift in the mid- to late twentieth century. One will recall the official "whitening" policies that state and federal governments engaged in during the early twentieth century and the widespread perceptions of these religions as primitive and barbaric (see Chapter 1). In just a few decades, the government leaped from attempting to eradicate these religions in favor of European culture to encouraging tourists to come to witness their "exotic" and "authentic" African practices. Kim Butler explains how racism remained (and perhaps remains) embedded in such government endeavors, arguing that while "government agencies were actively engaged in commodifying Afro-Bahian culture to promote tourism; they were also embracing a benign folkloric representation of African-based culture to publicly demonstrate Brazil's multiculturalism. Folklorization sought to freeze Africanisms as quaint and archaic holdovers from the past inconsistent with modern Brazilian society."[14]

In this chapter, we focus on two types of recognitions of Afro-Brazilian religions that illustrate the complex role of these religions in the public sphere: 1) statues, monuments, and public parks and 2) the designation of terreiros as intangible heritage. Regarding the statues or monuments to the orixás, Shirey describes them as "permanent advertising for one of the state's valued industries: tourism."[15] However, interviewing Candomblé adepts in 2001–2002 following the construction of some of the most notorious statues in Salvador, Shirey explains that "most respondents quickly asserted that the artworks in fact have nothing to do with Candomblé as a religion. They were described as merely superficial representations, created by an outsider for an audience of outsiders" that had no "sacred power."[16] Nevertheless, Shirey documented how many Pentecostals protested the inauguration of several prominent statues in Salvador around the turn of the twenty-first century and asserted that the statues were imbued with negative energy that could cause people to become physically ill and bring evil into the city. Within a few years after their installation and inauguration, however, Shirey argues that many Pentecostals had calmed down about the statues and started to see them merely as works of art.[17]

The perspective of Pentecostals appears to have gone through some evolutions during the past 20 years or so. Although they had supposedly begun to accept the statues shortly after their construction, in recent years, Evangelicals are again vocally and violently opposing the new construction and continued existence of these public depictions of Afro-Brazilian religions. More than the mere protests that Shirey documented, they are now vandalizing and destroying statues and monuments honoring these religions. Additionally, as the popularity of Afro-Brazilian religions continues to grow among white Brazilians and Black Brazilians continue to patronize Evangelical churches in large numbers, Evangelicals not only question Afro-Brazilian religions' status as heritage traditions but also increasingly claim their own space in the public sphere.[18]

During our field research, many of our interlocutors expressed concern and outrage about the recent vandalism and destruction of statues honoring Afro-Brazilian religions. While not necessarily contradicting Shirey's findings that the statues are essentially nonreligious sculptures, religious communities understood these attacks as extensions of assaults on themselves and their places of worship. Furthermore, some of them emphasized that while the statues may not be religious, many of them are built in spaces where devotees perform rituals and hold festivals.

Regarding the official recognition of Afro-Brazilian terreiros, scholars have made an interesting and critical distinction about government policies. Oftentimes, the terreiros that have gained heritage protection under IPHAN are the ones that "celebrate faithfulness to African legacy."[19] Additionally, those that are found in historic and centrally located areas are much more likely to receive the recognition of IPHAN and other government organizations. Otherwise, Stansky notes, "the destruction of sacred sites and terreiros continues until this day, especially in peripheral spaces where tourism is scarce or nonexistent."[20]

As we delve into these examples, it is important to note that even while the government and private businesses profit from the depiction of Salvador, Bahia, and/or Brazil as "African" and the celebration of cultural and religious practices from the continent, these celebrations often fail to trickle down to the individual level. It may be profitable and trendy to honor Brazil's African roots in public; however, actual devotees are often left hiding their association with these religions from their families and employers to avoid discrimination.[21]

STATUES AND PUBLIC PARKS

Brazil, especially the city of Salvador, is home to numerous public sites honoring Afro-Brazilian religions such as statues, monuments, and parks. What follows are short discussions of some of the sites related to Afro-Brazilian religions that we visited that have been either constructed or renovated using government funds and/or recognized by the government as heritage sites. Through them, we explore the process of public recognition of sacred sites and Candomblé leaders, as well as the acts of discrimination and violence that have demonstrated opposition. We begin with the Praça dos Orixás, which seems to have been one of the first public sites recognizing Afro-Brazilian religions in Brazil to suffer persecution.

Praça dos Orixás

As briefly introduced in Chapter 2, Praça dos Orixás (Plaza of the Orixás) is a 200 square meter area near Lake Paranoá in Brasília. Acclaimed Brazilian artist Tatti Moreno was commissioned to build sculptures of the orixás there around the turn of the twenty-first century. There are 16 sculptures in total, each approximately 4 ½ feet tall and seated upon a base. Most of the sculptures are placed around the border of the parking lot next to a grassy area near the lake's only beach. The shade of the trees and the capybaras roaming in the grass give the impression of a secluded park, although, in reality, the plaza is located in a central area of the Federal District, just a few kilometers from the seat of the federal government and the embassy sector. Since the 1960s, devotees of Afro-Brazilian religions have come to this beach to make offerings and to hold major celebrations such as the festival for Iemanjá on New Year's Eve.[22] In 2018, the plaza and the Iemanjá festival were declared intangible heritage by the Council for the Defense of Cultural Heritage and were included in the list of places and festivals that are protected by the Secretary of Culture.[23]

Almost since their construction, the statues of the orixás have been targets for vandalism. Attacks have ranged from minor damage like severing fingers or removing implements to stealing an entire statue and dumping it in the trash. At least three of the statues have been set on fire. In 2016, following a series of arson attacks that burned 13 terreiros in Brasília and the surrounding areas, vandals set fire to the statue of Oxalá, who is considered the orixá of peace. At the time of the arson, vandals had already severed the statue's arm.[24] When we visited the site nearly five years later, in December 2020, it had not been repaired. Devotees had wrapped the statue in white cloth to cover its charred body.

FIGURE 1: Burned statue of Oxalá in Plaza of the Orixás

Dique do Tororó

Dique do Tororó (a lake created by a dike) is the largest body of freshwater in the city of Salvador, Bahia. The site was created during the colonial era – between the end of the seventeenth century and the middle of the eighteenth century – as a defensive structure at the edge of the then capital of Salvador. In later years, it became a hub for the local population. People would collect water and social activities sprang up around it. Additionally, since at least the nineteenth century, devotees of Afro-Brazilian religions have used the Dique to perform rituals and make offerings, particularly for the orixá Oxum. In the mid-twentieth century, it was declared a protected "monument" by IPHAN.[25]

In the 1990s, the Dique was revitalized by the state government. As part of this refurbishing, in 1998, Bahian artist Tatti Moreno created a set of eight sculptures dedicated to the orixás Oxum, Ogum, Oxossi, Xangô, Oxalá, Iemanjá, Nanã, and Iansã that seem to float in the waters at one end of the Dique (Figure 3). Four other sculptures, representations of the orixás Oxumarê, Ossain, Logun-Edé, and Ewá were placed on land surrounding the lake. The statues are a multivalent ode to the city's rich Afro-Brazilian heritage. They are both an

FIGURE 2: Dique do Tororó with the soccer stadium in the background

FIGURE 3: Statues of Dique do Tororó

enticing vision for the tourist gaze and markers that activate the real spirituality of locals who pass by to admire or even leave offerings.

Evangelicals campaigned vocally against the inauguration of the statues, even staging a protest.[26] They argued that the government was infringing upon the principle of secularism by promoting Afro-Brazilian religions and that the statues did not represent them nor even a majority of the population of the city.[27] Some Evangelicals also contended that the state was promoting "a diabolical religion"[28] or even claimed to feel ill when near the statues.[29] Protestant councilmember Eliel Santana predicted that "nefarious events" (*acontecimentos nefastos*) would occur due to the installation.[30] When a large number of fish died as a result of the city removing oxygenating plants during the restoration process, some Evangelicals saw this as evidence confirming his predictions.[31]

Acts of racism and vandalism committed at this site continue in the twenty-first century. In 2014, Evangelical pastor Elionai Muralha focused his federal deputy campaign on eliminating all public references to the orixás in Bahia, including Dique do Tororó.[32] In October 2019, unknown persons severed the left arm of the Oxumarê statue that sits on the land surrounding the Dique.[33] No signs were left at the site to indicate why this particular figure had been targeted (aside from the ease of accessing statues on land versus those on the water) and the perpetrators were never caught. In December of 2020, on several occasions, we observed groups of Evangelicals gathered at the Dique near the statues of the orixás. They were handing out pamphlets about their faith and blocking or harassing individuals who approached the statues.

Pedra de Xangô

Pedra de Xangô (the Xangô Stone) is a site that has been recognized as cultural patrimony and integrated into city planning more recently. Pedra de Xangô is an ancient, geologically significant stone where some Afro-Brazilian religious communities gather for ceremonies and to make offerings to the orixá Xangô. The stone is on the historical site of the Quilombo do Buraco do Tatu.[34] It is located in Cajazeiras, in a part of the city that was considered wilderness until very recently.[35] However, in 2005, the government built a major thoroughfare, Avenida Assis Valente, right next to the Pedra de Xangô. This road connects four major regions of Salvador, Bahia: Fazenda Grande I, Fazenda Grande II, Boca da Mata, and Estrada Velha do Aeroporto.

Recent attacks against the Xangô Stone lay bare tensions between the city's efforts to recognize and protect Afro-Brazilian religions as cultural patrimony and increased racism against these faiths. For instance, in 2014, the governments of Brazil and Nigeria jointly funded a trip by the Alaafin (ruler) of Oyo, where he participated in a seminar titled "Brazil–Nigeria International Seminar for Preservation of Shared Cultural Heritage,"[36] and met with several government officials, including the Secretary of Policies for the Promotion of Racial Equality; the Minister of Culture; and the Governor of Bahia state.[37] In addition to the Xangô Stone, he also visited five historic Candomblé terreiros (discussed further in the next section), including Casa

FIGURE 4: Pedra de Xangô

Branca do Engenho Velho, Terreiro do Gantois, Casa de Oxumarê, Ilê Axé Opô Afonjá, and Terreiro Alaketu.[38] Just four months after the Alaafin's visit, vandals dumped 200 kilos of cooking salt and plastic bags on the Xangô Stone and the surrounding areas.

This appears to have been the first in what would become a series of major acts of intolerance against this sacred site. Four years later, in 2018, the monument was vandalized for a second time – covered in approximately 100 kilos of salt.[39] Like the 2014 attack, this vandalism followed just months after a Nigerian ruler, the Ooni (King) of Ifé, made an official visit to Pedra de Xangô as part of a trip that the governments of Brazil and Nigeria hoped would promote tourism and exchange between the countries.[40]

In 2017, the city designated the Pedra de Xangô and 17 surrounding hectares as a cultural heritage site and the city's first Environmental Protection Area.[41] When the city announced these recognitions, it also revealed plans to create a park to be known as the Parque em Rede Pedra de Xangô, which would include an amphitheater, bike path, and space for religious ceremonies, among other things.[42] During our visit in December 2020, the construction of the Pedra de Xangô park was underway (Figure 5). The area was cordoned off and seemed to have been recently excavated, with red earth exposed all around. None of the promised structures or the bike path had yet been completed. There were remnants of recent offerings for Xangô along the descending pathway through the stone. On this occasion, we spoke with

FIGURE 5: Construction underway at Pedra de Xangô Park

attorney and activist Maria Alice Pereira da Silva, who has written two books about the Pedra de Xangô.[43] She explained that although the park remains unfinished, the cultural and environmental protection of the Xangô Stone is clearly the result of more than a decade of activism by religious communities petitioning local and state officials to recognize the site.[44]

Mãe Stella de Oxossi

In addition to the cultural heritage and environmental protection of Dique do Tororó and Pedra de Xangô, the construction of the statues on the Dique, and creation of the Pedra de Xangô park, the government of Salvador has erected several statues honoring Candomblé leaders around the city. Perhaps the most conspicuous of these is the statue of Mãe Stella de Oxossi at the intersection of two major highways, at a highly visible crossroads between the city and airport (Figure 6).

FIGURE 6: Statue of Mãe Stella in Salvador

Maria Stella de Azevedo Santos, aka Mãe Stella de Oxossi, was born in Salvador on May 2, 1925. In 1976, she became the leader of Ilê Axé Opô Afonjá, one of the best known historic terreiros in Bahia, founded in 1910. Mãe Stella did a great deal of community service and became a powerful priestess, an iconic public figure, a renowned activist, and a model of civically engaged, militant Black womanhood.[45] She also spoke out against religious racism and attacked what she viewed as the blaspheming of Candomblé when ritual clothing and objects are used in tourism.

Mãe Stella passed away on December 27, 2018, at the age of 93. A few months later, on April 9, 2019, the city of Salvador inaugurated a statue in her honor, seemingly as a gesture affirming its support of her life's work against racism and religious intolerance.[46] The statue features a 20-foot-tall fiberglass representation of the orixá Oxóssi, designed by Tatti Moreno, who created the statues at Praça dos Orixás and Dique do Tororó. A life-size image of Mãe Stella, dressed in traditional Candomblé attire, sat upon a throne at Oxóssi's feet. Both sculptures were mounted together on a six-foot concrete base. At the time of installation, the mayor of Salvador, Antônio Carlos Magalhães Neto, expressed hope that the statue would become a popular tourist attraction.

However, just hours after the inauguration ceremony, Diogo Nobre, a young Evangelical man, posted a video on social media condemning the statue's installation.[47] Nobre claimed that God had spoken to him and promised to unleash his wrath upon Salvador, which had (according to Nobre) invited the devil into the city when it sponsored this homage. Witnesses informed the public prosecutor's office about Nobre's activities and expressed fear that his comments might incite violence against the monument.

In September 2019, vandals defaced the base of the statue with graffiti and tore off two of the plaques that identified the monument as an installation supported by the City of Salvador.[48] When we visited the site more than one year later, someone had poorly repainted the base of the statue to cover the graffiti; however, the plaques had not been replaced and there were obvious holes in the structure where the plaques had been. As we approached the statue, we were struck by the lengths to which the perpetrators must have gone to reach the site. The monument sits between two major highways. There is no parking in the vicinity and no other structures to conceal culprits. Even if they had arrived in the darkness of night, it seems certain that these airport-adjacent roads would have been occupied by at least a few cars and that the perpetrators would have been visible from the highway. However, such a bold attack should come as no surprise, as 2019 saw many similar assaults on representations of Afro-Brazilian religions. In fact, on the very same day the statue of Mãe Stella was attacked, a woman in the state of Santa Catarina repeatedly struck a statue of orixá Iemanjá with a sledgehammer in broad daylight on a busy road.[49]

Still, vandals were not finished with this site. The most recent attack occurred in the early hours of Sunday, December 4, 2022, when arsonists set fire to the statue, completely destroying the sculpture of Mãe Stella.[50] At some point before Dr. Boaz visited Salvador in May 2023, the municipality had removed the remnants of the sculpture from the base, presumably to restore it. However, this visit was more than six months after the arsonists destroyed it and the space where Mãe Stella had proudly sat upon her throne remained bare.

Mãe Gilda

In recent years, the city of Salvador also constructed a statue for Gildásia dos Santos e Santos, known in the religious community as Mãe Gilda de Ogum. The statue of Mãe Gilda is less visible than that of Mãe Stella; however, Mãe Gilda is one of the best known figures in Brazilian Candomblé and the fight against religious intolerance. Brazil's National Day to Combat Religious Intolerance is held on January 21 in homage of Mãe Gilda's passing and in remembrance of her iconic struggle against religious racism.

Mãe Gilda was initiated in Candomblé in 1976 and received the charge of iyalorixá in 1988. She was the leader of Ilê Axé Abassá de Ogum, located in the neighborhood of Itapuã in Salvador. In 1999, the Universal Church of the Kingdom of God took a photo of Mãe

Gilda that had been published in *Veja* magazine a few years prior and reprinted it in their own magazine, *Folha Universal*.[51] In the picture, Mãe Gilda is dressed in her priestly attire and surrounded by shrines of her orixás. The magazine used the image as an illustration for a story about how "charlatan sorcerers" were hurting the lives of their clients. The magazine had a circulation of 1,372,000 people. Mãe Gilda received harsh criticism from this unauthorized use of her image. Some members of her religious community saw the picture and thought that she had become a Christian and supported the Universal Church's derogatory perceptions of her faith. That same year, members of a different Evangelical church invaded and ransacked her terreiro.[52] In the midst of these attacks, Mãe Gilda's health deteriorated, and on January 21, 2000, she died of a heart attack at 65 years old.

Mãe Gilda's biological and spiritual daughter, Jaciara Ribeiro (Mãe Jaciara de Oxum), sued the Universal Church for moral damages and misuse of her mother's image and attributed Mãe Gilda's death to the stress of defamation.[53] In September 2008, after multiple appeals spanning nearly a decade, Mãe Jaciara received a final judgment against the Universal Church. The Superior Court of Justice ordered the church to pay Jaciara R$145,250.00 (around $29,000 USD) in damages and to print a retraction.

In 2007, Brazil's National Congress declared that January 21, the anniversary of Mãe Gilda's death, would be officially commemorated as the National Day to Combat Religious Intolerance (Dia Nacional de Combate à Intolerância Religiosa).[54] Today, several cities and states in Brazil celebrate this day by hosting forums for interreligious dialogue and marches in support of religious freedom, among other events. Several years later, in 2014, the Palmares Cultural Foundation and the City of Salvador installed a bust of Mãe Gilda (Figure 7) in Itapuã, a few minutes' drive from Ilê Axé Abassá de Ogum, at the entrance to Parque Metropolitano do Abaeté near Lagoa do Abaeté.[55] Similar to Dique do Tororó, this is a place with great significance as a natural resource, ceremonial space, and depository for sacred offerings to the orixá.

Figure 7: Bust of Mãe Gilda in Itapuã, Salvador

The bronze bust is 1.7 meters tall and sits on top of a white stone base that is 1.1 meters high. The entire structure is covered by a white tent. On the base of the statue, a plaque reads:

> Mãe Gilda. Daughter of Orixá Ogum, she was born on October 3, 1935, becoming the founder of Axé Abassa de Ogum. She died on January 21, 2000, despite living in a secular state, due to religious intolerance.
>
> We have many paths to follow in search of freedom and equality, in diversity.
>
> Kosi Mi Fara Owé (Yoruba Language)
>
> "Nothing in the world can harm me, we're [still] here."
>
> Salvador, November 28, 2014[56]

Less than two years later, in May 2016, the Mãe Gilda bust was desecrated. Unfortunately, the perpetrators were never identified or apprehended.[57] On November 28, 2016, Ilê Axé Abassá de Ogum, in conjunction with the Black Community Development Council,[58] the

State Secretary for the Promotion of Racial Equality[59] (SEPROMI), and the Interreligious Committee (Comitê Interreligioso) of Bahia, restored and re-inaugurated the monument. Reflecting on the significance of the restoration, Mãe Jaciara said that her mother's bust was "a symbol of our fight" and that it was "a way to say no to racism and to religious intolerance, which, in a veiled manner or not, has increased."[60]

On July 15, 2020, a man stoned the bust of Mãe Gilda, claiming that God told him to do so.[61] Police arrested him for violating the penal code, which prohibits destroying public property. The following day, Fabya Reis, Secretary of SEPROMI, visited the park and announced that her office would finance the restoration of the bust.[62] Mãe Jaciara once again denounced the violation of her mother's bust, explaining that it was not a mere act of vandalism but an act of religious intolerance and lamenting that in the two decades since her mother's death, "this hate doesn't stop."[63]

CANDOMBLÉ TERREIROS AS CULTURAL HERITAGE OF BRAZIL

Discrimination against Candomblé devotees and terreiros, including noise pollution allegations, also has a complex relationship with the visibility of Afro-Brazilian religions and the recognition (or lack thereof) of terreiros as cultural heritage sites. The oldest terreiros are the most likely to be recognized, particularly at the federal level. Most of these terreiros were founded by African religious communities in what were then rural areas outside the historic city center of Salvador. In part, they sought distance from the city as a way to protect themselves from persecution by police and other authorities. In the twenty-first century, long after the metropolitan area has greatly expanded and these historic terreiros now reside in the center of the city, Candomblé communities are increasingly seeking recognition by local, state, and federal governments. In this section, we consider how tombamento and other public recognition offers protections to certain historic Candomblé terreiros and yet leave other, unrecognized ones more vulnerable to attack, including noise complaints.

IPHAN explains that Candomblé terreiros "house a symbolic universe rich in traditions such as dances, songs, poetry (*oriquis*), myths, rituals and spatial organizations that keep alive the ancestral memories of Africans."[64] In the entire country, only nine Candomblé terreiros have been recognized through tombamento by IPHAN. All nine of these terreiros are located in the northeastern region of the country; eight are located in the state of Bahia and one in the state of Maranhão. These include:

- Six terreiros in Salvador: Casa Branca do Engenho Velho, Ilê Iyá Omim Axé Iyamassé (Gantois), Ilê Axé Opô Afonjá, Ilê Maroiá Láji (Alaketu), Bate-Folha, and Ilê Axé Oxumarê
- One terreiro in Itaparica, Bahia: Omo Ilê Agboulá
- One terreiro in Cachoeira, Bahia: Zogbodo Male Bogun Seja Unde (Roça do Ventura)
- One terreiro in São Luís, Maranhão: Casa das Minas Jeje

The six terreiros in Salvador that have been recognized by IPHAN can be divided into two categories – those founded in the nineteenth century and those founded in the twentieth century. The four terreiros founded in the nineteenth century – Casa Branca, Alaketu, Terreiro do Gantois, and Casa de Oxumarê – were established in adjacent territories – what would become the neighborhoods of Federação, Brotas, and Engenho Velho da Federação. In the nineteenth century, Federação and Engenho Velho were located in a marginal or peripheral area, far from the "administrative center of the ancient city of Salvador, undervalued because of its hills bordered by valleys and entrances of difficult access."[65] Historian Lisa Castillo notes of Brotas: "With an enormous geographical area, Brotas was nonetheless the city's least populous parish, consisting mainly of plantations and a few tiny hamlets."[66]

The placement of these terreiros seems to have been intentional. Samuel Gordenstein argues that most of the well-known communities were founded

> in the semi-rural neighborhoods of Salvador, on properties with extensive wooded patches and waterways that were inhabited by some of the divinities being worshiped, and which provided the botanical resources necessary for many ritual aspects. These locations were also isolated enough to muffle the noise from the singing and percussion instruments that are integral to the religion, and to provide the privacy for the ritual dancing and other activities frowned upon by the conservative sectors of society and repressed by local police.[67]

The terreiro communities' narratives of their histories seem to support this. Casa de Oxumarê's own website recounts that it was relocated to the current site in 1904 because the area was heavily forested and provided a way to "hide" the terreiro from police and other aggressors.[68] Terreiro do Gantois's website also explains that the area where they built their community was chosen because it presented difficult access for police.[69] Some of these terreiros were founded by African-born religious leaders and became spiritual and cultural refuges, which one could argue were similar to quilombos. However, it was not long before they were swallowed by the burgeoning city of Salvador.

By the late nineteenth and early twentieth century, Salvador had begun to expand and engulf these once rural areas. Ironically, official sources identify the establishment of these terreiros as a major influence in the development of these neighborhoods into urban areas. Some of the founders of these first terreiros purchased their lands from plantation owners. In the case of Federação, sources indicate that the only significant structure at the time of the neighborhood's founding in 1889 was Terreiro do Gantois and the cemetery of Campo Santo.[70] In the twentieth century, several radio and television stations moved into the neighborhood, as well as three university campuses.[71]

Today, these neighborhoods and historic terreiros are located in the heart of the city of Salvador, north of trendy coastal neighborhoods like Barra, Ondina, and Rio Vermelho, and right off of major roadways such as Avenida Anita Garibaldi and Avenida Vasco da Gama.

At the time of the last census, Brotas was the most populous neighborhood in Salvador, with more than 70,000 inhabitants.[72] Federação has a population of slightly more than 36,000 people, nearly 80% of whom declared their race to be Black or brown in the last census. Engenho Velho da Federação is home to around 24,500 inhabitants, nearly 90% of whom are Afro-Brazilian.[73]

As Federação and Engenho Velho da Federação developed in the twentieth century, Candomblé terreiros in Salvador were established in other neighborhoods that helped lead the extension of the city. The other terreiros protected by IPHAN provide great examples. Ilê Axé Opô Afonjá was founded in 1910 by Mãe Aninha (Oba Biyi) in the neighborhood of Cabula in the district of São Gonçalo do Retiro. It is located approximately 6 miles northeast of Federação and Engenho Velho. Terreiro Bate Folha, one of the oldest of the Angola nation, was founded in 1916.[74] It is situated on 15 hectares of land in the neighborhood of Mata Escura, approximately 1.5 miles from Ilê Axé Opo Afonja, slightly further northeast of Federação and Engenho Velho.

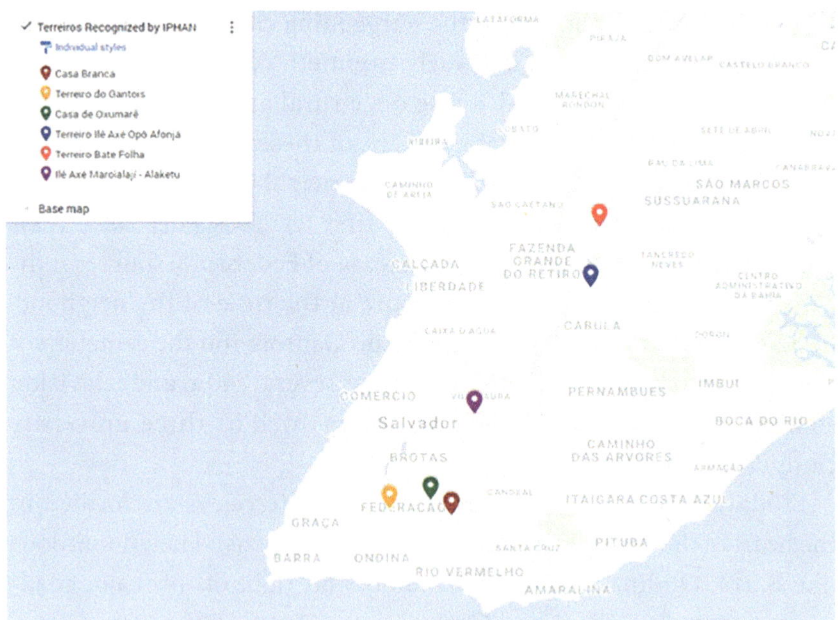

FIGURE 8: Map of Salvador terreiros recognized by IPHAN

DISCRIMINATION AGAINST HISTORIC TERREIROS

In April 2021, we had the opportunity to speak with Desirée Tozi, who is the Director of the Department of Cooperation and Development at IPHAN, about the benefits of cultural heritage recognition for Afro-Brazilian religions. Desirée explained that the registration and tombamento processes can be beneficial to terreiro communities because "it brings a new status, a status of public and private interest... in a certain way that makes it legitimate for the Brazilian state to apply financial resources to protect the construction, carry out renovations, to be able to dedicate public resources to the private [sector]."[75] She added that the communities understand that it is a way "to bring material protection" to their terreiros and that it "brings public visibility which in and of itself protects from aggression, from religious intolerance, from racism." Therefore, she explained that terreiros are looking to be recognized as cultural heritage by the municipal, state, and federal government for more than "just protecting cultural assets," but also "to protect and preserve their way of life."

Despite the hope that historic terreiros will be shielded from religious racism, similar to the protected sites and monuments discussed previously in this chapter, the terreiros recognized by IPHAN and parallel state and local institutions have experienced discrimination and violence in recent years. The discussion of a few examples, focused primarily on places we visited, is useful to understand how these supposedly protected spaces remain vulnerable to religious racism.

Casa de Oxumarê

The oldest Candomblé terreiros in Salvador did not escape the twentieth-century persecution discussed in Chapter 1, even though they built their communities in peripheral areas, on land that was difficult for police and other government authorities to reach. Baba Pecê, leader of Casa de Oxumarê for the last 30 years, observed that Afro-Brazilian terreiros have always suffered persecution. In our interview with him, he explained that in the early twentieth century, terreiros had to request a license for music ceremonies because if they didn't, the police would come and take their drums.[76] Authorities would puncture drum skins and even burn these sacred instruments. Memories of persecution remain vivid in the minds of the older Candomblé communities in Brazil, augmenting anxieties about recent forms of intolerance and aggression.

Casa de Oxumarê, despite its protection from IPHAN, has suffered multiple attacks in recent years. Like Mãe Gilda, Baba Pecê has had his image co-opted and used for unauthorized purposes. A local television station in Itapuã (a city within the greater municipal area of Salvador), took an interview of him and made a buffoonish voiceover with clear racist overtones to make it seem like he was commenting ridiculously on the Bahia football team losing a game. In a different kind of attack, Baba Pecê reported that Christians have gathered at the entrance of the terreiro and harassed people entering, telling them that they need to listen to the word of Jesus. (This is similar to what we observed of Evangelicals gathered at the Dique do Tororó.) Additionally, unidentified persons threw stones into the terreiro and broke sacred objects located right outside the entrance. In yet another kind of violence, the exterior wall of the terreiro was defaced twice, most recently in 2018. First, vandals painted a menorah and the Bible verse "The lord is my shepherd, he will never fail me" over a mural of orixá Oxumarê. The following year, unknown persons wrote "Jesus is the Way" in black paint on the same wall.[77]

Some recent instances of religious racism have come from the government. Ekedi Rose de Ogum, an important leader within Casa de Oxumarê, noted that the city of Salvador wanted to remove the terreiro to make room for the construction of a shopping center, a road, etc. The whole project was never completed, but the limited work that has occurred disrupted and took land from the terreiro. They had to fight very hard to stop the construction and intrusion on their property. On part of the land that had once belonged to the terreiro, newcomers to the area built an Evangelical church. The church acquired loudspeakers, which they have used to blast Christian music directly into the terreiro as a way to proselytize and disrupt ceremonies and other functions at Casa de Oxumarê. When we spoke with Ekedi Rose in January 2021, she explained: "We are watching the construction continue and the law has not budged to help us. It remains uncertain if we will be able to protect ourselves from this encroachment."[78] In all of these ways, despite its history and recognized status from IPHAN, even Casa de Oxumarê is vulnerable.

Despite remaining vulnerable, we observed that historic terreiros like Casa de Oxumarê seem less likely to suffer the types of noise pollution charges that we are examining in this project. When we asked Baba Pecê about such complaints from neighbors, he replied that there were some who were bothered by the sacred drumming and others who were not. There have been times when the police arrived and investigated noise complaints; however, unlike other smaller and less well-known terreiros, the police left shortly after realizing that they were just having a religious ceremony and nothing out of the ordinary was going on. He even reported that the police would sometimes become "security," actually protecting the ceremony and conversing with community members before departing.

Roça do Ventura and Terreiro Icimimó

Aside from the terreiros in Salvador and Casa das Minas in São Luís (discussed in Chapter 2), there are only two Afro-Brazilian religious sites that have been recognized through tombamento by IPHAN. One of those is Terreiro Zogbodo Male Bogun Seja Unde, aka Roça do Ventura Terreiro, which was founded in 1858 and is an important terreiro from the Jeje-Mahi nation.[79] It is located in the city of Cachoeira, considered the capital of the sugar-producing interior region of Bahia state that generated wealth and necessitated the importation of the Africans who founded the religions under discussion in this book. IPHAN's protection includes not only the community's buildings but also its large surrounding natural site, including multiple sacred trees and a stream.

In 2013, just before Roça do Ventura's tombamento by IPHAN was finalized, the community was attacked by arsonists.[80] Unknown persons set fire to the site, destroying around 600 meters of vegetation, including at least 50 sacred trees. Part of the reason that the damage was so extensive was that firefighters initially refused to respond and left the devotees to try to extinguish it themselves.

Such attacks on terreiros in Cachoeira and surrounding areas have been woefully common in recent years. One of the other most notable examples is Terreiro Ilê Axé Icimimó Aganjú Didè, located in a rural area of Cachoeira known as Terra Vermelha (Red Earth). Although it has not yet been recognized by IPHAN, Terreiro Icimimó was recognized as a cultural heritage site at the state level by the Instituto do Patrimônio Artístico e Cultural da Bahia in 2014. It is over 100 years old; the founder purchased the land for the terreiro in 1913 and it opened to the public in 1917.[81]

Terreiro Icimimó has suffered frequent attacks from a paper and bamboo company known as the Penha Group. In February 2019, employees of the Penha Group claimed that the terreiro's historic lands belonged to the company and threatened the religious leader, Pai Duda.[82] The state public prosecutor's office (Ministerio Publico) came to the defense of Terreiro Icimimó, issuing a recommendation that the Penha Group stay away from the terreiro and that the military police respond immediately and arrest company employees who ignored this recommendation.[83]

Later that year, in November 2019, unknown arsonists set fire to the property, destroying a large area of vegetation, including sacred plants and trees.[84] Like Roça do Ventura Terreiro, firefighters failed to respond for hours, enhancing the damage. Although it does not appear to have been proven, Pai Duda strongly suspects that the Penha Group was behind the attack. This suspicion seems logical considering that seven months later, in June 2020, company employees broke through the fence, invaded the terreiro lands, and threatened Pai Duda once again.[85]

We had the opportunity to visit Terreiro Icimimó and speak with Pai Duda in January 2021. At this time, he still felt certain that the terreiro was under threat and that harassment would not stop.[86] He was right. In September 2023, representatives of Terreiro Icimimó posted on social media that men on horseback sent by a paper company interested in acquiring the land had been seen repeatedly on the property. They claimed that several recent trespasses, burnings of plant life, and even the destruction of sacred stones have been at the hands of these individuals or others sent by this company.[87]

Public officials confirm that the kinds of attacks suffered by Roça do Ventura and Terreiro Icimimó are common in Cachoeira. Hilton Coelho, who is a member of the Special Commission for the Promotion of Equality and Human Rights of the Legislative Assembly of Bahia, told reporters that private companies in Cachoeira were engaging in land grabbing schemes targeting Afro-Brazilian terreiros.[88]

MUSEUMS AND CIVIC ORGANIZATIONS

Many of the more recently founded terreiros that we visited were finding their own ways to achieve state recognition by creating community and civic organizations, museums, libraries, art galleries, and markets on terreiro grounds. Terreiro Mokambo (Onzó Nguzo Za Nkisi Dandalunda Ye Tempo), founded in the Vila Dois de Julho neighborhood of Salvador in 1996, is a prime example. Its leader, recently deceased Pai Anselmo, built a museum on the compound to honor the knowledge and heritage of people of African descent. In 2013, they received a R$89,000 (~ $16,000 USD) grant from IPAC to expand the museum's library and educational center, and to host guided tours and research workshops.[89] Four years later, this barely 20-year-old terreiro was recognized through IPAC's tombamento process.[90]

It is ironic that these museums within terreiros sometimes include items (drums, ritual sculptures, etc.) that were at one time confiscated and held by police. For example, the crown jewel of Terreiro Mokambo's museum is a ritual chair (Figure 9) called Jubiabá that was confiscated in 1920 from an ancestral terreiro, São Jorge Filho da Goméia, and lived for nearly a century in a police evidence locker before being returned to its rightful owners in 2015.

Another striking example is Casa do Mensageiro, aka Ilê Asé Ojisé Olodumare, founded in 2004 in the state of Rio Grande do Norte and relocated to its current location in Barra de Pojuca, Bahia, in 2015. In 2019, this community suffered a severe incident of violence, when armed assailants invaded the temple during a ceremony, robbed devotees of their valuables, and pistol whipped the babalorixá. While carrying out the attack, the robbers referred to adepts as macumbeiros and admonished them for participating in a Candomblé ceremony.[91]

FIGURE 9: Photo of Jubiabá ritual chair, Terreiro Mokambo

We visited the terreiro in December of 2020, nearly two years after the attack. The community proudly showed us the museum that they had opened in November of 2020, on the terreiro grounds. The museum features sacred artifacts, sculptures, photos of the community in ceremony, and photos of spiritual ancestors of their leader,

FIGURES 10 & 11: Museum at Casa do Mensageiro

FIGURES 10 & 11: (Continued)

Pai Rychelmy. To reach the terreiro from Salvador, it is necessary to drive approximately 90 minutes to the northeast to the small town of Pojuca, which is home to slightly more than 40,000 people. From there, one has to navigate dirt roads without the benefit of GPS, which can be unavailable in the area.

CONCLUSION

Through this discussion of statues, sacred sites, and historic terreiros, one can see the complexities surrounding public recognition of Afro-Brazilian religions. Although devotees represent a minor segment of the population, the government has sponsored the preservation of sites of worship like Praça dos Orixás, Pedra de Xangô, and Dique do Tororó and the construction of statues honoring Afro-Brazilian orixás and religious leaders like Mãe Stella and Mãe Gilda. Even historic Candomblé terreiros, once built on the peripheries of the city to avoid police harassment, are now seeking and receiving protection from the government that once persecuted them. Tombamento, the creation of museums, and other forms of official recognition appear to defend terreiros against some forms of religious racism (especially noise pollution complaints) but do not insulate them from other forms of harassment, discrimination, and violence. These complex tensions between religious racism and the marketing of Afro-Brazilian religions as the cultural heritage of Brazil form the backdrop of complaints about noise pollution and other forms of discrimination against Afro-Brazilian sacred music. There is at once a reliance upon and a rejection of the sounds and sights of Africana religions in the public sphere in Brazil.

CHAPTER 4

Macumba Boa é Macumba Longe: Noise Complaints, Biased Neighbors, and Structural Discrimination

In the course of our research, we were introduced to a phrase or proverb that speaks volumes about Afro-Brazilian religions and their precarious position in Brazilian society: "macumba boa é macumba longe," which could be translated as, "Good macumba is distant macumba." However, because the phrase is used by devotees and by individuals who discriminate against Afro-Brazilian religions, it can mean a variety of things. According to Ilzver Matos, an attorney from Acaraju, Sergipe, who has worked on "noise pollution" cases, there are three main ways to interpret the phrase[1]:

1. "It is good to be in nature, in a place where we have all that we need to accomplish our ceremony." Ilzver explained that this is how his terreiro would think, as it is located inside the city of Aracaju. "There is nature where we are, but real estate speculation is arriving fast. If the city officials don't protect the area, it will quickly be lost to us as a sacred space."
2. The further away macumba is, the better. This is a white or Christian perspective that has to do with Afro-Brazilian religious communities being pushed off their land. This echoes information from earlier chapters in this book that document the movement of terreiros in Salvador and Rio de Janeiro fleeing religious persecution by police.

3. There is a third, more figurative, interpretation of "macumba boa é macumba longe," which has to do with the closeness of Brazil to Africa in terms of ancestry and identity. Whitening has long been a part of Brazilian national identity formation.[2] By the end of the eighteenth century, Africans and their descendants already formed the majority of the Brazilian population. As we discussed in Chapter 1, Brazil attempted to physically and culturally whiten the nation in the late nineteenth and early twentieth centuries through encouraging immigration from Europe and prohibiting African cultural practices. Religious racism today seems to be a new chapter in the age-old conflict over how much of an African diaspora nation Brazil really is. The desire of mainstream Brazil to distance itself from Africa and Blackness manifests in attempts to control, push to the periphery, and ultimately eradicate Afro-Brazilian religion as a stain on the purity of the Brazilian nation, which, from the mainstream perspective, imagines itself more white than Black. Of course, this desire for whiteness continues alongside and is in competition with the Brazilian government and tourist industry's ongoing capitalization on marketing Brazil as an African heritage site.

One should keep this phrase, "macumba boa é macumba longe," in mind as they are reading this chapter, in which we explore complaints against Afro-Brazilian religious communities for "noise pollution." Leaders are being arrested for "disturbing the peace" or "disturbing society." They are frequently sentenced to community service or even prison terms. These complaints often arise in small cities or in satellite cities on the borders of larger metropolitan areas. In many of the situations that we investigated, Afro-Brazilian communities had intentionally relocated to these more rural, secluded regions precisely to acquire more space, escape urban sprawl, and conduct rituals and ceremonies undisturbed. Still, their tactics have not been enough to avoid persecution by their neighbors.

There are two sets of actors who play central, intersecting roles in these noise pollution cases: neighbors and the government. We begin with two examples that highlight the discriminatory actions of neighbors in these cases. Then we discuss three cases that, in addition to providing other examples of neighborhood discrimination, also illustrate the abuses of the government in investigating and adjudicating these disputes.

THE ROLE OF NEIGHBORS

Many of these cases seem to follow a familiar pattern – Candomblé religious leaders establish their terreiros in areas of the city that are less developed and purchase tracts of land to support their religious practice. After years or even decades of hosting religious communities, these onetime outskirts develop into new residential and commercial centers as the city grows. As part of this expansion, Evangelical neighbors move in and complaints about Candomblé ceremonies begin. Two cases from the city of Lauro de Freitas in Bahia provide excellent examples.

Lauro de Freitas

The city of Lauro de Freitas is founded on lands that were once occupied by the Tupinambá people.[3] In 1552, Portuguese colonists took control of the region and established it as the parish of Santo Amaro do Ipitanga. Over the following centuries, the parish developed and the population of Portuguese colonists and enslaved Africans grew. However, in the nineteenth century, a devastating cholera outbreak killed a large portion of the population and there were few people living in the parish until the mid-twentieth century.

During the second world war, the construction of an air base brought a new influx of young men to the area. Some of these men got married and settled near the air base with their families. By 1962, it had grown large enough that residents petitioned to form their own municipality, which they named Lauro de Freitas.

In the 1990s, the city continued to grow.[4] A variety of businesses, such as condominiums, bars, restaurants, shopping malls, and banks moved into the area. Today, Lauro de Freitas spans an area of approximately 60 square kilometers and has a population of just over 170,000 people.[5] It is considered part of the greater metropolitan region of Salvador. In 2015, *Istoé* magazine named Lauro de Freitas the best Brazilian city to live in.[6]

Statistics from 2019 indicated that 85% of the population of Lauro de Freitas are people of African descent.[7] Despite the unwelcome atmosphere that the following cases suggest, the official website for the city notes that Indigenous and African culture have greatly influenced the area. It lists Candomblé terreiros, capoeira groups, and samba dancers as part of the city's rich heritage.[8] It also states that there are more than 400 terreiros registered in the city.[9]

Case of Pai Anderson

In a February 2021 interview, Pai Anderson de Oxalá, leader of Ilê Axé Alá Obatalandê, shared a moving story of a noise pollution-related incident of religious racism directed against his community in 2009. The terreiro has been in its current location in Lauro de Freitas since 2007. Pai Anderson explained that they had moved to that location precisely to have more ample space and avoid any issues with noise complaints. For two years, they played their atabaques and held ceremonies with no issues. However, in 2009, while having a ceremonial drumming, Pai Anderson's terreiro was "invaded by city officials who falsely claimed to be military police in order to stop the proceedings."

The invasion happened in two parts; the first incident occurred on a Saturday and the second on the following Sunday. During the Saturday invasion, Pai Anderson was *manifestado* (experiencing the presence of the orixá in his body), so he did not see what happened. The ogans and other authorities from the terreiro received the officers and after a time, the officers left. On the next day (Sunday), the ceremonies continued at 1 pm, and by 5:30 pm or so the officers had returned. Pai Anderson recounts the events as follows:

> I saw something strange happening near the entrance to the terreiro. When I approached, I saw a police vehicle. I asked the officers why they

> were there. They said they had come the day before and given a notification/warning. They said that their current visit was a second warning and if they came a third time, they would shut down the terreiro outright. I explained to the officers that they would never dare to invade another religious community's space in this way, especially not Christians and especially not white people. The officers were very aggressive and disrespectful. I told them to leave my property. They refused to leave the premises, claiming that it was a public space. I clarified that in fact it is my own private property and furthermore that this was no bar or nightclub, but rather a sacred space, a temple holding a religious function. They said they would not leave. They didn't confiscate our atabaques only because I refused to let them. I was very upset. We started to video what was happening as a way to defend ourselves and our rights. The video footage of the incident got a lot of attention around the world.

At the time of the invasion, they had 500 or more visitors, including religious leaders from various traditions at the celebration. The guests included small children as well as elderly persons who were 70 or 80 years old. Pai Anderson asked us to "imagine how disturbing and odd it would be to have such a religious ceremony interrupted in this way."

Pai Anderson described the invasion of the terreiro as "absurd," explaining

> our terreiro is officially registered and everything is in order legally. The law in Brazil gives our religion (Candomblé) and ALL religions the right to worship as we choose. Our terreiro has an established calendar of celebrations. We don't play all day every day, but rather on certain occasions throughout the year. So this invasion came as a big shock.

He also expressed frustration about the biases in the entire process, referring to the claims of noise pollution as "unfounded." He stressed the lack of objective evidence for the complaint, observing that "No one ever measured the decibel levels of our acoustic drum music and singing." He was convinced that their ceremonies were not bothering anyone because "the nearest neighbors are quite a distance away. We use no amplification, no speakers."

The true motivation of the complainants was very clear to Pai Anderson. Without hesitation, he told us,

> The complaints come from newcomers who are affiliated with Neo-Pentecostal churches in the area. Once they arrive, they realize there is a terreiro here. They get uncomfortable with our music but not with the amplified Christian church music [likely referring to the common sound of vehicles fitted with loudspeakers driving slowly through neighborhoods blasting church music or sermons – something that several informants mentioned in our discussions about "noise pollution"]. And they denounce us anonymously to the authorities.

He lamented the clear discrimination against Afro-Brazilian religious communities but expressed his resolve to keep fighting against religious racism, adding, "The church music plays loud and no one is offended, no one silences them. But our atabaques also should not and will not be silenced."

Case of Pai Vilson

Vilson Caetano de Sousa Jr. holds a PhD in anthropology, is a professor at the Federal University of Bahia, and is the babalorixá of Ilê Obá L'Okê. In an interview in January 2021, he recounted to us how his terreiro was harassed by a neighbor over the course of more than five years. By lodging fictitious or exaggerated complaints to the authorities, this person was able to harness the power of the state to attack Afro-Brazilian religions.

Ilê Obá L'Okê, or Casa do Rei e Senhor das Alturas, is a Candomblé terreiro that has been located in the city of Lauro de Freitas for more than ten years. Between March 2014 and August 2019, the temple struggled to defend itself against legal attacks by a neighbor who purported to represent the entire community, claiming "nobody wants a terreiro in this area."[10] The case is instructive because the starting point is clear antipathy toward Candomblé. This individual meticulously sought out various ways the terreiro could be vulnerable to petty legal violations that could see it shut down and forced to leave the area.

According to Pai Vilson, the controversy began because of his efforts to build physical representations of Africa that would challenge preconceived notions of a continent of poverty and misery.[11] He arrived in Lauro de Freitas in 2004 and began renovations on the inside of the terreiro in 2011. He built elaborate sculptures of the orixás. He intentionally chose to depict the orixás as Black skinned with African features, including the facial scarification practiced by some Yoruba people.[12] These representations contest more common public monuments to the orixás, which depict these African deities as white or racially ambiguous. Pai Vilson's focus on making the terreiro appear beautiful and inviting while challenging misconceptions about Africa reminded us of other communities' efforts to transform part of their sacred space into a museum or cultural center. In fact, he shared that part of the goal was to represent aspects of Africa that most people would not have learned in school.

Pai Vilson explains that the terreiro had existed in this location in Lauro de Freitas for ten years without incident, until he began work on the exterior of the building. The front wall of the terreiro is adorned with Yoruba words, relief sculptures of elephants, chameleons and other symbols, African masks, and crowned Black men and women in honor of the terreiro's patron deity Oxalá, orixá of peace and wisdom. Palm fronds in the doorway delineate holy ground. All of this stands in stark contrast to the bland buildings close by.

When Pai Vilson put the Yoruba name and artwork on the front of the terreiro, a neighbor began to complain. He told Pai Vilson that he had no problem with them practicing their religion behind closed doors but when they put up the artwork and signage they were "institutionalizing" or "officializing" their religious space. This was an issue because Candomblé temples could not be located in residential areas, the neighbor claimed. Pai Vilson responded by pointing out to the neighbor that there were other non-residential buildings, including churches, on the same street. The neighbor insisted that no one

FIGURE 1: Exterior of Terreiro Ilê Obá L'Okê or Casa do Rei e Senhor das Alturas

wants to live next to a Candomblé terreiro and that the presence of this community devalued neighboring properties.

After this encounter, city officials received a series of anonymous complaints about the terreiro, which Pai Vilson suspects originated from the same neighbor. The first complaint claimed that the terreiro was renovating their space without a permit. According to Pai Vilson, there were no renovations underway. The second complaint asserted that the terreiro was not properly handling rainwater drainage. The third report to city officials complained about noise pollution. Pai Vilson expressed confusion about the basis for such a complaint, explaining that "our atabaques, sacred drums through which we communicate with our divinities, are not able to produce enough decibels to justify such an accusation."[13] He speculated that the noise complaint may have been in response to fireworks, which are occasionally used in ceremonies.

Frustrated by the persistent harassment, Pai Vilson drove to the city office where the noise complaint had been filed and demanded to know the identity of the complainant. City officials refused to disclose the name of the person making the complaints but admitted that the same individual had been to their office several times. The officials told Pai Vilson that they had advised the complainant that his efforts to close the terreiro would not be successful because "After all, Candomblé is a religion and people have the right to practice it. Moreover, since the Candomblé community didn't play their drums every day, he should try to have a harmonious coexistence with the terreiro."[14]

Despite the clear response of this public office, someone continued to file complaints about the terreiro. In addition to repeating the initial accusations about unpermitted renovations and noise pollution, the next wave of complaints included new alleged infractions, such as the breeding, keeping, and sacrificing of animals, odors from ritual meal preparation and refuse, and the unsightliness of offerings supposedly left outdoors around the neighborhood.[15] The community received repeated notifications from city officials, ordering them to respond to these allegations, and underwent multiple inspections by city authorities. By the time that we spoke with Pai Vilson, most (if not all) of these complaints had been resolved and the city had determined that none of the allegations had any merit. However, the community had suffered years of near constant persecution.

Eventually the neighbor took to filming the terreiro's activities with a drone. This last invasion was such an indignity that Pai Vilson felt forced to lodge his own complaint against this neighbor, which resulted in a restraining order against this person, barring them from disturbing the terreiro's activities. In Pai Vilson's estimation, the fear of Candomblé and its drums sparked a whole slew of false accusations in an attempt "to shut down the terreiro and move it to another space in the city," which, he explains, "has happened with many communities who have been pushed to peripheral areas marked by violence and lack of basic infrastructure."[16] He feels that his preparation as a scholar was his salvation, because it allowed him to navigate the legal systems, research laws, and write on his own behalf. He says, "If we had not been prepared, we would have been vulnerable."[17] Although not totally satisfied with the outcome and lack of more rigorous punishment,[18] Pai Vilson feels pleased that at least, "Our drums will finally have peace."[19]

Analysis of the Role of Neighbors

The cases of Pai Anderson and Pai Vilson in the growing city of Lauro de Freitas illustrate some of the important characteristics of the role of neighbors in noise pollution cases in Brazil. One of the key points is that both religious leaders told us that one of the reasons that they established their terreiros in Lauro de Freitas is because it is a suburban area that afforded them more space and where they could create some distance between themselves and their neighbors. Both asserted that they were too far away from their nearest neighbors and/or that the way that their buildings were constructed would have prevented their ceremonies from bothering the neighbors. But this didn't stop the harassment.

A second observation is that Pai Vilson and Pai Anderson both reported that they were surprised when the authorities came to notify them of the noise complaints and other violations with which they were charged. In one sense, this surprise or indignation seems to have stemmed from the fact that Brazilian law, as both men pointed out, grants freedom of religion to all. They stressed that they had complied with all the relevant laws such as the registration of their terreiro but that did not guarantee them the rights afforded to other religious communities.

The religious leaders' surprise about the complaints also tells us something important about the relationship with the neighbors prior to the filing of the charges. Aside from Pai Vilson's neighbor making discriminatory comments and asserting that the terreiro was not allowed to exist in the neighborhood, there seems to have been little to no communication from the complaining neighbors before the authorities arrived at their door or issued formal notice of the complaint. This suggests that the neighbors were not interested in a peaceful resolution to the alleged problems.

Along these lines, both men indicated that the complaints against them were at least partially fabricated. Pai Vilson described numerous allegations that were so ludicrous that he could not even, at times, pinpoint what exactly the neighbor meant (i.e., complaining about unpermitted renovations when no renovations were taking place). Pai Anderson discussed how his new Pentecostal neighbors lived too far from the terreiro to have genuinely been disturbed by the drumming; however, their religious views led them to try to use the authorities to persecute the terreiro. Both men questioned how deeply anyone could have been inconvenienced by their celebrations, noting that the atabaques are not played every day.

Finally, Pai Vilson and Pai Anderson both describe a pattern of persecution –over the course of several days or even years – in which repeated complaints are lodged to attempt to drive the terreiro to shut down or to move. As both men stated in their interviews, this is treatment that is unique to Afro-Brazilian religious communities. These neighbors would not and do not question the presence of churches in their communities or call the authorities to claim that they are being disturbed by Christian gatherings. Pai Anderson notes that this is particularly discriminatory because of the loud speakers that the churches use to amplify their services.

For all of these reasons – the false allegations, the lack of communication before lodging a complaint, the disparate treatment of terreiros and churches, etc. – we can see evidence of bias in the actions of the neighbors. This is just the first stage in a multifaceted problem. Government authorities compound the discrimination that Afro-Brazilian religious communities experience with their own biased responses to the problem.

THE ROLE OF GOVERNMENT

After community members have mobilized police to enforce noise laws, various branches of government have acted to silence the atabaques. Judges have sentenced religious leaders to excessive and embarrassing punishments for minor (perhaps fabricated) infractions. Judges have also imposed strict limits on when ceremonies can happen, sound decibel levels, and even the number of drums permitted. Other authorities have raided Afro-Brazilian religious ceremonies and forced devotees to stop playing their drums. All of these things greatly impact religious communities and impose restrictions on them that are different from those faced by other faith communities. The story of Pai Fabricio in Ilhéus (Bahia), Pai Joselino's terreiro in Aracaju (Sergipe), and the case of Centro Espírita Ilê Axé e Sangô in Belo Horizonte (Minas Gerais) demonstrate how these cases regularly unfold.

Pai Fabricio

In 2013, Pai Fabricio Leal Nascimento, a Candomblé leader, was arrested in the city of Ilhéus, a historic town in the southern part of Bahia, located about 400 miles from the state capital, Salvador. He was charged with violating the federal penal code, which, in a chapter of crimes against "public peace," prohibits disturbing anyone's work or tranquility by "abusing sound instruments."[20] Court records indicate that Pai Fabricio was supposedly performing Candomblé rituals in his residence that "disturbed the tranquility and quiet of the neighbors" by inviting throngs of people to drum and sing loudly.[21] In the court case against Pai Fabricio, the victim is listed as "Society."

As a penalty, the Public Prosecutor's Office (Ministério Público) proposed that Pai Fabricio complete 210 hours of community service within 180 days (a local reporter claimed that this proposed sentence would include sweeping the street).[22] They also asked that he refrain from doing any activity related to Candomblé in his home, especially using sound-emitting instruments, including atabaques and other drums, burning anything that produces odor or fumes, or sacrificing animals. Pai Fabricio rejected this proposed punishment; therefore, the judge ordered several government agencies to go to the home to conduct further investigation about whether having religious services in the space would, in fact, disturb the community. A local news story quoted Pai Fabricio as having said,

> Since when is lighting candles for our orixás, in the interior of our homes and singing our prayer songs disturbing public order? If we have our instruments like the adjás and atabaques, evangelicals also have theirs, such as microphones and drums.[23]

Pai Joselino

The case of Pai Joselino in Sergipe's capital, Aracaju, illustrates both government and citizen-led efforts to silence Afro-Brazilian religious practice.[24] Over the course of two decades he has struggled to defend his terreiro from harassment and exercise his right to practice Candomblé freely. In 2001, despite the fact that it was not late at night, police came to his door to demand that he stop a ceremony that included drumming. He went to the police headquarters later and found out that this interruption was brought on by a neighbor's complaint. This was Pai Joselino's first encounter with religious racism. In this instance, the neighbor moved away and the situation resolved without further incident.

Pai Joselino's second experience with religious racism took place in 2008 after the so-called Law of Decibels[25] was passed, limiting the volume at which drums were allowed to play. Another neighbor had moved into the same place as the one who had previously filed a complaint. This neighbor was nice for a time, even having Joselino do spiritual work for her. Then all of a sudden, he learned that she had filed a complaint, stating that the terreiro's drumming was bothering her. As a result of complaints and various occasions of police coming to his home (usually as festivities were wrapping up), Pai Joselino was called to the Public Ministry. He jokes gravely that since he had no money for a lawyer, "Olorum [god] and Ogum [a warrior orixá] came with me instead." The agent informed him that he would either need to stop playing drums or adjust to the decibel requirements. Pai Joselino replied that there was no way to adjust to those requirements and still play. There was no way to clap softer for the *nkisi* (spirits) than what they had already been doing. There was no way for the sound of the drums not to travel. "Drums have no volume button to turn down," he said. The official responded that Joselino was very bold (*muito atrevido*) and that the terreiro would be shut down unless or until adjustments were made. He was given 90 days to comply.

When we interviewed him in March 2021, he expressed his frustration with the encounter.

> I told them I couldn't [adjust the sound]. To construct sound proof walls would require a large sum of money, which I simply did not have and could not possibly raise. As a way to help me, some friends with a little knowledge about dampening sound made the suggestion of putting egg cartons up, closing windows and other openings, as a way to, hopefully, meet the decibel requirements. I scraped together money and hired a lawyer. With his help, we learned that the neighbor who was complaining had family inside the Public Ministry, and for this reason their minor complaints were being given so much weight. Eventually, the case was shelved (*arquivado*) because there was no evidence and the woman's story was shaky. At first, she alleged that my terreiro played drums seven days a week (*domingo a domingo*), 24 hours a day. Of course, no Candomblé terreiro plays that often or much. I explained that in my case, I couldn't even if I wanted to because I have a job as a public functionary in addition to my work in the

> terreiro. Her nonsense accusation and the family connection between the complainants and Public Ministry officials made them shelve the case.

During that time that he and his lawyer were investigating the case, Pai Joselino did not play drums for fear of arrest or other reprisals against his congregation, which was composed mostly of elderly members. Celebrations for several deities, including the important feijoada de Ogum, were canceled due to the silencing. At the time of our interview in 2021, Pai Joselino seemed regretful that he did not ignore the complaint and play anyway; however, at the time, his desire to keep his followers safe made him cooperate with authorities.

In 2009, the same woman filed a new complaint against Joselino for disturbing the peace, using the same argument as before. This precipitated a series of visits to the police station and hearings before judges that lasted until 2012. At every turn, officers asked if he wanted to make an arrangement or agreement (*fazer acordo*) with the complainant. He explained,

> I said no because I'm not the one who needs to make an arrangement or change. It is my right to practice my religion (which includes these drums). This woman wants me to let go of my drums, to stop playing. But my religion cannot exist without the drum. It's the drum that calls the spirits.

Since Pai Joselino did not want to make a settlement, his case was passed on to the Civil Crimes Division. Again he hired a lawyer. At the last hearing in December of 2012, Joselino achieved a small victory. After his lawyer explained his position in the case, the judge asked the complaining neighbor if she wanted to go forward and press charges. The neighbor responded that she wanted Joselino's terreiro closed outright. The judge beat her gavel and said, "It won't stop. It's his right. In fact, he could bring a case against you right now for religious intolerance." At the time, Joselino wasn't interested in bringing a case. However, reflecting back on the situation during the interview, he wondered, "Maybe it was a mistake not to."

In 2020, during the COVID-19 pandemic, the same neighbor came to Pai Joselino's door while he was holding a ceremony (*borí*) with just a few initiates and officiants. She asked him to stop the ceremony because she wanted to rest. Pai Joselino explained that it was, at the latest, 7 pm. Frustrated by more than a decade of harassment from this openly bigoted neighbor, he decided to take action. He told us, "So, I went and filed a complaint of my own against her. This has stopped her; she is no longer bothering us."

Centro Espírita Ilê Axé de Sangô

In 2015, neighbors petitioned the government (the Ministério Público) to do something about the noise at Centro Espírita Ilê Axé de Sangô, in Santa Luzia – a small city in the greater metropolitan area of Belo Horizonte (the capital of Minas Gerais). In September of 2016, government officials came out and measured the decibels of "noise" coming from the terreiro. The limit for the area was 50 decibels; the sound readings came back at 80.7.[26] In response, the Ministério Público coordinated (and perhaps imposed) an "agreement" (Um Termo de Ajustamento de Conduta, or TAC) on this terreiro that it would only hold ceremonies on Wednesdays from 7 to 10 pm and on one Saturday of the month from 3 to 8 pm. The city also limited their music to a certain decibel level and to the use of one of the sacred drums (atabaques). Typically, three are required for ceremonies. The "agreement" even prohibited "silent" ceremonies outside of these dates and times. If it violated any of these rules, the Center could be subject to a fine of R$100 (~$20 USD) per violation.[27] These restrictions would be in place until the Center was able to construct soundproofing to muffle the noise. Ironically, this Center was located in a very poor and peripheral location in the city of Belo Horizonte; therefore, it is unlikely that the sounds of the temple were actually disturbing anyone. Instead, according to a representative of Cenarab, an Afro-Brazilian religious organization that assisted with the Center's case, the temple was being persecuted by the neighbor who initiated the complaint because of religious intolerance.[28]

The owner of the building, Aílton da Costa Silva, initially agreed to these restrictions but signed the "agreement" without legal counsel. Later, Silva discovered that it would cost R$30,000 (~$6,000 USD) to construct the soundproofing.[29] The renovations would have included substantial modifications to the building, such as moving and removing walls.[30] They were unable to afford these changes. As time passed and the burdens of construction became more apparent, the Center began questioning the accord. One of the leaders of the terreiro, Pai Luiz Oxossi explains, "There is no Candomblé without the three atabaques. It would be like a mass ceremony without the priest or a Catholic church without the church bell."[31]

In October 2017, the Conselho Nacional do Ministério Público held an administrative proceeding to determine whether the "agreement" should have been made and could be enforced against the Center.[32] Hedio Silva Jr., a famous attorney who represents Afro-Brazilian religions on a variety of cases regarding religious racism, argued that "agreement" was unconstitutional according to article 170, section 5 of the state constitution, which prohibits the government from requiring any kind of license or permit for the operation of a religious temple. He also pointed out that the willingness to dictate how religious services are conducted is a type of selective attack against Afro-Brazilian religions. Similar to Pai Luiz, Silva contended that it would be akin to requiring the Catholic church to use grape juice instead of wine for the eucharist in response to arguments that wine might lead to child alcoholism. Such an invasive restriction, Silva argued, would never be imposed on the Catholic church, a powerful institution, based on such a fanciful argument. But this Council was willing to dictate the practices of a *macumba* temple based on flawed evidence and an aversion to Afro-Brazilian religion. Silva affirmed, "This is called religious intolerance, there is no other legal expression that can describe conduct like this."[33]

Despite these forceful arguments, the Council refused to reopen the case, essentially leaving the "agreement" in place. Not long thereafter, in 2018, the Center was closed and the property owner, Aílton, died from a heart attack.[34] When we spoke to Túlio Aguiar, a representative from Cenarab, he informed us that this was just one noise pollution case out of dozens, reported and unreported, that have targeted Afro-Brazilian religious communities in recent years.

Analysis

These examples underscore important trends in the government's mishandling of these cases. Many cases, like the charges against Pai Joselino and Centro Espírita Ilê Axé de Sangô, begin with a community petition seeking to restrict the religious practices at an Afro-Brazilian religious temple or to remove the temple from the community altogether. Following these complaints, authorities will often provide neighbors with a way to continue their harassment of Afro-Brazilian religious communities by creating a fixed penalty (often a substantial fine) for subsequent violations. This can be used to intimidate these communities by threatening them with additional complaints that will trigger burdensome fines. In some cases, authorities even explicitly empower neighbors to make such complaints in their decision.

For example, in August 2016, Tat'etu Josué d'Ogum of Ilè Asé Oxum, Obaluayê e Ogum, a Candomblé temple in Cafelândia, São Paulo, was sentenced to 28 days in prison for violating a criminal law about noise restrictions.[35] After imposing this severe penalty, the judge also distributed a letter to the neighbors of the terreiro that said that the temple could play drums between the hours of 9 am and 10 pm with a maximum noise level of 50 decibels. The letter specified that if someone was offended by the sound coming from the temple, they could lodge a complaint and the temple would be fined R$1,000 (~$200 USD).

We were unable to speak with Tat'etu Josué d'Ogum directly or find a copy of his case; however, other sources report that the letter authorized neighbors to file a complaint (and thus trigger a hefty fine) regardless of whether the temple exceeded the miniscule decibel level permitted in the order.[36] A neighbor feeling "bothered" by the sounds was enough to warrant a report and likely constitute a violation.

This case exemplifies several of the other recurring problems that emerge when Afro-Brazilian religious worship is framed as noise pollution. First, it shows religious leaders being treated like criminals for having ceremonies that neighbors or authorities deem too noisy. Sometimes, like in the case of Pai Joselino (and the case of Pai Anderson described in the previous section), complaints take religious leaders by surprise. The first time they realize there is a problem might be when the police show up at their door. Second, while the hours that Ilè Asé Oxum, Obaluayê e Ogum, was permitted to play drums may seem reasonable, there are serious questions about the consistent application of the law to all community members no matter their religion. It is discriminatory to single out Afro-Brazilian religious temples for more restrictive noise regulations than the law otherwise imposes. Additionally, sounds from these temples should not be treated differently than sounds from a house party, barbeque, or church. The decibel levels permitted in this case (and some of the others that we examined) are comparable to the sounds from a large office (50 dB), sewing machine (60 dB), dishwasher (55–70 dB), freeway traffic (70 dB), or a noisy restaurant (85 dB), all of which constitute an impossibly low threshold for Afro-Brazilian religious celebrations where music takes place.[37] Finally, in addition to these restrictive rules, the judge delivered authorization to neighbors to persecute the temple if they merely felt bothered (regardless of the decibel levels).

Ilè Asé Oxum, Obaluayê e Ogum does not seem to be the only Afro-Brazilian religious community that has been subjected to such arbitrary restrictions. Other cases suggest a pattern of ignoring official guidelines for determining whether a noise violation has occurred in allegations against Afro-Brazilian places of worship, therefore allowing cases to proceed based solely on unsubstantiated reports.[38] One will recall that Pai Anderson emphasized that one of the reasons that he believes the police mishandled his case was that they failed to take a decibel reading of their singing and drumming when they came to harass him about the supposed noise complaints. There are several other accounts of similar situations.

In 2013, a neighbor filed a noise complaint against Centro Umbanda Cachoeirinha de Xangô in Londrina, Paraná. The Center had been located at this site for ten years and regularly held services from 8 pm to 10 pm on Fridays. When a neighbor repeatedly called the police to complain about the sound of the drums, the leaders suspected that religious racism was behind the allegations. However, authorities imposed a R$500 (~$100 USD) fine based only on the neighbor's claims, without measurements to prove that the sounds exceeded the legal limits.[39] The Center contested the issuing of this decision without evidence, noting that they even had a permit to operate in this space. They organized a protest, calling on their supporters to dress in white and gather in front of the court where the case was being heard. They stressed that they had functioned in this same place for over a decade and had always had the respect of their neighbors, except for this one person.[40] One of the center leaders, Claudia Ikandayô, told reporters: "We are going back to the age of Black people in slave quarters, when we had to go to the middle of the forest to play our drums and worship our orixás. We are tired of being slaughtered and demonized."[41]

Similarly, in 2017, Babalorixá Edson de Omulu, leader of Tenda de Umbanda e Caridade Caboclo Flecheiro, was sentenced to 15 days in prison for "disturbing the peace of others."[42] (This sentence was later reduced to community service.) The case appears to have been based primarily, if not entirely, on the complaint of a neighbor, José Roberto Monteiro de Lemos. While Lemos claimed that noise from the temple disturbed him late at night through the early hours of the morning, Baba Edson asserted that the services only took place from 5 pm to 8 pm. Additionally, a representative of the Office of Legal Advice to Popular Organizations (Gabinete de Assessoria Jurídica às Organizações Populares) went to the temple to observe their monthly drumming services. She reported that they did not emit much noise during these ceremonies – they only used two small drums, chanted, and clapped.[43]

Advocates pointed out that Baba Edson's case seemed to be contrary to the state laws governing noise pollution and "disturbing the public." This law, passed in 2005, listed several types of noise that were exempt from provisions about noise pollution such as the sounds emitted by ambulances, fire trucks, or security alarms.[44] In 2010, legislators had amended this statute to include sounds produced "by religious manifestations, as well as church bells and liturgical instruments used in the exercise of religious worship or ceremony."[45]

In addition to showing the bias of the legal system against Afro-Brazilian religions, such cases demonstrate the problem with courts allowing witness testimony, particularly that of a single complaining neighbor, to form the entire basis of a noise complaint. In many instances, religious leaders indicate that neighbors complain about the sounds at their temples while not appearing bothered by similar noises from other local events. Additionally, the neighbors report hours and activities that differ from when religious communities state that they have ceremonies. One must recall that in Pai Joselino's case, the neighbor claimed that he was holding ceremonies seven days a week, despite the fact that no Candomblé temple has religious services that frequently. Later, this neighbor's bias became apparent when she stated outright that her goal was to see the terreiro closed. Even in the case of Centro Espírita Ilê Axé e Sangô, where there were multiple signatories on the petition complaining about noise pollution, Attorney Silva pointed out that the original two complainants were Evangelicals (implying that their motive may have been religious racism), and that the exact address and actual proximity of the original complainants and other signatories is unknown.[46]

Ilzver Matos, who has worked on such "noise pollution" cases, confirmed that officials in Sergipe often initiate a trial process based on the crime of breaking decibel levels, but no measurement is taken at the time with a decibel meter.[47] To address this issue, the Associação Brasileira de Normas Técnicas established a set of protocols (beyond decibel measurement), which includes accounting for obstacles, direction of the sound, etc., and making a series of calculations based on these factors. Sometime thereafter, a case took place with a terreiro in Laranjeiras in which a judge refused to proceed with claims of noise pollution because the protocols were not followed. There were no precise measurements, no testimonies, no evidence of a complaint that represented a majority of the community. The case was dismissed based on these procedural errors. Ilzver reports that a transformation occurred due to this experience. On paper at least, officials in Sergipe are not to be sent out in response to individual complaints alone. Authorities are required to first conduct an investigation to learn whether or not the peace is really being disturbed.

However, in other states, such protective protocols may not have been introduced. Without objective measurements and other evidence of the purported "disturbance," biased people are able to mobilize authorities to harass devotees of Afro-Brazilian religions. When these complaints do not represent a majority of the neighborhood in question, as is often the case, Candomblé and Umbanda communities are still treated as less valuable than one or two neighbors.[48]

In cases like those of Baba Edson and Tat'etu Josué, neighbors' complaints have led to criminal charges. In others, they have led to limitations on the hours of ceremonies and the numbers of drums used, as well as fines. They can also impose other financial burdens. Religious communities may feel pressured or even be required to install costly insulation or make other repairs to their temples to reduce the decibels emitted from the space because, as Pai Joselino pointed out, there is no "volume button" on the drums. They cannot just play them more softly. As in Pai Joselino's case, the inability to afford these repairs can leave devotees scrambling to try makeshift methods like closing doors and windows or putting up egg cartons to try to meet the decibel requirements in an affordable way. Eventually, unable to find an affordable solution, temples like Pai Joselino's and Centro Espírita Ilê Axé e Sangô are often forced to shut down or relocate to a different area where they can have greater distance from their neighbors.

In 2013, Ronaldo Pelli wrote an article titled "Religious Intolerance in the Land of the Festivals," which, in part, describes the similar plight of an Umbanda leader, Maurício dos Santos Mota, in the northern state of Maranhão.[49] According to Pelli, Mota signed an agreement with the State Public Ministry stating that he would only hold religious celebrations for his community, the Spirit of Umbanda Center of Our Lady of the Candelaria, on Fridays from 6 pm to 9 pm. Mota also agreed that he would not use "traditional musical instruments" during these celebrations. Perhaps most troubling, Mota agreed to move the Center from "the place it had long occupied to move to another, far more remote and worse place."[50] Although framed as an "agreement" or contract between Pai Maurício and the State Public Ministry, Pelli suggests that consent was likely coerced. He notes that if Pai Maurício failed to follow the terms of the agreement, he "would be subject to legal consequences and a police investigation would be set in" motion.[51] The threat of police investigation can be very serious for Afro-Brazilian religious leaders, who have often been arrested due to noise complaints and who (as the next chapter explores) have suffered physical violence at the hands of officers who have arrived to investigate these complaints.

During our interview, Ilzver discusses a similar pattern following a case in Sergipe in 2016. On a Saturday evening at 8:30 pm, neighbors called the police to report that an Umbanda center in Acaraju was "disturbing the peace." When the police arrived, they arrested the leader for violating local noise ordinances, and they seized some of the instruments that were being played in the ceremony, including the atabaques and the agogô.[52] In 2021, almost six years after the incident took place, Ilzver reported that just 15 days earlier, he had spoken with the leader of the center and learned that he was moving to another, less central location. Ilzver explained that on the one hand, it's a good thing. But on the other hand, the place he is moving to has no infrastructure for what he wants to do. Thus, twenty-first-century noise complaints form a pattern of forced displacement with ever more dire consequences for Afro-Brazilian religionists.

Observing this forced movement, we are reminded of the adage "macumba boa é macumba longe" discussed in the introduction to this chapter. Fear of police raids and other discrimination continues to push Afro-Brazilian places of worship to the peripheries of cities. However, unlike the early communities who were able to escape into the wilderness, fewer and fewer parts of Brazil are undeveloped and able to provide refuge. Ilzver Matos recounted an issue with his own community that illustrates this problem. He said,

> I come from an era in which we practiced our religion in the center of the city [Aracaju]. There was a spectacular crossroads at the corner of our house where people would leave offerings, hold ceremonies, sacrifice bulls, roosters, etc. Right in the center of the city! Not long ago our terreiro was looking for a place to conduct a ritual, somewhere not crowded that was clean, and we could not find anywhere. We had to go somewhere much further out than what we were accustomed to. I think it is problematic that the city does not consider [protecting or preserving] the spaces that have traditionally been used for ritual. [As described in previous chapters, as the city grows it devours sacred spaces of Africana religions.] For example, we have always used mangrove swamps (*mangue*) for ceremonies. That is where the organic remnants of the parties (animal parts, etc.) would be taken, returning them to nature. We ended up losing those spaces because the city grew into or grew over the places that we used for our ceremonies.[53]

In fact, Matos mentioned studies, such as one conducted by Professor Jucara Reigo in Salvador, that show that Afro-Brazilian terreiros have lost 98% of their ancestral land over time.

However, distance from central areas and from one's neighbors does not guarantee that Afro-Brazilian temples will be free from noise complaints. One will recall that Pai Anderson, Pai Vilson, and the Centro Espírita Ilê Axé de Sangô were already located in peripheral areas of the city when the complaints against them took place. Similarly, following his arrest for noise pollution, Tat'etu Josué d'Ogum (discussed previously) posted a video on YouTube showing the area where his terreiro is located.[54] The video footage revealed a desolate area with several empty lots surrounding the terreiro. Surely if this is not "far enough" for Afro-Brazilian religious temples to operate freely, nowhere is.

CONCLUSION

After describing several examples of noise pollution complaints and exploring the multitude of biases – from neighbors, police, judges, and others – that are operating in these cases, it is important to make a few final observations that help place them into better context. First, noise complaints and subsequent restrictions on religious practice often go hand-in-hand with other types of harassment and discrimination. In the case of Centro Espírita Ilê Axé e Sangô, the religious leader reported that someone threw eggs at their car, someone called the owner a "black macumbeiro," and someone threw stones on the roof of the terreiro. Tat'etu Josué d'Ogum reported that his wife was called a monkey and a witch in front of the terreiro and told that in a different situation she would have been "burned at the stake."[55] "Justice is not being just with us," he claimed, adding that gay members of the group have been insulted, called "macumba fags" and other slurs.

Similarly, devotees of Terreiro Santa Luzia in Teresina, Piauí, suffered two attacks prior to neighbors filing noise complaints against them in 2019. First, in 2017, unidentified persons set fire to the terreiro, causing minor damage before the flames were extinguished.[56] Shortly thereafter, an unknown person destroyed some of the temple's sacred objects. In these cases, complaints of noise pollution form part of a pattern of religious racism.

Second, it is essential to contrast the situation of Candomblé terreiros who have been accused of noise pollution against a common new form of religious racism where Evangelical churches literally bring their services to the door of Afro-Brazilian religious communities. One will recall that in Chapter 3, Baba Pecê and Ekedi Rose of Casa de Oxumarê described how an Evangelical church purchased loudspeakers and aimed them at the terreiro, intending to disrupt their rituals and ceremonies. Unlike Afro-Brazilian religious communities, who are charged with noise pollution merely because the sounds of their ceremonies are (allegedly) perceptible outside the terreiro walls, Evangelicals are practicing their religion in public spaces and are intentionally trying to disturb others.

Patricia Zappone, a lawyer-practitioner who lives in Brasília, serves as an advocate for devotees of Afro-Brazilian religions. In an interview in December 2021, she explained that she has had people come to her several times with cases where people are living close to an Evangelical church that is playing their music until late at night (i.e., 3 am); they can't sleep, so they go to the police (*delegacia*) and report them, to make the church install acoustic barriers to dampen the sound. In one case, however, the noise was no mere accident. An Evangelical neighbor "placed the speakers on the wall facing the terreiro and turned them on. When the person was doing a ritual, [the neighbor] turned them on! So [the terreiro community] was listening to the Evangelicals." The religious leader called and told her that they couldn't take it anymore so they called the police who, thankfully, removed the speaker from the wall.

In fact, many of our interlocutors recounted stories of Evangelical churches intentionally using noise to attack terreiro communities. Ana Paula Mendes de Miranda, a scholar-devotee who lives in Rio de Janeiro, explained to us how such encounters can be very traumatic for the community.[57] She described an incident in which she was at a terreiro and the people from a nearby church came to the front of the terreiro and began to sing and pray very loudly. She described the situation as "very scary" although the church members would say "We're not doing anything... We're just here praying." However, Ana Paula explained that the sound was "unbearable" because the "prayers" made it difficult for the terreiro members to communicate with one another. "Everyone is saying, 'I can't understand anything,' more or less. So [the church members] sang and prayed very loudly to drown out the sound of the drums. This is very common. I call it an act of symbolic violence."

Ilê Axé Oyá L'adê Inan, a Candomblé terreiro located in the Santa Terezinha neighborhood of Alagoinhas, Bahia, provides another example of how terrifying the intentional sonic attacks of Evangelical churches can be.[58] In 2019, at least 40 people from a local Neo-Pentecostal church gathered to perform an "exorcism," shouting "Satan will fall!" and "Lord, intervene and close the house of evil!" at the door of the terreiro at midnight. At the time, there were only two elderly women alone in the terreiro, Mãe Rosa and another religious leader. It appears that the church members waited until the women were alone – after participants in the weekend ceremonies had returned to their respective homes – to gather up their bibles and begin praying and shouting at the gate of the terreiro. The women, terrified, hid inside the temple until the "exorcism" ended. After it was over, Mãe Rosa was rushed to the hospital with a suspected heart attack. She suffered physical and psychological symptoms for months.

This leads us to the final point. These noise complaints and the police harassment that results from them can have dire consequences for devotees of Afro-Brazilian religions beyond arrest and physical violence from the authorities. As mentioned previously, the leader of Centro Espírita Ilê Axé de Sangô died from a heart attack in 2018. When we spoke with Túlio Aguiar, he attributed the leader's death to the strain of religious persecution.

Over the last few years, this has become a woefully common cycle in Brazil. Religious leaders are suffering such severe trauma from religious persecution that they are suffering heart attacks and other serious health complications, which sometimes lead to early death. As discussed in Chapter 1, in 2000, Mãe Gilda died from a heart attack after the Universal Church of the Kingdom of God published a defamatory article about Candomblé using her image and after members of another Evangelical church invaded her temple. In 2015, 90-year-old Mãe Dede de Iansã suffered a heart attack and died while members of an Evangelical church, Casa de Oração Ministério de Cristo, gathered outside her temple in Bahia for an all-night "vigil," praying for god to burn the site to the ground.[59] One has to keep in mind such dire consequences as we explore cases of religious racism and the official responses to them.

Thus far, we have seen how discrimination against Afro-Brazilian religions and their sacred music takes many forms. It comes from the harassment of neighbors who continue to try to push these religious communities to the peripheries of ever-growing cities. It comes from state legislators who implement statutes that specifically target Afro-Brazilian religions and other government officials (i.e., city authorities and judges) who selectively enforce laws to limit the time, duration, and format of religious ceremonies. And it comes from Evangelical churches who use targeted noise pollution to harass and intimidate

Afro-Brazilian religious communities and force them out of their terreiros. It leads to the arrest of religious leaders, the changing or silencing of ceremonies, and severe health consequences, even death, for religious leaders who carry the weight of sustained persecution.

In the next chapter, we will explore more case studies of religious racism related to complaints of noise pollution. That chapter reveals even more violent methods of religious racism, as we discuss drug traffickers whose extremist Evangelical ideologies lead them to threaten, bully, and physically attack Afro-Brazilian religious communities until they have successfully silenced the atabaques.

CHAPTER 5

Visibility and Violence: Evangelical Drug Traffickers and Other Assaults on Devotees

> These attacks are not because of the toques, not because of the sound, but due to the representation (visibility) of [Africana] religions.
>
> – Babalorixá Alan Crave

In September 2019, authorities in Rio de Janeiro reported that Evangelical drug traffickers had threatened at least 200 Afro-Brazilian terreiros in the state since the start of the year.[1] The severity of these attacks varied greatly. In some cases, the traffickers allowed devotees to stay in the community but prohibited public displays of these religions, prevented devotees from wearing religious attire, and/or restricted the hours and types of ceremonies that could occur. In other instances, the traffickers forced adepts out of the communities through threats and violence. They invaded temples, held priests at gunpoint, physically assaulted devotees, and destroyed their temples.

This includes at least 21 traffickers who organized a group called Bonde de Jesus (Jesus Tram) in the neighborhood of Parque Paulista in Duque de Caxias, Rio de Janeiro.[2] The group was directed by Álvaro Malaquias Santa Rosa, a leader of the gang known as the Terceiro Commando Puro (TCP), who has been ordained as an Evangelical pastor. Santa Rosa ordered the group to attack Candomblé terreiros in the city. The victims of these assaults included an 84-year-old mãe de santo who, in July of 2019, was forced to destroy her own orixá shrines and then the traffickers demolished the rest of the temple.[3]

In this chapter, we explore how, in some neighborhoods and cities, Afro-Brazilian religions are under threat of complete eradication. In cases like those just described, drug traffickers in Rio de Janeiro are converting to extremist sects of Evangelical Christianity and barring Afro-Brazilian religions from the territories they control. This chapter explores this terrifying issue and its connection to sacred music – one of the first religious practices that must be modified or suppressed to appease the traffickers and hide from their violent assaults. It also underscores how these incidents are part of larger waves of violence against Afro-Brazilian religious communities that are occurring throughout the country.

EVANGELICAL DRUG TRAFFICKERS

Christina Vital Da Cunha, who conducted some of the first studies on the phenomenon, explains that "Evangelical drug traffickers" (*traficantes evangélicos*) are drug traffickers who

> 1) attend evangelical services; 2) participate in church campaigns and currents; 3) make contributions to churches through direct donations to leaders or through tithing; 4) approach the evangelical network to ask for protection and deliverance from evil; 5) promote and finance evangelical events in the favela; 6) hold thanksgiving services to celebrate their birthdays and/or their families' birthdays; 7) have walls and billboards painted with biblical messages in the favela.[4]

Evangelical drug traffickers are common in some of the cities of Rio de Janeiro and in informal settlements or "shanty towns" known as favelas.

As of 2010, around 22% of the population of Rio de Janeiro lives in a favela.[5] These communities have been in existence in Rio de Janeiro since the late nineteenth century. They originated as informal housing for migrant laborers who arrived in Rio to work. However, they became more organized over time, with the residents of the favelas forming associations to govern their community. Additionally, "[s]ince the city and state governments failed to extend many public services to the favelas, community members, led by their local associations, banded together to provide sanitation, medical care, and transportation to their friends and neighbors."[6]

In the mid-1980s, Brazil, especially Rio de Janeiro, became a major player in international drug trafficking. The favelas and other poor communities in Rio de Janeiro became and continue to be areas plagued by violence, that which results from both drug-related crime and police violence (see Chapter 6 for further discussion of the latter). Over time, drug trafficking gangs took over the governance of favelas from the residents' associations.[7]

Evangelical Christianity became increasingly popular in Brazil in the late twentieth century and found a large support base in Brazil's poor communities, including the favelas and among the drug traffickers. One of the central teachings of many Evangelical churches in Brazil is that they are in a "spiritual war" against Satan and that Afro-Brazilian religions are affiliated with the devil and other evil forces. As we will discuss in this chapter, Evangelical drug traffickers are carrying out threats and violence against Afro-Brazilian religious communities, claiming that they are ridding their territories of "evil."

Although, outwardly, many of the drug traffickers will state that they do not want Afro-Brazilian religious communities operating in their territory because they view these people as devil worshippers, scholars and devotees have explained that the situation is much more complex. Dr. Rosiane Rodrigues de Almeida, an iyalorixá who has conducted extensive research on this subject, explained to us that one of the reasons for the connections between the churches and the drug traffickers is that the churches launder money for the traffickers, which is essential to the traffickers' continued existence. On the other hand, "the terreiro doesn't launder money from crime… It's not even because we're nice, no. It's because we don't have [money]."[8] She explains that terreiros are not recognized as religious temples in the same way as churches so they cannot accept donations without declaring them in the way that churches can. So, from the traffickers' perspective, she asks "What are [terreiros] good for? They will just get in the way of our [drug trafficking] business."

Another reason that traffickers prefer churches to terreiros is because churches operate for the people within the local community. Terreiros, on the other hand, pull people from different cities and states. Iyá Rosiane explains, "the flow of people in and out makes it difficult to control the territory, because you don't know who is entering. If it's my filho de santo, or if it's a guy in disguise, an undercover police officer who's going there."[9] Additionally, "the beat of the drums makes it difficult to perceive the police invasion in the favela."[10]

The first case of traffickers expelling Afro-Brazilian religious communities that Iyá Rosiane has uncovered occurred over two decades ago in 2001.[11] The victim was Baba Talabí, who had run a terreiro in the Carobinha favela in Campo Grande, West Zone of Rio, since 1990. A pastor built a church on the same street where Baba Talabí lived and where he had built his terreiro. The pastor began converting some of the drug traffickers and this seems to have emboldened the pastor. He began placing loudspeakers facing the terreiro every time Baba Talabí had a ceremony. Baba Talabí went to the pastor and tried to reason with him, explaining that they didn't have to have a conflict, each could honor god in their own way. Within hours, the traffickers showed up at Baba Talabí's place with guns and ordered him to leave within 24 hours. If he did not, the traffickers said that they would kill Baba Talabí and everyone else. Iyá Rosiane's description of Baba Talabí's case and explanations about why the traffickers are bothered by atabaques helps lay the groundwork for understanding how the notion of "noise" and "sound" play a role in this form of religious racism.

ILHA DO GOVERNADOR AND THE ORIGINS OF EVANGELICAL TRAFFICKERS

Aside from Baba Talabí's case, one of the earliest sites where Evangelical traffickers began attacking Afro-Brazilian religious communities was Ilha do Governador, which is one of approximately 100 islands in the

Bay of Guanabara in Rio de Janeiro State.[12] In 1570, it was named Ilha do Governador because the first governor of Rio built his home there.[13] The island was initially used for agricultural production, especially sugarcane farming. By 1820, the population of the island had grown to more than 1,600.[14] In the mid-twentieth century, the construction of a major bridge allowed greater movement between Governador island and mainland Rio, increasing the residential population. During the second world war, the western part of the island (that is closest to the mainland) became the site of an important military air base, Base Aérea do Galeão. After the end of the war, a commercial airport was built next to the military air base. It is now known as Aeroporto Internacional do Rio de Janeiro/Galeão – Antonio Carlos Jobim[15] – one of the largest and busiest international airports in Brazil. There is also a residential section of the island that, at the end of the twentieth century, was estimated to be composed of 22 favelas and four "irregular subdivisions."[16] The current population of Ilha do Governador is unknown but is likely in the 200,000–500,000 range.

In the mid-twentieth century, which one will recall was an age of growth of public celebrations of Afro-Brazilian religions in Rio de Janeiro, there are multiple records that suggest that Ilha do Governador was a central gathering site. In *Revista da in Semana* in 1943, journalist Renato de Alencar recalls that adepts of Afro-Brazilian religions, especially Umbanda devotees (*umbandistas*), would convene at Pedra da Onça, on the top of Bananal Hill on Ilha do Governador to celebrate the New Year.[17] Historian Joana Bahia interviewed Afro-Brazilian religious leaders about their memories of the development of religious communities in Rio and their ceremonial practices in the mid-twentieth century. Bahia explains that "Many pais de santo refer to Ilha do Governador in their memories of childhood and adolescence from the 1950s onwards."[18] Newspapers of the time, such as *Jornal do Brasil,* corroborate these memories. For example, on December 30, 1966, there was a record of 400,000 *umbandistas* and 18,000 *tendas* (worship tents or centers) in Ilha do Governador, Paqueta, and Sepetiba celebrating the new year.[19]

However, by the early twenty-first century, Ilha do Governador had become one of the first locations where drug trafficking leaders targeted Afro-Brazilian religions due to Evangelical Christian extremism. After forming a relationship with Pastor Sidney of the Igreja Assembléia de Deus Ministério Monte Sinai, Fernando Gómes de Freitas ("Fernandinho Guarabú"), commander of the Terceiro Comando Puro in Ilha do Governador, began showing extremist tendencies. He ordered the construction of signs around Morro do Dendê, the island's largest favela, that told inhabitants that the community "belonged to Jesus," and he had bible verses painted on the walls. He prohibited residents of Morro do Dendê from wearing necklaces or bracelets associated with Afro-Brazilian religions. He also ordered the closure of the ten terreiros that had been operating in the favela.[20]

More than 15 years later, Evangelical drug traffickers continue to harass devotees of Afro-Brazilian religions on Ilha do Governador. In March of 2021, we interviewed Mãe Pauli de Oxumarê, a Candomblé priestess who resides and worships on Ilha do Governador, about her experiences with the traffickers. Mãe Pauli had been initiated in Candomblé for 37 years at the time of the interview.

When she moved to Ilha do Governador, Mãe Pauli was aware of the problem with Evangelical drug trafficking gangs. The previous owner of her terreiro had already been warned to stop their singing and drumming and had moved because of threats to her wellbeing. Therefore, Mãe Pauli knew that she would have to be careful and clever in order to keep worshipping. She started having ceremonies that were very small, with just a few people – mostly family and friends, "to not give it too much visibility." Mãe Pauli implemented another precaution that was particularly creative and daring in order to have worship and still protect herself and her followers. During ceremonies, she placed speakers in front of her home and blasted Christian music to disguise the Afro-Brazilian worship happening inside.

Additionally, Mãe Pauli carried out the ceremonies without much "noise," limiting the duration of the celebration and limiting the use of atabaque, singing, and dancing. She gave as an example the curtailed and relatively quiet Olubajé ceremony she performed for orixá Omolú. Normally, Olubajé is a very elaborate ceremony with ritual meals, drumming, dance, and spirit possession of devotees accompanying various key moments of observance. Mãe Pauli had drummers play only the most representative rhymes and songs. According to her previous instructions, when she was mounted by her orixá, Oxumarê, the drummers only played a short time so that her patron orixá could *tomar run* (dance in dialogue with the drums, especially the lead drum, and receive its blessings) at least momentarily. The usual intense, extended drumming, dancing, and singing was curtailed like other aspects of the ceremony in order to avoid conflict and violence.

Iyá Rosiane documented more than 300 terreiros in a different part of Rio de Janeiro that were engaged in similar tactics to avoid problems with the traffickers.[21] For instance, one of her interlocutors described holding ceremonies with drumming at 8 am during a workday, when the traffickers would be sleeping. Iyá Rosiane describes these as terreiros that are "functioning precariously." She explains that these communities are deeply impacted by the traffickers because they are being forced to change practices to avoid detection and devotees might be unable to attend ceremonies because they cannot be held during the weekends when the traffickers are more likely to notice them.

The stakes in continuing to "precariously function" are high, even life and death. Iyá Rosiane shared a personal story that further illustrates the seriousness of the situation. Iyá Rosiane and a friend were on the way to Mãe Pauli's house. They were coming back from a *macumba* and so were already *vestida de macumbeira*, with white clothes, headwraps, bead necklaces, and other visible signs that they were devotees of Candomblé. While they were in a taxi cab, they realized they couldn't arrive at Mãe Pauli's place dressed that way or they would be killed. They took off their ilekes and they changed clothes in the back seat of the cab as they rode, warning the driver, "Don't look back because there are two naked ladies in the back here!" While Iyá Rosiane and Mãe Pauli laughed at this memory during the interview, Mãe Pauli pointed out that it was deadly serious at the time.

Eventually, Mãe Pauli found the pressures of the traffickers' threats to be too much, and she closed her terreiro and told the other devotees in her community that they had to find their own way to continue their worship. She moved all of her orixá shrines and other religious items into her sister's home in Guanabara, a different neighborhood on Ilha do Governador from where her terreiro was located. Today, Mãe Pauli practices Candomblé as a more intimate, family religion within the home where she and her sister live. She no longer holds public festivals or ceremonies. Even though the area where she lives is still controlled by Evangelical drug traffickers, they do not live close to her and she feels free to engage in these small-scale religious rituals.

Iyá Rosiane told us that this was a common trend in Rio de Janeiro. Candomblé is returning to a "family religion" with just a few people practicing together. Mãe Pauli agreed, explaining that it is difficult to be a religious leader who is tasked with taking care of 20 or 30 people in their community. In these uncertain times, one never knows when something is going to happen, when someone is going to show up at the terreiro and tell them to shut down. She asked us to imagine being in the middle of a ceremony when people are singing and drumming, and some people are possessed. Then armed strangers arrive, interrupt the ceremony, and tell them to stop everything. That is what is happening, Mãe Pauli explained.

Iyá Rosiane has collected data showing that, in addition to the multitude of terreiros that had directly been closed by the traffickers and hundreds that are "functioning precariously," dozens have shut down simply out of fear that armed men will show up at their door.[22] However, both Iyá Rosiane and Mãe Pauli stressed that this decision to close one's terreiro is not a simple one. Like most religious leaders, they worry about where and how devotees who frequented their temple (who may or may not be godchildren of the religious leader) will continue to worship. Additionally, Afro-Brazilian terreiros are typically more than just a building or structure where worship takes place. Devotees have planted herbs, trees, and sacred materials in the earth to sanctify the space and have often created shrines that might be embedded within the structure of the terreiro itself. These steps make it very difficult to simply abandon a space – leaving behind sacred artifacts in the ground and structure. They also make it time consuming and costly to open a new terreiro in another location.

Mãe Pauli expressed concern that her experiences and those of Afro-Brazilian religious communities on Ilha do Governador are not unique. In various neighborhoods in Brazil, especially in the state of Rio de Janeiro, discrimination and violence are a big problem. Traffickers are entering temples and destroying everything, including shrines and other sacred objects. She explained that drug trafficking gangs control different communities throughout the state of Rio. One has to know what areas are strictly controlled by drug traffickers and which gang rules each community.

Like most recent news reports suggest, Mãe Pauli indicated that the TCP is the most discriminatory toward Afro-Brazilian religions. Regions controlled by the Comando Vermelho, such as Sepetiba, are not seeing similar attacks; devotees can play their drums and wear religious attire without harassment. In cities like Nova Iguaçu and Duque de Caixas, there are a lot of neighborhoods controlled by the TCP where devotees are having similar difficulties to those faced by Mãe Pauli. They cannot play their atabaques for fear of the traffickers so they are holding only small, closed ceremonies and clapping out sacred rhythms with their hands.

NOVA IGUAÇU

Although most of the earliest and most famous trafficker attacks against Afro-Brazilian religions occurred on Ilha do Governador, similar activities have been reported in many different parts of the state. Many of these attacks are occurring in an area known as Baixada Fluminense – a region located directly north of the city of Rio de Janeiro that encompasses some of the largest cities in the state. One of the most impacted areas is Nova Iguaçu.

Nova Iguaçu is a city of approximately 800,000 people – the fourth largest in the state of Rio. Like most of the major cities in Rio, it was historically inhabited by Indigenous populations but slowly began to be occupied by Europeans in the sixteenth and seventeenth centuries. In 1833, the municipality of Iguassú was formally incorporated (later renamed Nova Iguaçu).[23] Initially, Nova Iguaçu encompassed a very large part of the Baixada Fluminense; however, several cities such as Duque de Caxias and Belford Roxo split off from Nova Iguaçu during a population boom in the mid-to-late twentieth century and became large cities in their own right.

Today, at least five Umbanda and Candomblé communities in the state of Rio de Janeiro have sought protection as cultural heritage sites through IPHAN. Of these, at least four are currently located in the cluster of cities that span from Nova Iguaçu in the west to Duque de Caxias in the east.[24] Furthermore, in 2009, IPHAN and its state counterpart (IPAC) published a report titled "Terreiros de Candomblé do Rio de Janeiro," which examined 32 terreiros that, although not protected by IPHAN, represented part of the National Inventory of Cultural References (INRC).[25] Of these, 13 are in Nova Iguaçu, Duque de Caxias, or São Gonçalo, where communities are under threat from Evangelical extremists. Many others are in neighboring peripheral areas that experience similar problems with Evangelical traffickers but that we will not specifically address in this chapter.

Despite the early presence of Candomblé temples in this area and the prevalence of communities that are considered cultural heritage sites, the religious affiliation of Nova Iguaçu has shifted. In 2010, nearly 300,000 residents (37%) self-identified as Evangelicals and another 266,000 self-identified as Catholics (33%). This represents a significant departure from the national population of Brazil, which is 22% Evangelical and 65% Catholic. Fewer than 15,000 (1.8%) declared an affiliation with Afro-Brazilian religions.[26]

Nova Iguaçu has the unfortunate distinction of being a city that started a colossal wave of Evangelical trafficker violence against Afro-Brazilian religions, which began in the middle of 2017. Between July and early September, the traffickers destroyed at least seven terreiros in Nova Iguaçu.[27] Two of these attacks would become particularly visible in the media and among Afro-Brazilian religious communities because the traffickers recorded the assaults and someone (likely the traffickers themselves) began sharing the videos on WhatsApp and other messaging and social media platforms.

The first of these recorded attacks took place in August of 2017. The identity of the victim and the religious community has not been disclosed, but the recording shows a man, likely a babalorixá, standing in the ruins of what appears to be part of an Afro-Brazilian terreiro. The man has dozens of ilekes in his hands and he is slowly breaking each one. The person behind the camera, who never shows his face in the video, yells at the man "É só um diálogo que eu tô tendo com você. Da próxima vez eu mato" (It's just a dialogue that I am having with you. The next time, I kill). As the off-camera voice issues this threat, a baseball bat appears in the corner of the screen and shakes in the direction of the babalorixá. Ironically, the baseball bat had the word "dialogue" written on it, suggesting that such threats of physical violence are a common form of "dialogue" that the attackers have with their victims.

After shaking the bat and warning the babalorixá that subsequent "dialogue" would result in his death, the traffickers tell him that the area that they are in is under the control of the TCP and that they did not allow *macumba* in the areas that they control. Presumably referring to the ruined place of worship that he is standing in, the traffickers admonish the babalorixá for praying in a "dog house." The attackers instruct him to continue destroying the ilekes and also order him to break some "Satanic" bottles (presumably ritual containers) sitting outside the ruins. As the video comes to an end, the traffickers issue another threat that if he rebuilds this space, they will kill him.

The following month, in September 2017, the traffickers carried out another assault in Nova Iguaçu. This attack targeted an iyalorixá, Mãe Carmen de Oxum, who later shared the details of her experience after she had safely fled the area. Her interviews with reporters and the video of the attack paint a grim picture of what happened that day.

The attack began when Mãe Carmen was returning from the market with several companions. Seven people, armed with baseball bats, iron bars, and guns, surrounded the group and ordered Mãe Carmen's associates to lay on the ground. Two of the attackers pointed their guns at the companions while the others led Mãe Carmen into her terreiro.

The traffickers began filming Mãe Carmen when they reached a room where she had several shrines set up on pedestals and candles were burning. Like the first video, the attackers remain off-camera as they harass and taunt Mãe Carmen, calling her the "devil's chief." They point at the shrines and give her instructions to break them one by one, meanwhile telling her that only the blood of Jesus has power. The short video ends when the last of the shrines has been knocked to the floor, but the ordeal did not end there. Mãe Carmen reports that the attackers identified themselves as representatives of one of the drug cartels (she does not name which one) and told her that they were following the instructions of "the man who did not want macumba" (*do homem que não queria macumba*). Far from receiving support and sympathy from her community, Mãe Carmen asserts that some of her Evangelical neighbors clapped and shook hands with the traffickers as they were leaving.[28]

Nova Iguaçu made the news again in May 2019, when the Commission to Combat Religious Intolerance reported that Evangelical traffickers had targeted 100 terreiros in the state of Rio de Janeiro in the five months since the start of the year. Nova Iguaçu had one of the highest concentrations of attacks – at least 15 terreiros were located in the city.[29] Among the communities targeted in these 2019 attacks was a terreiro known as Ilê Asé Togun Jobi in Parque Flora, a large community that sits on approximately 1200 square meters of land and has more than 20 rooms. In 2017, the traffickers had invaded this space and destroyed shrines, furniture, musical instruments, and other important items. In 2019, the traffickers not only re-invaded the space but also took it over as their headquarters for several months. They evicted the Afro-Brazilian religious community, destroyed their sacred objects, and painted "Jesus is the owner of the place" (*Jesus é o dono do lugar*) on the outside wall of the terreiro.[30]

In January 2021, we spoke with babalorixá Alan Crave from Nova Iguaçu, who shared his thoughts about the danger posed by Evangelical traffickers in the city. He refers to the situation as a holy war (*guerra santa*) declared by some of the traffickers against Africana religions, with the specific aim of eradicating Candomblé and Umbanda terreiros from particular areas. He points to communities such as Parque Flora in Nova Iguaçu and certain neighborhoods of Duque de Caxias and Ilha do Governador where terreiros were completely closed and not allowed to function. He explains that some of the traffickers joined segments of Evangelical Christianity that carry out a kind of "Satanization" (*satanização*) or "demonization" (*demonização*) of Candomblé. He argues that this is entirely against the character of Christianity, but that some Evangelical or Neo-Pentecostal factions embrace traffickers and support this radical view.

He frames the overall situation as a struggle for control over marginalized territories and their inhabitants. But in his view, spiritual control is not the only, or even primary, form of domination in question. To be certain, salvation and social need are posed as reasons for church intervention. In these marginal communities, there is a deficit of education, public health services, and safety. Perceived spiritual need and acute social need are what allow the Evangelical Christians to enter and gain power by offering needed services and spiritual rescue. But according to Baba Alan, the real aim is financial – specifically the collection of funds by the church. For this reason, he calls out the contradictory notion of drug traffickers as "soldiers of Christ" (*soldados de Cristo*) in this imagined holy war.

Baba Alan explains that Candomblé terreiros have a social welfare component that conflicts with the church's dominance. The representation of Candomblé symbols in this context contests the primacy of the church. For example, when terreiros hold an important ceremony for the orixá Ogum, the bean stew associated with it (known as *feijoada de Ogum*) is afterward distributed to the community as part of the ritual. Baba Alan emphasizes,

> We don't want anything in exchange for the food. This bothers the leaders [of the church] who want to maintain control of the community and manipulate people. At the end of the day, these attacks are not because of the toques (drumming celebrations), not because of the sound, but due the representation (visibility) of [Afro-Brazilian] religions.

He reports that his own terreiro, Casa das Águas, has never had direct problems with traffickers because it is located near the center of the city, where extensive police presence and protection exist. If you are closer to the center of the city, Baba Alan argues, there is more vigorous police presence and you are more protected from attack than on the periphery. It is ironic that in various regions of Brazil, terreiros have repeatedly moved to the peripheries, in part to escape the police and in part because they are looking for more land. But once relocated to the peripheries, they remain in danger, under attack.

SÃO GONÇALO

In Chapter 2, we discussed how São Gonçalo is considered to be the birthplace of Umbanda. Nevertheless, in May 2019, the Commission to Combat Religious Intolerance reported that Evangelical traffickers had targeted 100 terreiros in the state of Rio de Janeiro since the start of the year. São Gonçalo was one of the top five locations suffering the most attacks. At least ten terreiros were attacked in the city during this five-month period.[31]

São Gonçalo is the second largest city in the state after Rio de Janeiro and the 16th largest in the nation. In 2010, it had a little fewer than 1 million people. Of these, 417,577 (41.8%) were Roman Catholic and 325,310 (32.5%) were Evangelical. Although São Gonçalo is very historically important to the development of Umbanda, a mere 15,652 people claimed affiliation with Afro-Brazilian religions at the time of the 2010 census.[32] In May 2011, *Rio On Watch* reporter Samuel Lima explained that São Gonçalo was known as "the city with the most churches per square kilometer in Latin America."[33] Lima identified at least one pastor, Luiz Cláudio of the Ministério Resgatando Almas, who was a former drug trafficker and focused his ministries on converting local drug traffickers and other persons who had been involved in violent crime.[34] Based on these descriptions and statistics, it is no surprise that Evangelical churches are carrying out threats and violence against Afro-Brazilian religious communities in São Gonçalo. Babalorixá Alexandre Savi spoke with us about his experiences with Evangelical traffickers there in March 2021.

Pai Alexandre was the leader of a terreiro that was open for 18 years.[35] His terreiro was located right next to a Neo-Pentecostal church; however, he says that he never had a problem with the church. He was a good neighbor. He did favors for community members, such as giving sick people rides to the hospital. There were one or two people who didn't like him, and their complaints seem to have caused the traffickers to target him. The traffickers arrived at his door carrying high caliber firearms. They spoke politely but firmly, saying that they were not kicking him out but that they "didn't want any more macumba" in the area. Pai Alexandre immediately said "fine" (*tudo bem*) because, he explained, it is impossible to reason with the traffickers. Any other response from him would have been met with violence.

The traffickers told Pai Alexandre that he could continue to live at his terreiro. Social gatherings like barbecues were permissible but any kind of *macumba* would not be tolerated. All religious objects and paraphernalia had to be removed within 30 days. There was a meeting of the 17 terreiros in his community but he wasn't present because he was traveling. The other terreiro communities were asking if he got evicted but he says that he wasn't really ousted. He simply decided to gather all his things and leave. He left all his sacred belongings in the terreiro. He relocated to a different neighborhood called Maria Paula, also in São Gonçalo. He hasn't been back to his terrerio for three years. He is overcome with emotion when he talks about how traumatic this experience was. He says he wouldn't wish it on his worst enemy.

When we spoke to Pai Alexandre, we also had the opportunity to meet with Pai Gilmar de Iansã (Gilmar Hughes), a babalorixá and activist who is the undersecretary of the Coordination for the Defense of Diffuse Rights and Combating Religious Intolerance (Codir) of the City of Niterói – which is located right next to São Gonçalo. Pai Gilmar helped advocate for Candomblé devotees in São Gonçalo, including assisting in brokering a deal between a religious leader, Mãe Dalva, and local traffickers. We were not able to meet with Mãe Dalva; however, Pai Gilmar's description of her situation sounded similar to the kind of concessions that Afro-Brazilian religious leaders were asked to make in Pai Alexandre's neighborhood.

Aware of recent efforts by the government of Rio to create a police force that would respond to these widespread attacks against Afro-Brazilian religious communities, we asked Pai Alexandre and Pai Gilmar about the feasibility of notifying police and asking them to help intervene in these conflicts with the traffickers. They stated emphatically "No, definitely not!," explaining that this is not how things work in Brazil.

OTHER FORMS OF VIGILANTE VIOLENCE

Traffickers are not the only ones enacting vigilante violence against devotees of Afro-Brazilian religions. In the 500 cases of religious racism in Brazil analyzed in the International Commission to Combat Religious Racism's 2022 report, approximately 63% involve physical violence against devotees and/or their places of worship.[36] Methods of violence include arson, bombing, physical assault, shooting, stabbing, stoning, and murder, among others.

Sometimes perpetrators try to justify violence against these religious communities based on complaints about noise. For example, on January 19, 2019, unidentified persons stoned Templo de Culto à Ògún e Yemojá in Campo Limpo Paulista, São Paulo, for 20 minutes while they were having a religious gathering.[37] The leader of the terreiro, Pai Beto, reported that the stoning caused damage to several cars and injured one person. He expressed concern that the attacks showed no regard for the vulnerable people who attend their temple, including children, the elderly, and a person in a wheelchair. Reports are somewhat unclear, but Pai Beto suggests that at least one of the perpetrators was a neighbor who had repeatedly harassed the temple on the basis of noise complaints.

Pai Beto argued that the neighbor's complaints and violence must be based on religious intolerance and not legitimate concerns about noise. The neighbor who was complaining about noise, Pai Beto explained, was located 15 meters from the temple while there was a much closer neighbor, whose home was only 2 meters away, who was not bothered by the "noise." Furthermore, before the January 2019 attacks, Pai Beto had already made significant adjustments to the temple to show respect to his neighbors and avoid potential complaints. Specifically, he adopted the custom of ending Saturday services by 10 pm and installed new soundproofing material on the walls.

In February 2020, there were two back-to-back attacks related to supposed "noise pollution" in two separate states. The first took place on February 3, in Ribeirão Preto in São Paulo.[38] The religious leader, Solange Brito, explained that she had been holding Umbanda meetings at her home on Monday evenings for about six months. Their meetings started at 8 pm and lasted until 10 pm or 11 pm. During the meeting on February 3, someone threw a small explosive device over the wall that surrounds the house and it landed in the middle of the group, near a baby who was sleeping in its stroller. As the devotees tried to leave the space, a group of attackers started cursing them. Then they began physically assaulting them, hitting adepts with sticks and stones, as well as punching and kicking them. A 25-year-old, who is Brito's son, was beaten so badly that he was rendered unconscious, several of his front teeth were knocked out, and he suffered a seizure. Emergency crews arrived and transported him to the hospital, where he was admitted for treatment.

Brito reports that this was the fourth time that these attackers had thrown bombs into their space since they began holding meetings in September. The aggressors were members of the neighborhood, who complained about the sound of the atabaques used in the ceremonies. Similar to the traffickers mentioned previously, these assailants also said that they don't allow macumba in their community.

A few days later, on February 7, 2020, another violent attack occurred at Centro de Umbanda Caboclo Sete Flechas in the Fátima Alto neighborhood of Caxias do Sul in the state of Rio Grande do Sul.[39] The leader of the Umbanda center, 32-year-old Joanatan Freitas Pereira, had begun holding weekly ceremonies in the building approximately two months earlier in December 2019. These ceremonies typically began at approximately 8 pm and lasted until around 11 pm. On this occasion, around 15 people were still gathered in the Center at approximately 11:15 pm on a Friday night. The ceremony had already ended and half of the participants had gone home. Suddenly, a neighbor stormed into the Center armed with a machete and a revolver. He shouted at them to "Stop that noise!" and then fired six shots into the Center from the entrance. Pereira and the other adepts hid in the bathroom until the shooting ended and the neighbor had left. Pereira filed a complaint against the neighbor with the police but no information has been released about an arrest.

CONCLUSION

Acts of violence against Afro-Brazilian religious communities are common throughout the nation. As one can see from the examples described in this chapter, these attacks are sometimes preceded by noise complaints or accompanied by exclamations about not wanting to hear or see Afro-Brazilian religions in the neighborhood. This demonstrates the paradoxical space that African-based religions have in Brazilian society. While they are tourist attractions in the northeastern part of the nation, they are frequently a much-less celebrated minority religion in other regions. While a statue of Jesus towers over the city of Rio de Janeiro, drug traffickers and other extremists are forcing devotees to abandon all visible and audible sounds of their faith, including wearing white clothes and sacred necklaces, as well as singing and the playing of drums.

Although the widespread persecution by Evangelical drug traffickers is most common in the state of Rio de Janeiro, recent informal conversations with religious leaders have suggested that the problem is spreading to other regions. In particular, in July 2021, we met a babalorixá who lives in a region of Salvador that is largely controlled by drug traffickers. To protect his safety in this volatile situation, we will not list his name or the community where he resides.

This babalorixá explained that some of the traffickers from Rio de Janeiro had fled to Salvador and were planting roots in his neighborhood. The traffickers were not yet issuing open threats to the Afro-Brazilian religious leaders in their territory or overtly trying to shut the terreiros down; however, they were lingering outside the terreiros, harassing devotees as they entered for spiritual consultations or ceremonies. As one can imagine, the mere surveillance of the traffickers is enough to deter some devotees from returning to the terreiro. Especially if they live in the same community as the traffickers, the devotees become concerned that if an Evangelical trafficker observes them coming and going from an Afro-Brazilian religious community, they might become the target of further harassment or violence. In this way, the traffickers are subtly intimidating the terreiros and discouraging them from operating in the traffickers' territories. With increasing numbers of like-minded traffickers, he is concerned that their harassment will turn to physical violence in the near future.

Additionally, some of the areas that have been most impacted by Evangelical trafficker violence, government authorities have compounded the problem by committing their own acts of discrimination. For instance, in 2016, the U.S. Department of State's International Religious Freedom Report for Brazil states that Rio de Janeiro

> completed demolition of the home where Brazilians founded the African-originated religion known as Umbanda. The city first scheduled demolition of the house in 2011. The CCIR (Commission to Combat Religious Intolerance) stalled complete demolition for five years while it led preservation efforts, lobbying the city mayor, the governor of the State of Rio de Janeiro, the Office of the President, and the Institute of National Historic and Artistic Heritage. The Office of the President has yet to deliver on promises to build an Umbanda Museum at the site.[40]

Presumably, this refers to the house of Zélio Fernandino de Moraes, the medium in São Gonçalo who is credited as the founder of the religion in 1908. This destruction of such an important historical and spiritual site reinforces comments by informants about how the government has no regard for Afro-Brazilian religions.

Another act of government discrimination occurred in Nova Iguaçu in August 2018, the year after the first wave of trafficker attacks. The city government erected a sign that reads: "Welcome to Nova Iguaçu. This city belongs to the Lord Jesus" (*Bem-vindo a Nova Iguaçu. Essa cidade pertence ao Senhor Jesus*).[41] This seems to taunt religious leaders who have been forced at gunpoint to destroy their own temples and others who have been evicted under threats of similar violence. It also contradicts the fact that Brazil is a secular state (has no official religion).

Government discrimination like the destruction of the site where Umbanda was founded and the declaration that a city plagued by Evangelical trafficker violence belongs to Jesus underscore the vulnerable position of devotees of Afro-Brazilian religions and the multitude of actors who compound the attacks against these communities. In the next chapter, we will explore how police violence also poses a threat to devotees of Afro-Brazilian religions and can prevent them from reporting cases of religious racism to the authorities.

CHAPTER 6

Vagabundos and *Macumbeiros*: Over-Policing of Afro-Brazilian Religions

On August 17, 2018, at approximately 10 am, police officers were on the ground in the neighborhood of Liberdade in the city of Salvador, Bahia, looking for drug dealers. There were also five police helicopters flying overhead, searching to see where they might be hiding. The police focused on one of the oldest Candomblé communities in Brazil, Terreiro Vodun Zo, which is located in this area. The religious leader, Doté Amilton, noted that part of the reason may have been that this terreiro is the only place with large amounts of green vegetation in Liberdade.[1]

At the time that the helicopters were searching the area, Doté Amilton was sitting in the central room of the terreiro (where we later conducted an interview with him), talking with visitors from France and Germany. The helicopters were noisy and he could not hear when the military police arrived at the temple. Suddenly, three military police officers broke down the back door.

One of Doté Amilton's godchildren was inside the temple, near where the police barged in. The police called the *filho de santo* a "hoodlum" (*vagabundo*) and told him to get out. The filho de santo called for Doté Amilton, who went to the area where the police and filho de santo were. The police told him that the neighbors had said that the "hoodlums" (in this case, referring to the drug dealers) were inside the terreiro. The police yelled at Doté Amilton and others present, cursing and intimidating them, and ordering them to leave the premises. Doté Amilton told the military police, "No, you are the hoodlums here," and advised them that they were violating sacred space and that they were the ones who should leave. During this exchange, one of the officers pointed a gun in Doté Amilton's face.

The police continued searching and entered part of the terreiro where only initiated devotees are allowed to go.[2] When we spoke to him more than two years later, Doté Amilton told us that to date, there has been no resolution to this violation of the terreiro. He explains that the issue did not yield more backlash or serious investigation "because this didn't happen to an Evangelical church." Such a comment, especially when considered in light of the intricate connections between drug traffickers and Evangelical churches discussed in Chapter 5, really highlights the biases against Afro-Brazilian religious communities. It is telling that Doté Amilton believed that there would be outrage if the police had searched an Evangelical church for drug traffickers in this violent fashion but neither the public nor the police appear to have felt that such an invasion of a Candomblé terreiro was unreasonable.

Although not occurring in response to a noise complaint, this incident helps explain one of the last remaining components of these cases and how they represent a form of discrimination against Afro-Brazilian sacred music. To fully understand these cases, one must also become familiar with the immense problems with police brutality in Brazil. This chapter examines these cases from the micro to macro level – first providing a few examples of police violence in response to noise complaints, then discussing other cases where police officers have discriminated or committed violence against devotees of Afro-Brazilian religions, and, finally, placing all these cases in the context of police brutality against poor and Black communities.

POLICE VIOLENCE AGAINST AFRO-BRAZILIAN RELIGIOUS COMMUNITIES

In the 2022 database for the International Commission to Combat Religious Racism, which identifies 500 cases of discrimination against Afro-Brazilian religious communities, there are at least 15 cases involving police harassment, invasion, and violence. These cases begin in many different ways, but one of the most common is when the police arrive to investigate a noise complaint. Three of these cases stand out.

Case #1: Pai Diego

The first example is the case of Pai Diego, which was described briefly in the Introduction but will be discussed here in greater detail. Pai Diego's terreiro is located in the small town of Iturama (population around 38,000 people) in the western region of Minas Gerais.[3] At the time of our interview in 2021, the terreiro had been in this location for six years. However, Pai Diego had been initiated for ten years to Logun Edé and Ifá (the latter in the Yoruba lineage from Nigeria).

Pai Diego reported that they had consistently had problems with a certain neighbor for some time; this neighbor had called the police repeatedly to interrupt their worship. Pai Diego explained, "The first times he did this, we always just stopped. But at a certain point, I got fed up." The incident in question took place in September 2018, when the community was initiating an iyawó to Oxum. Pai Diego recounted the events as follows:

> At 8:23 pm, police came to my home and demanded we stop the ceremony, saying that the "neighbors" [implying there were multiple people] were complaining, when in fact it was this ONE person alone. Everyone else in the neighborhood was okay with our practicing Candomblé. We kept going in order to give the iyawó their sacred name. Unfortunately, the police returned at 9:20 pm, entered the place, and took our atabaques. There were four police vehicles (*viaturas*) with ten officers. Their treatment made me feel like a criminal, like someone who had truly threatened society. It was very strange (*constrangedor*). There is a video of me asking the police "Are we in another world?"

Pai Diego's disbelief partially stemmed from the fact that it was contrary to local regulations. He explained "In our municipality, there is a law that protects Candomblé worship and music until 10 pm. They invaded at 9:20 pm." He also expressed outrage at the consequences for the religious community. "There were children who were frightened. I spent a lot of money for the event: the ritual officiants, the food, all the expenses during the week of work initiating the new devotee." In later communications, he told us that he had paid around R$90,000 for the initiation, which he could not complete because of this police interruption.

Pai Diego's ordeal did not end there. The three atabaques that the police had seized were taken to the police station (*delegacia*). "The officials claimed that I needed to pay a fine equivalent to a *cesta básica*[4] that the judge would determine." Meanwhile, videos of the police invading the terreiro and seizing the atabaques began circulating on the internet. Pai Diego contacted an attorney and they started preparing their case.

Pai Diego recounts,

> I was taken by Deputy Edson Moreira – a deputy at the civil, state, and federal levels – to his office in Belo Horizonte and the office (*correduria*) of the Military Police. There, I spoke with Paolo Alto, who told me that the police had acted incorrectly because liturgical instruments must not be taken from places of worship. Sacred instruments can only be removed with authorization from the priest who cares for them. This is because religious objects and instruments like atabaques have been granted protected status (*tombado*) as cultural or historical patrimony.

Pai Diego explained, incredulously, that despite this seemingly encouraging meeting, "Still my atabaques were not immediately returned to me. Instead they were transferred to the forum where guns, knives, and other illegal objects used in crimes are kept. My sacred instruments were kept there!" Therefore, he proceeded with the legal case.

> It was determined by the judge that religious intolerance was happening because, first, in order to establish a legitimate case of disturbing community peace, there needs to be complaints from multiple community members. Unless this is true, such a violation cannot exist. Second, drums and sacred objects cannot be removed from places of worship.

> Third, the municipality gives us the right to carry out whatever religious practices we want until 10 pm on weekdays, and until 11 pm on Saturdays and Sundays.

After this ruling, Pai Diego recounted, "I was called to go to the forum (storage) to retrieve my atabaques and my case was dropped." He ended up not having to pay a fine to get the drums back because the police were deemed to be in the wrong. By the time that he was called to the forum, the atabaques had been locked up for 15 days. The drums had to be reconsecrated after they were returned. However, Pai Diego expressed relief: "They had not been punctured or damaged, thankfully."

When we asked if there was any kind of response or follow up from the police, Pai Diego told us

> Yes, one commander came and talked with all the neighbors who all said they had no problem with us. He came to me and apologized in the name of his battalion and assured me that this would never happen again. He said he would have a meeting with his staff to orient them about Candomblé, etc. in order to avoid incidents like this.

He also explained that, initially, his attorney planned to sue to recoup monies lost due to the cancelation of the initiation. However, "since the case was resolved, we decided not to pursue it further. But there was no punishment for the police." He seemed to regret not taking further action, lamenting, "Unfortunately, the police officers involved in these cases have little or no understanding of Candomblé, atabaques, etc."

Later in the conversation, we talked more generally about noise complaints and what causes them. Pai Diego highlighted the hypocrisies of his case. For instance, in response to our queries about the nature of the neighborhood and whether there were any other religious communities that might make noise, Pai Diego told us, "Seven days after my case, I recorded a video of the Evangelical church 40 meters from my home. They were in the streets with microphones and musical instruments. I didn't make a fuss, but I made note of it. They do this and no one says anything, no police come." Pai Diego also stressed that there was only a single neighbor who complained and it was not the one who resided closest to the terreiro who was bothered. "My neighbor directly to the left of my place was okay, but the complaining neighbor who lives 30 meters away, he had a problem."

Additionally, trying to understand the progression of this conflict with the neighbor and whether Pai Diego had experienced any other neighborhood disputes, we asked some questions about what had happened before the night that the police invaded and took the atabaques. He told us that before this incident,

> there was a case with another neighbor, but we were able to talk it out. I explained that they could come to me instead of calling the police. I understand that it is possible for me to actually be disturbing someone. That people can have work the next day or what have you. The place where musical ceremonies happen in my barracão (part of the terrerio) is open. So we talked. In his case, he had been taking medicine and the music bothered him on that occasion. Now we are great friends.

When we asked if Pai Diego had ever been able to talk with the neighbor who called the police in the incident in question, he replied that he had not. He had tried to talk to him but the guy was drunk and a conversation was not possible.

When we asked Pai Diego whether he planned to change his ritual practice in order to avoid these kinds of complaints, his response demonstrated the profound impact of this ordeal. He replied,

> I think religious intolerance will be hard to stop. Humanity is regressing. Many religions plant hate in their teachings so that just wearing white can expose you to hate. There is no way to play quietly, so unfortunately,

we can't do that. I will change the schedule or timing of when we play. Also, on occasions when ceremonies will go beyond protected time limits, I will request a special charter (*alvará*). The bad thing is that, as a practitioner, you become afraid. I'm not sure what was worse, seeing my atabaques taken or seeing my five-year-old son cry because they were being taken.

Pai Diego was the only religious leader who we were able to speak with directly who had had his drums confiscated in recent years (of course, many older terreiros had experiences with this in the nineteenth and twentieth centuries). However, other records reveal that this case is not unique and, sadly, some communities have suffered more physical violence than that reported by Pai Diego.

Case #2: Tenda de Umbanda Caboclo Pajelança

One of the earliest cases of this kind affected Tenda de Umbanda Caboclo Pajelança, which is located in Jaraguá do Sul – a small city of a little more than 180,000 people in the northern area of Santa Catarina. At around 8 pm on June 26, 2010, 12 military police officers invaded this Umbanda temple.[5] The officers were heavily armed with pepper spray, stun guns, pistols, and shotguns. At the time, the devotees were having a ceremony for the *pretos velhos* and dozens of adepts were gathered in the temple. The police ordered them to shut up and freeze, threatening to deploy their weapons against anyone who did not comply. The ogan, a minor, asked why the police had invaded the temple. However, officers responded by ordering him to be silent and then damaged his atabaque. The officers handcuffed and arrested the ogan, as well as some of the regular members who were in attendance, and took them to the police station. When the temple leader, Dona Cristiane, arrived at the police station, the officers showed her a petition signed by the neighbors seeking to close the center and move it to another location.

After this incident, the military police asked for 40 days to conduct an investigation. Leaders of the temple felt that this timeline was excessive because of the numerous eyewitnesses who reported the police abuses. Devotees sought the assistance of Attila Nunes and Attila Nunes Neto (two prominent politicians from the State of Rio de Janeiro who are also adepts of Umbanda), who wrote a strong letter to the governor demanding his intervention. On July 12, 2010, the governor called the legislators and denounced the police actions as "absurd" acts of violence. Nevertheless, the municipal authorities arrived to inspect the property and ultimately demolished it. The temple relocated their headquarters to Pena (also in Santa Catarina) to avoid religious persecution.[6]

The situation in Santa Catarina does not seem to have improved in recent years. In 2018, José Aparecido Félix, a president of the Fórum Itinerante Afro-Religioso de Santa Catarina, reported that devotees experience persecution every time they play their drums.[7] Although appearing to speak generally about the discriminatory climate of Santa Catarina and Brazil, Félix specifically identified Jaraguá do Sul as a site of continued concern.

A leader of another organization of Afro-Brazilian religions, António Piasson, claimed that the discrimination was so prevalent that devotees were leaving the city and going to other places to live and practice their religion. He reported that the military police had prohibited an Umbanda terreiro located there from playing atabaques during their meetings because of the constant noise complaints from neighbors. Félix explained that this was part of a series of interventions that the police had made at this terreiro over the years. He also told reporters: "For us, [the atabaque] is an essential instrument, it is our voice. Banning the atabaques is like removing the Eucharist from Catholic Mass. The atabaque is one of our liturgical instruments."

Case #3: Terreiro in Mato Grosso do Sul

The most recent case took place in the city of Corumbá, in Mato Grosso do Sul. Corumbá is a small city of 103,703 people, located in the northwestern part of Mato Grosso do Sul, directly on the border with Bolivia.[8] The population of Corumbá is slightly more than 70%

Afro-Brazilian. It houses more than 21% of the state's 7,389 devotees of Afro-Brazilian religions. They represent approximately 1.5% of the city's population.

Those Afro-Brazilian religions are extremely visible in Corumbá. According to local devotees, there are 490 registered terreiros in the city and an unknown number of informal, unregistered ones.[9] In total, some media sources suggest that there are approximately 1,200 terreiros in the city, or one per every 83 people.[10] There is an area of approximately 1.5 hectares of protected land known as O Vale dos Orixás that the city donated to Candomblé and Umbanda terreiros for them to practice their religion, including to make public offerings.[11] Nevertheless, an Umbanda community in Corumbá recently suffered a very violent invasion by police officers.

On October 31, 2021, the military police in Corumbá responded to a noise complaint from a neighbor with regard to an Umbanda ceremony.[12] According to members of the terreiro, a military police vehicle arrived and negotiated with the terreiro that they would eat cake and wrap up the ceremony soon. Everything seemed resolved. However, soon after, a second vehicle arrived and these officers entered the terreiro aggressively, striking participants with truncheons and cursing them as thugs, degenerates, and so on.

The police claim that when they arrived at the scene, they had an encounter with the owner of the Umbanda house, who was leaving the space. They assert that she was disrespectful so she was placed under arrest. After this, the police argue that the other devotees got belligerent and started cursing at the officers, and that this was the reason for the police violence. Six devotees were taken to the station to give statements.

Videos posted on social media seem to confirm at least part of the religious community's version of events, showing two police officers standing at what appears to be the doorway of the Umbanda center, swinging batons (or a similarly shaped object) at devotees, while one of the devotees shouts "religious intolerance is a crime." The police then pushed their way into the Umbanda center and the participants fled from the doorway into an interior room, which appears to have been where they were holding a ceremony. In the commotion, at least two of the atabaques were knocked to the ground and rolled about the floor.

After we learned of this incident in a news story, we made numerous efforts to try to reach out to the victims of this police invasion, to talk about their experience, to discover what had transpired following the arrest of the religious leader, and to determine whether the police officers who conducted this raid were investigated and/or reprimanded for their actions. Aside from a few articles that largely reported identical facts about the incident, there was little media attention about this shocking case. None of the sources identified the names of the religious leaders or the community, making further investigation difficult.

Experiences like those of Pai Diego, Tenda de Umbanda Caboclo Pajelança, and the Umbanda temple in Mato Grosso do Sul seem to be extreme cases. This suggests that they could be the result of the actions of a few especially prejudiced officers. Still, we can identify an overall pattern and tendency to harass Afro-Brazilian religions. For example, in 2009, at least six police officers invaded at least six Candomblé terreiros in the Maceió region of Alagoas and threatened to force them to cease their entire religious services if they didn't stop playing their instruments.[13] In the sixth incident, which took place in September of that year, the police invaded the terreiro of Pai Francisco in the neighborhood of Jacintinho. This time, instead of just issuing threats, the police seized the atabaques and other instruments. Like Pai Diego, Pai Francisco had to go through formal proceedings (in this case, petitioning a judge) to retrieve these sacred instruments.[14]

These cases illustrate some important points about how police officers themselves are committing acts of discrimination and violence when responding to noise complaints against Afro-Brazilian religious communities. In these cases, the police treated religious leaders and other devotees as criminals – calling them delinquents and lowlifes, sending multiple officers to respond to non-violent complaints, and using force against community members to disperse the ceremonies. They have disrespected the sacred atabaques – knocking them to the ground in the case in Mato Grosso, damaging them in the case of Tenda de Umbanda Caboclo Pajelança, and seizing them in the cases of Pai Diego and Pai Francisco. This type of aggression is not only an excessive response to a civil dispute but also represents a continuation of the forms of violence enacted against these religions in the nineteenth and twentieth centuries, when authorities not only seized ritual objects from the terreiros but kept them for decades in police custody or burned them in the street.

OTHER CASES OF POLICE DISCRIMINATION AND VIOLENCE

There are numerous other cases documenting police discrimination and violence against Afro-Brazilian religious communities. Although a full examination of all of these cases is outside the scope of this project, a brief discussion of some of them can help illustrate a few trends that provide context for noise pollution cases. The first of these is that while complaints against Afro-Brazilian religious communities (such as noise complaints) frequently receive an immediate and severe response, devotees of these religions are turned away or dismissed when they seek to report discrimination or violence against them.

One example took place in the city of Mário Campos in Minas Gerais. In October of 2016, a group of individuals, including a retired military police officer, armed with guns, axes, and a chainsaw invaded an Umbanda temple.[15] They began threatening to kill the devotees, asserting that they did not want *macumba* in their territory. When the devotees called the police on the invaders, the police refused to protect the devotees, even though they witnessed some of the threats. Instead, they just told everyone to calm down. Likely emboldened by the lack of intervention, the assailants returned the next day, using further threats and causing physical damage to the property. This demonstrates the lack of trust in police from two levels – the retired officer who attacked them and the current officers who refused to intervene.

In another instance, in January 2020, pai de santo Marcus Vinício Valente de Oliveira went to the police station in Nilópolis, Rio de

Janeiro, to report a case of religious intolerance that involved music with discriminatory references to Afro-Brazilian religions. However, when he arrived, the inspector refused to allow him to file the necessary forms. The inspector was the only other person in the station when Oliveira arrived. When Oliveira explained the problem, the inspector identified himself as an Evangelical, contending that all kinds of insults to Christianity occur without them being considered religious intolerance. He offered the specific example of a controversial Netflix special, *The First Temptation of Christ*, that depicted Jesus as homosexual. In this inspector's view, it would seem, if Jesus himself could be disrespected this way, surely no "macumbeiro" deserved to file a claim.

While the inspector in Oliveira's case offered a very specific reason for refusing to assist him, tales of similar rebuffs are common. During our fieldwork, our interlocutors constantly recounted incidents where they had waited in long lines, been given the wrong forms, or sent to different stations when they tried to file a discrimination claim with the police or other government authorities. One particularly poignant story came from Babazinho de Oxalá, whose terreiro in the Federal District was attacked three times in a row.[16] In the third attack, the perpetrators completely burned the terreiro and Babazinho had to close it down. He spoke of multiple attempts to go to the police to report the crimes. On one of the first attempts, he explains, "the police chief said that it was silly that I was registering a complaint because I was just making him waste the paper and that [the complaint] would be kept in a drawer." On another occasion, he arrived at the police station, and "When I got there, there were three agents, one drunk and two sleeping, you know? And then I think that those who were sleeping, I think they were bothered to have to get up and assist me. [The agent] said [filing a complaint] was nonsense once again and that it would come to nothing." Telling us that up until the date of our interview, he hadn't received a response to his complaint and no one had been arrested, Babazinho said, "that's what the agent said at the time, right? ... It came to nothing, right?"

By contrast, when devotees of Afro-Brazilian religions have complaints registered against them, they frequently suffer harassment from the authorities. For example, in 2017, when police officers arrived to investigate a noise complaint at an Umbanda ceremony in São Paulo, they wrote down the license plate numbers of the people who were present at the ceremony. They allegedly planned to use this information to issue fines to the devotees, but the adepts feared that the information about their religious affiliation would be used to harass them.[17] The following year, in 2018, police officers and city environmental authorities arrived at Terreiro Rêi Hungria in Aracaju, Sergipe, claiming that they had received reports that "black magic" and mistreatment of animals were taking place in the temple. The officers searched parts of the terreiro that are considered off-limits to non-initiates and seized the animals that were going to be used for an annual festival.[18] Most recently, in 2020, an iyalorixá in Rio de Janeiro told the media that the police had harassed her terreiro multiple times since the start of the Covid-19 pandemic even though the temple was not open to the public and the devotees who were present were wearing masks and practicing social distancing. These police encounters occurred even after a municipal order identified religious services as "essential activities" that could remain open during the pandemic.[19]

Another significant observation about such cases is one that can be seen in the invasion of Vodun Zo, discussed in the Introduction. Police officers (and other officials, as well as some segments of Brazilian society at large) falsely associate Afro-Brazilian religions with criminal behavior, especially trafficking illegal drugs. Several cases in the ICCRR database document police officers invading Candomblé terreiros, claiming that they are searching for drugs or drug traffickers that they believe have been hidden inside.[20] For instance, police invaded Ilê Axé Torrun Gunan terreiro in Salvador da Bahia, in January 2018, purportedly searching for drug traffickers who they accused the devotees of hiding. In the process of searching the temple, officers fired four shots, some of which hit and damaged the exterior walls. They also threatened to shoot some of the devotees. As in the case of Vodun Zo, the police entered sacred areas that uninitiated persons are barred from accessing. One of the religious leaders began filming the police, asking them if they would behave the same way toward a church. Ultimately, the leader was charged with contempt and resisting arrest.[21]

A more egregious case took place in Ilhéus (also in the state of Bahia), a few years earlier. Approximately eight police officers invaded the Dom Helder Câmara settlement, claiming that they were looking for drugs and weapons that were supposedly hidden there. When the police arrived, the community was having a religious ceremony and there were approximately 50 families present, including children. The religious leader, Bernadete de Souza, was in trance, possessed by the orixá Oxossi. They officers grabbed her by the hair, dragged her out of the temple, and threw her on top of an anthill. They claimed that such force was necessary because they needed to expel the "devil" (referring to Oxossi) from her body. The officers were also aggressive toward other devotees – pepper-spraying some adepts and holding others at gunpoint. Officers asserted that they were merely trying to ensure that no one interfered with their activities.[22] However, the extent of the force that they used to conduct the search and the references to Oxossi as the "devil" contradict the officers' claims. Instead, they used their positions of power to enact violence against devotees of Afro-Brazilian religions while displaying the same Christian biases that Evangelical extremists have used to attempt to rationalize their attacks on these communities.

These cases involving searches for drugs and traffickers are particularly disturbing in light of the growing relationship between Evangelical Christianity and organized trafficking groups. As discussed in Chapter 5, drug traffickers in the state of Rio de Janeiro have converted to extremist sects of Evangelical Christianity, in some cases, under the leadership of traffickers who have been ordained as pastors. Some of these groups are barring other religions from the territories that they control and committing violence in the name of Jesus. Nevertheless, police officers are not invading Christian churches (even those known to be frequented by traffickers) and accusing them of hiding drugs or suspected criminals. Instead, many officers continue to stereotype Afro-Brazilian religions as more prone to violence and crime.

This bias may be partially derived from a growing connection between police officers and extremist Evangelical churches and sects. The most widely known example of this affiliation began in 2018, when the Universal Church of the Kingdom of God (Igreja Universal do Reino de Deus) created a program for police officers called Universal in Police Forces (Universal nas Forças Policiais).[23] The mission of this program is to promote "the teachings of the Bible in the forces of Public Security, Armed Forces and government agencies." Any instance of such close affiliation between government authorities and a particular religious institution would seem to threaten the safety and security of a purportedly secular state. However, the affiliation between the police and the Universal Church is particularly problematic because the latter has repeatedly published biased materials about Afro-Brazilian religions and promoted discrimination against them. In the ICCRR database, there are also several examples of members and leaders (including pastors) of the Universal Church participating in attacks on these religions.[24] Therefore, if the church's claims that it reached more than 1 million people through this program are correct, there is a potential for very significant negative impact on the already tenuous relationship between the police and Afro-Brazilian religious communities.

THE BROADER CONTEXT OF POLICE VIOLENCE IN BRAZIL

We chose to devote an entire chapter to violence and policing of Afro-Brazilian religions because this represents an important component of the problem of discriminatory noise complaints and the suppression of Afro-Brazilian sacred music. These cases of police violence against devotees of Afro-Brazilian religions are part of a larger pattern of police brutality against poor and Black communities. This systemic and significant problem is often rooted in anti-Black racism that, as we have discussed previously, is inextricably connected to discrimination against Afro-Brazilian religions. Therefore, it is important to understand the broader context of police violence and to explore how it might impact the relationship between Afro-Brazilian religious communities and the police.

Two particularly significant incidents of "police" violence occurred in Brazil in the last few years. The first took place on November 19, 2020, on the eve of the Day of Black Consciousness, which one will recall is the largest holiday celebrating Afro-Brazilians (see Chapter 2).[25] João Alberto Silveira Freitas, a Black man, was shopping in a Carrefour supermarket in Porto Alegre, the capital of the state of Rio Grande do Sul. Responding to an argument between Freitas and a Carrefour employee, two white security guards removed Freitas from the store and began violently attacking him near the entrance. After they knocked him to the ground, security camera footage shows one of the officers continuing to beat Freitas, including administering blows to the head, while the other knelt on his back and neck. Freitas begged for help, but no one moved to intervene and the officers did not back down. This went on for several minutes before Freitas died. Official reports indicated that Freitas died of asphyxiation.

Occurring less than six months after the strikingly similar murder of George Floyd in the United States, the death of this Black man caused by a white security officer kneeling on his neck spurred massive protests across Brazil. Many of the protestors invoked the language and organization that has been in the forefront of protests against police brutality in the United States – Vidas Negras Importam (Black Lives Matter). Even though the perpetrators in this incident worked for a private security firm, reports emerged that one of them was an off-duty military police officer. One must also recall that the death of Travyon Martin, which led to the founding of Black Lives Matter, occurred at the hands of a private citizen (a neighborhood watch representative). Whether the assailants have official policing authority or not, such incidents draw public attention to the undue criminalization and demonization of Black people and the often-deadly consequences of this discrimination.

The second incident took place less than six months later, on May 6, 2021, in the state of Rio de Janeiro. Approximately 200–250 police officers entered the favela of Jacarezinho, allegedly executing arrest warrants for 21 people on charges of drug trafficking.[26] However, media reports characterize the invasion as retribution for the death of a fellow officer earlier that morning.[27] The officers were heavily armed and "supported by at least one helicopter and armored vehicles."[28] According to Human Rights Watch, the arrest warrants were based solely on photos uploaded to social media showing the accused individuals with drugs and guns.[29]

Before the raid ended, 28 people (one officer and 27 residents of the Jacarezinho) were dead. Police claimed that there were no innocent bystanders harmed in the raid; however, the information that reporters gathered about the victims contradicted this story. Only three of the people killed were among the 21 alleged drug traffickers listed in the search warrant. Two of them, including a 16-year-old boy, had no criminal record, and 11 of them had only been arrested for minor, non-violent offenses (i.e., pickpocketing) years earlier.[30] This was the deadliest police raid in the history of the state. Media outlets emphasized that deaths at the hands of police officers represented 83% of gun-violence deaths in Jacarezinho in the preceding five years.

The incident in Jacarezinho is representative of police brutality in Brazil, especially in the state of Rio de Janeiro. One can understand the scope of the issue better by comparing the situation in Brazil to the more internationally known situation in the United States. In 2019, police killed 1,009 people in the United States.[31] Many have denounced this figure as excessive and called for defunding or abolition of the police. However, that same year, police killed 1,814 people in the state of Rio de Janeiro alone. Around this same time, in 2018, records show that police killed more than 5,000 in the entire nation of Brazil.[32] In 2019, this number increased dramatically to 6,357 people, or more than 17 people per day.[33] Thus, there are at least 5–6 times more police killings occurring each year in Brazil than those taking place in the United States. Meanwhile, the population of Brazil is significantly smaller – about 212 million people versus approximately 331 million in the United States.

Like the United States, the problem is not just about the number of people who are killed by police each year; it is also about the circumstances surrounding their death. Human Rights Watch reports that many of these are not merely issues of excessive force; rather, they are executions – individuals who have been shot in the back while running from the police and targeted when they are unarmed.[34] A large percentage of the cases that they reviewed also showed injuries at point-blank range and/or in the back of the head/neck – shots that are inconsistent with the police allegations that they killed the "suspects" in a shootout.[35] Police will also sometimes transport the victims (already deceased) to the hospital to destroy the crime scene and may plant weapons on them to support the supposed necessity of their actions.[36]

Furthermore, multiple studies suggest that police officers in Brazil are killing Black people at rates that are disproportionate based on their percentage of the population. For example, the population of Rio de Janeiro is, similar to the national population, approximately 50% Afro-Brazilian (if one includes individuals who self-identified as brown and as Black). By contrast, the United Nations Working Group of Experts on People of African Descent referenced a statistic in their 2014 report on Brazil that indicated that "police homicides were twice as high as officially reported and that, in the majority of the cases investigated (64%), the victims were shot in the back at close range – and most of these victims were of African descent."[37] The following year, in 2015, the report of the U.N. Special Rapporteur on Minority Issues provided more detail – indicating that 80% of the victims of police violence in Rio were Black.[38] Human Rights Watch agrees, reporting that approximately 77% of the people killed by police officers in 2016 were Black men.[39]

There are many factors that lead to this violent style of policing and the targeting of Black people. One of the most significant is a culture of us-versus-them that is cultivated between the police and the residents of poor communities. The police officers are taught that the only way to control crime is to execute the people who commit crime.[40] The problem becomes cyclical because studies have shown that officers will cope with their role in violence against these communities by dehumanizing them and viewing them as criminals.[41] Stated differently, the police officers shoot in the first place because they are taught that the only way to deal with crime is to kill the people who commit crime and then they justify these killings by viewing the victims as criminals.

The Working Group on People of African Descent adds:

> The police is responsible for maintaining public security as asserted in the Federal Constitution, yet institutional racism, discrimination and a culture of violence lead to practices of racial profiling, over-policing, blackmail, torture, extortion and humiliation particularly against Afro-Brazilians. The use of force and violence for crime control and public security has become accepted by society at large because it is perpetrated against a sector of society whose lives are not considered as valuable. The Group views this as the fabrication of an internal enemy which justifies the use of military tactics to control criminal behaviour and reduce public and private liberties.[42]

Again like the United States, "prosecution of police brutality cases in Brazil is practically nonexistent."[43] For instance, Human Rights Watch reports that only four of the 3,441 cases of police killings that occurred between 2010 and 2015 resulted in the attorney general filing charges.[44] Moreover, there is rampant corruption within the police forces that are supposed to secure the favelas. In 2015, investigators from Human Rights Watch heard first-hand accounts of police officers taking payments from drug traffickers to not carry out raids on certain favelas.[45] Thus, in addition to fearing that police may commit violence against civilians, there is also concern that they are in league with the perpetrators of violent crime.

Because the police are able to kill with such impunity and allegations of corruption are so widespread, people are hesitant to report police abuses. They are afraid of retaliation that could follow.[46] Specifically, the Working Group on People of African Descent explains,

> According to civil society sources, 80% of robbery victims in Rio did not register the crime with the police because they were afraid to interact with police officers. Again, according to civil society, 76% of citizens thought that the police force is directly involved with death squads terrorizing Afro Brazilian communities suggesting that institutional racism leads not only to incarceration but also to excessive use of force and violence.[47]

Furthermore, other studies have shown that military style operations, like the one in Jacarezinho, not only have a negative impact on community trust of the police, but they also do nothing to improve public safety. In fact, they may encourage youth in the favelas to join gangs because of their frustration with the police.[48]

Human rights experts have taken particular note of how mistrust of police has impacted Afro-Brazilian religious communities. For example, in 2015, the Special Rapporteur on Minority Issues expressed concern

> that community members report widespread impunity surrounding attacks on their person, places of worship, or instances of discrimination, including against children in schools. Lack of responsiveness to complaints filed, or failure to investigate allegations, further contributes to a sense of marginalization and discrimination on the part of the communities. Moreover, the lack of accountability and trust in law-enforcement services has meant that followers of Afro-religions report feeling unsafe in their neighborhoods and cities. The Special Rapporteur notes the need for police and judicial training in order to better ensure that the rights of Terreiros and their followers are protected.[49]

Therefore, when one thinks about these high-profile incidents and overall statistics, it becomes clear that there are two distinct but cyclical problems leading to the relatively unchecked violence against Afro-Brazilian religious communities, especially in the state of Rio de Janeiro. One part is the radicalization of the traffickers (and other Evangelical Brazilians) and the incitement to attack Afro-Brazilian religious communities discussed in Chapter 5. The other part is the fear and mistrust of the police that prevents victims of violence from reporting the crimes against them.

CONCLUSION

A conversation with Ekedi Jandira of Terreiro Bogum in February 2021 got us thinking about noise pollution cases and the broader problem of police violence in Brazil in a different way. In the middle of commenting on cases of noise pollution, Ekedi Jandira paused to mention that both Afro-Brazilian religious communities and Christians organize walks – the former hosts an annual walk against religious intolerance and the latter a "Walk for Jesus." Ekedi Jandira asserted that when the Christians hold their "Walk for Jesus," they leave an "absurd amount of garbage" in the park and street. However, she explains, "We didn't complain. We didn't take it there, understanding that someone would have to bring it up. [However, the responsibility] should be the municipality's, not ours."

After relaying this story, Ekedi Jandira returned to the topic of noise pollution. She explained that people call the police to try to get the terreiro to stop playing their atabaques, complaining that they create a disturbance. By contrast, when cars stop in front of the terreiro, playing loud music, "especially when it's time for religious ceremonies, we ask them to turn down the sound, that they show respect." She added "living in a community where there are other people, other communities, other cultural forms of sociability, is not easy, but we manage to dialogue with the community, very calmly."

The contrast between these stories makes a subtle but important point. Neighbors are calling the police to try to intervene in non-violent complaints against Afro-Brazilian religious communities such as noise pollution, construction without a permit, drainage issues, and environmental pollution. Religious leaders and other members of the terreiro communities, on the other hand, are often having a dialogue with their neighbors to try to resolve problems of noise pollution. Or, in the example of the Evangelicals polluting the park and street during their walk, they leave it up to the government to notice the problem and resolve it. Although there are certainly instances where Afro-Brazilian religious communities have called the authorities to complain about noise pollution and other non-violent offenses (we mention a few of these in the next chapter), we observed a general pattern of neighbors, especially Evangelical ones, appearing more prone to call the police against Afro-Brazilian terrerios than neighbors are to call the police against a Christian church to complain of similar disturbances.

These differences in who makes complaints reminded us, in some ways, of the better known phenomenon of "racialized emergency communications" in the United States. This term refers to stories that frequently go viral about people, who are usually white, calling the authorities to report non-white (usually Black) people for "suspicious" behavior or non-violent offenses. One of the most famous of these incidents was an encounter between a white woman, Amy Cooper, and a Black man, Christian Cooper (no relation), in Central Park in New York City in May 2020. Amy became agitated because Mr. Cooper asked her to put her dog on a leash – a request that was consistent with park regulations. Mr. Cooper began recording the exchange, and Amy warned that she was going to tell the police that there was an African American man threatening her life if he didn't stop filming their interaction. Amy made two false calls to 911, alleging that Mr. Cooper was threatening her and her dog, although the recording clearly showed that he was not saying anything threatening to her nor taking any steps to approach her. Particularly in the wake of the death of George Floyd, many viewed Amy's warning that she was going to call the police and the two actual calls as threats or attempts to mobilize the police to harm a Black man who had broken no laws and posed no danger whatsoever.

Although the timing of this incident made it particularly well known, numerous other similar cases have occurred in recent years. In April 2018, a white woman in Oakland, California, who became known on the internet as BBQ Becky, called the authorities to report a Black family for barbequing with coal at a public park. She told the dispatcher that she was "really scared" and to send someone quickly. Later that year, another white woman, who became referred to as Permit Patty, threatened to call the police on an 8-year-old Black child for selling water on the street without a permit.[50] Recent studies have discussed how, because they simply do not want Black people in their space, white people are summoning the police as their personal army to forcibly remove these individuals.[51] Although their real concerns are racial, these individuals often frame their complaints as a "public good," claiming that they are reporting suspicious persons or enforcing rules that are meant to protect the community. Because of rampant problems with police bias in the United States, the (sometimes intended) byproduct of such calls is that they make Black people more vulnerable to potential violent encounters with the police. Such interactions can encourage or coerce Black people to avoid certain public spaces and move from certain residential communities because they fear this type of unwarranted surveillance and potentially lethal police interactions.

One can think about the criminalization of Afro-Brazilian terreiros in a similar way. From our research and the observations of our interlocutors, it seems clear Afro-Brazilian religious communities are targeted while Evangelical churches are not, even though both might comprise Black congregants who "make noise" as part of their worship. One of our central arguments is that this is because religions like Candomblé and Umbanda represent Blackness – a rooted, African Blackness – in a way that Evangelical churches do not. This seems to remain true regardless of the actual racial makeup of Afro-Brazilian religious communities and despite the popularity of Evangelical churches among Black Brazilians.

So, like the "racialized emergency communities" in the United States, neighbors call the authorities on Afro-Brazilian religious communities to report "suspicious behavior" (i.e., that drug dealers might be hiding on the premises) or minor infractions (i.e., noise pollution). Although there is often only one neighbor who is concerned about the terreiro, that neighbor frequently asserts that they are acting on behalf of the public good or representing a larger collective. Sending police in for minor complaints stigmatizes Afro-Brazilian religious communities in public perception as "criminals." This is particularly true when multiple police cars arrive to investigate and religious leaders are arrested, led away in handcuffs, and sentenced to terms of imprisonment for such violations.

In addition to the legal consequences of being found guilty of violating noise ordinances, these complaints also expose devotees to potential police abuses in the moment that the police are responding to the call. In a climate of such rampant police violence, particularly against Black Brazilians, devotees understandably fear that encounters with the police will result in violence against communities who practice religions of African origin. In the previously described instances, one can see that such fears are grounded in reality. Devotees have been physically assaulted by officers and/or held at gunpoint and their sacred instruments have been confiscated or damaged. Such discrimination, or threats thereof, can intimidate Afro-Brazilian religious communities into changing their ritual practices or leaving the neighborhood. Like "racialized emergency communications" in the United States, noise complaints in Brazil might be intended to have precisely this result.

CHAPTER 7

Moving Forward: Devotees and Activists Speak Their Minds About Religious Racism and the Future

In the preceding chapters, we have provided an overview of religious racism against Africana religious communities in Brazil, especially the persecution of sacred music. From our scholarly (and somewhat outsider) perspectives, we see the following as being some of the key trends and takeaways:

- Discrimination against Afro-Brazilian sacred music is occurring on multiple fronts, involving multiple actors. From the neighbors who file complaints of "noise pollution" to the drug traffickers (and others) who use threats and violence to prohibit sacred music to the police who seize atabaques and assault devotees to the judges and other authorities who limit the hours and dates of ceremonies, there are numerous ways in which Afro-Brazilian religious communities are under attack. (See Chapter 4.)
- Africana religions are both celebrated and reviled in Brazil. While statues, monuments, and sacred areas publicly honor these religions and government organizations designate terreiros themselves as part of the cultural heritage of Brazil, there are still segments of the population who are actively trying to remove these religions from public sight and sound, and even to eradicate them entirely. (See Chapter 3.)

- Larger, well-known Afro-Brazilian religious communities (particularly those recognized as heritage sites) are still the targets of discrimination; however, they often have more leverage and political clout to prevent noise complaints and similar minor legal charges from being taken too seriously. In cases where the authorities do investigate these communities and violate devotees' rights (i.e., Vodun Zo, Chapter 5), they are in a better position than other terreiros to draw public scrutiny to such invasions.
- Noise pollution controversies are part of a continuing dispute over space and belonging. Afro-Brazilian religious communities initially chose to live on the peripheries of the city and in remote regions to avoid persecution. However, some communities have become central fixtures of the cities as the population has grown and the cities have expanded. Intolerant persons would like to see Afro-Brazilian religions expelled to the peripheries once more, and they use legal harassment (like noise complaints) to attempt to coerce temples to shut down or relocate. Moreover, particularly in the case of Evangelical drug traffickers, some are claiming that certain neighborhoods belong exclusively to Christians (or "to Jesus") and are committing violence against other religious temples that operate in the territories that they claim or control. (See Chapters 4 & 5.)
- Noise pollution cases are rarely about "noise." Even when Afro-Brazilian religious leaders take substantial measures to ensure that the sound levels at their temples do not bother neighbors (e.g., reducing the length and frequency of ceremonies, moving to peripheral areas, installing special insulation, etc.), they are still the target of complaints. Allegations of noise pollution are often lodged by prejudiced neighbors, who sometimes admit to being particularly bothered by the type of sound emanating from Afro-Brazilian temples (drums and animal noises) and to a desire to convince the community to relocate out of the neighborhood (Chapter 4).
- Government authorities are often part of the problem. They impose restrictions on Afro-Brazilian temples that differ from the treatment of other religious communities (e.g., limiting the

length, day, and type of ceremony that can occur; see Chapter 4). They have also committed acts of violence when investigating noise and other minor complaints (seizing or damaging the atabaques, arresting religious leaders, physically assaulting devotees; see Chapters 4 & 6).

While we hope that there is some value to these observations and conclusions that we have developed through our research, to close this book and to talk about the ways to address noise pollution, as well as the larger problem of religious racism, we turn more directly to the words and ideas of Brazilian religious leaders and activists. The following is a series of (translated) quotes from our interlocutors that speak to the major themes and issues that came up in our research. We have organized these quotes into different sections based on the series of questions that we asked in our interviews or on common reflections/observations that surfaced in multiple interviews.

HOW DO WE UNDERSTAND RELIGIOUS INTOLERANCE/ RELIGIOUS RACISM TODAY?

In our field research, we frequently asked whether our interlocutors believed that discrimination against Afro-Brazilian religions was a big problem in the twenty-first century, and if so, what was fueling this issue. We also asked about terminology used to describe this discrimination, especially whether they prefer the term "religious intolerance" or "religious racism," or some other phrase entirely. Such questions yielded responses that help understand how some devotees and activists understand the current climate in Brazil.

First and foremost, many people indicated that they preferred the term "religious racism" for the reasons that we discussed in the Introduction. A lot of devotees and activists reject the phrase "religious intolerance" because they understand its opposite to be mere "tolerance" of them and their religion. Many people were in agreement that they are seeking "respect" and that this term signified a lot more than "tolerance."

Both Túlio Aguiar and Ekedi Rose argued that discrimination against Afro-Brazilian religions is a form of racism because it is a type of structural discrimination. Ekedi Rose cited a lot of different forms of racial discrimination that continue to exist in Brazil today that, in her view, can be traced back to colonial structures. She bluntly summarized "There is no legitimacy for Black people [in Brazil]." Túlio Aguiar likewise discussed a series of different forms of structural racism in Brazil, but he also specifically mentioned the pervasive discrimination against drums. He explained that this is not just a problem in Brazil but also abroad.

Along similar lines, Mãe Jaciara had some strong words about the role of politics in discrimination against Afro-Brazilian religions.[1] Her ideas reflected on some of the paradoxes that we discussed in Chapter 3 about the public representations of Afro-Brazilian religions versus the discrimination against them. She stated that "Bahia, as much as it is the city of all orishas, of all colors, of all saints, is still far behind." (She is referencing the fact that Bahia is known as the "Bay of All Saints.") She made a similar observation at another point in the conversation, stating: "I think we need to put more representations in spaces of power. The political voice is important." Mae Jaciara lamented,

> Bahia is 90% black, but who is in power? Whites. Who is in the city hall? White people. Who is the governor? A white person, who doesn't go to the terreiro, who doesn't know what's [happening in] the favela ... So, like that, we are ... seen as folklore.

Another common reason that some people use the phrase "religious racism" is that they regard discrimination against Afro-Brazilian religions as a form of persecution of Black people/people of African descent. Mãe Baiana, a well-known religious leader and activist who lives in Brasília, said that the term "religious racism" is more accurate because Candomblé "is a religion that comes from Black people." Pai Richelmy of Casa do Mensageiro was one of few interlocutors to state that he regarded both "religious racism" and "religious intolerance" as appropriate terms. He felt that religious intolerance "can be used in general terms, because it is not just Candomblé that suffers, other religions also suffer intolerance." Religious racism was appropriate because Candomblé "is a black religion, so it is a religion that carries a stigma." He added that while religious intolerance can be used "in a broader way," the "religious racism that we suffer, has the issue of color, has the issue of the [African] origin of these spiritual processes."

Although not directly engaging with debates about the use of the term "religious racism," many religious leaders emphasized the role of race in discrimination against Afro-Brazilian religions. For instance, Pai Carlos Brottas in Cajazeiras, Bahia, said "why [is] our religion so massacred, so attacked?" Answering his own question, he explains "it was the religion of the macumbeiro, the sorcerer, the witch. Because it is a black religion."[2] Baba Pecê agreed that "all this persecution is because [Candomblé] is a religion that comes from Africa – that's all it is." Doté Amilton expressed a very similar opinion: "A person's color is not important. … It's racist because I am from 'macumba,' I am from Candomblé, I am from the devil." He provided the example of the four police officers who invaded and desecrated his temple. All four of them were Black. He explains that they were Evangelicals so they did not have respect for Afro-Brazilian religions.

Because of the central role that Evangelicals play in discrimination and violence against Afro-Brazilian religions, Doté Amilton argued that there is no difference between religious racism and religious intolerance. He explained, "color doesn't exist for Evangelicals. Only Jesus exists. Color doesn't mean anything to them. It doesn't matter if you are Black, white, whatever." This easily transitions to the next point.

Another common theme was that the growth of Evangelical Christianity in Brazil, especially extremist sects, was at least partially at fault for religious racism. For instance, Mãe Pauli, who spoke to us about the drug trafficking violence in Rio, said "Evangelical churches are very intolerant and are participating directly in religious intolerance. The Catholic church or Catholic people not so much." She was careful to clarify, "Not all Evangelicals but some of them." Similarly, when we asked if religious racism or intolerance was a big problem in

Brazil, Baba Pecê replied that the growing presence of Neo-Pentecostal churches has led to increased and bolder acts of intolerance. He observed, "It's a fever. It used to be just talk but now it's real violence."

Iyá Rosiane who, as mentioned previously, has carried out substantial research on communities impacted by Evangelical drug traffickers in Rio de Janeiro, connected these religious animosities back to race. She argued that part of what is happening is based on "the idea that slavery was good for Blacks, which is an idea that has been spread precisely by the Pentecostals of the movimento negro ('Black movement')." This reminded us of public statements from a few Black people in the United States and other countries who have expressed similar sentiments about slavery. For instance, in 2018, news broke that Florida State representative Kimberly Daniels had publicly thanked God for slavery, stating that "If it wasn't for slavery, I might be somewhere in Africa worshiping a tree."[3]

Another interesting observation about the role of Evangelical Christians in religious racism came from Ekedi Rose, who told us that Protestants who attack Candomblé are people who converted to Christianity from Candomblé. They are people who blame their poverty and lack of opportunity on the fact that they have been practicing these African religions. Doté Amilton had a personal story that seemed to reinforce this argument. He spoke about his own brother, who grew up in the terreiro with Doté Amilton but now refuses to deal with him after becoming an Evangelical.

Ilzver Matos agreed, stating,

> We could talk about the growth of Evangelism; how they are occupying positions of power and passing laws that favor their position. We are currently in conflict with a Neo-Pentecostal city councilperson (*vereador*) who is creating a Religious Liberty law in Aracaju. It is a dangerous law for terreiros and other groups (referring to LGBTQ communities, among others), but it's making progress. So, there is a lot in the way of creating state and local organizations to protect terreiros.

A third theme that our interlocutors highlighted is a series of structural problems that prevent both noise complaints and cases of religious intolerance from being handled properly. Mãe Jaciara suggested that the rampant discrimination and violence against Afro-Brazilian religious communities was partially an issue with the Brazilian penal code. She argued "it is really a question of having stricter laws." She stated bluntly, "There is no effective law that makes the oppressor afraid to oppress us."

Others focused on more procedural issues with police forces and other offices. When asked about whether DECRIN, a special police force in Brasília that was implemented to respond to crimes of intolerance, was helping respond to the problem, Mãe Dora told us, "It depends. I think these kinds of organizations are tightly linked to whoever is in power in government at the time. For example, if you go to report an incident, the first thing they will do is try to frame it as related to anything *but* racism." In the end, she seemed to have lost hope in the office, explaining, "So many friends who went through the process ended up very disappointed because nothing gets done. No one gets arrested or fined. This shows me that a white mentality – that sees us Candomblecistas as eccentric, folkloric, etc. – controls the process."

Other religious leaders agree. Pai Vilson, in an essay describing his legal case, succinctly explains,

> Racism, as well as the Brazilian state's lack of familiarity, sensitivity, and experience with issues related to Afro-Brazilian communities, has been an obstacle to curbing crimes of racism and religious intolerance and putting into practice legislation that provides for punishment of those crimes.

Likewise, Baba Pecê noted "there is no competent body [organization responsible] to hear cases of religious intolerance. They think it is just a fight between neighbors." Referring to a special government office in the state of Bahia that can assist with cases of discrimination against Afro-Brazilian religions, he added "SEPROMI has only existed for the past few years. Some of these incidents happened before that."

Pai Carlos Brottas also spoke about the procedural difficulties with the Brazilian justice system. Pai Carlos had aggressive land speculators invade the boundaries of his terreiro and destroy 8,000 square meters of land, including sacred groves and trees. He described the process of going to the police station (*delegacia*) to try to report the crime. He said that "They receive us very well, accept our complaint and talk to us. They are very kind people. Now the follow up, that gets difficult." He had similar issues with the Ministério Público (the Public Prosecutor's Office). Pai Carlos explained, "the Ministério Público has the power to forward that complaint of ours to the judiciary. In my case, it didn't happen. It was very well received. It was very well heard." However, two years later, there was no resolution to the case.

Another great example is a story recounted to us by Ilzver Matos about a noise complaint against a babalorixá he knows. The police arrived initially saying they wanted to stop the sound. Some attendees spoke out saying this was a sacred ceremony, that it could not be interrupted, etc. It was a huge party for orixá Exu. There were a lot of people, lots of alcohol, and people talking and singing at once. It was a noisy scene that outside observers (neighbors and police) did not see as a "religious ceremony." So, the police, untrained and uninformed, simply assumed their historic role as repressors, supported by the noise complaint. Ilzver reports that this happens a lot.

In the same conversation, however, Ana Paula Miranda explained that such issues with police vary from state to state. She noted that unlike Sergipe, "in Rio such calls are treated like 'feijoada' (not taken seriously). It would be a waste of the police's time and, in fact, outside their true function to deal with such claims." She added "It could happen in Rio that police react [to a noise complaint]; but it would be the initiative of an individual officer, not the political plan of the police force."

PREDICTIONS FOR THE FUTURE

One of the common questions that we asked devotees and activists during our field research was, in terms of religious racism, "What will things look like ten years from now?" The nearly universal response was *muito pior* – much worse. Sometimes, as in the case of Mãe Pauli, such a question caused a moment of pause and reflection, but did not yield much explanation of why the future looked so bleak. Perhaps in those cases, the gravity of the examples of recent discrimination and the lack of a concrete plan to combat violence against Afro-Brazilian religions seemed to speak for itself.

In other circumstances, our interlocutors identified exactly why they had little hope for change. This often seemed to center on political concerns. For instance, Túlio Aguiar predicted that things were going to get worse in Brazil "Because it is not really a democracy but a theocracy." He mentioned the political alliance known as the "Evangelical Caucus," which is at the disposal of intolerant persons, and expressed concern that there were so many people who identify as Christians and have money in their hands. Aguiar asserted that there has never been, in the history of Brazil, a government that was so openly Christian. And they don't give people of the terreiro access to education and power.

Similarly, when asked about how religious racism might develop or resolve over the next ten years, Baba Alan reflected on the danger of increased radicalization and the need to cleave to the [political] center, because "the center is where dialogue happens." He remarked that Brazil is a radically polarized country where the discourse of hate is becoming normalized in society. He worries that, "If we can't find a way to meet in the middle, these groups [traffickers] are going to find more support, more force [to engage in the fight] … They have an important ally which we practitioners of Africana religions do not, which is guns!"

Others, while expressing their fear for the future, reminded us about the strength and power of their religion. For example, Baba Pecê admitted that he is afraid and imagines that ten years from now, things will be much worse. Nevertheless, in the spirit of hope, he added that every day, he asks the orixás to give them the strength (*força*) to continue defending their religion and their ancestral legacy. Ekedi Jandira, of Terreiro Bogum, similarly said that "We really believe that one day our ancestors will bring about a revolution … I really believe in Xangô [orixá of justice]. I believe that one day this revolution, this uprising will happen."

WHAT WOULD HAPPEN WITHOUT THE DRUMS?

Before embarking on our field research, we were very much aware of the history of religious racism in the Americas and the extreme impact that it has had on religious communities such as those of the "silent" or "whispered" Candomblé in Alagoas following the Quebra de Xangô. We frequently had conversations with religious leaders about whether they or other communities were changing their musical or ceremonial practices to avoid or respond to noise complaints (aside from those incidents in which communities were ordered to make such modifications). Before long, these conversations about what was happening in practice led to a much more theoretical question – can Afro-Brazilian religions exist without drums?

Many religious leaders highlighted the adaptability of Afro-Brazilian religions and the determination to survive. For instance, Baba Pecê reflected on the history of persecution, explaining that there was an era (likely referring to the late nineteenth and early twentieth centuries) when Candomblé communities were not able to play the drums. Sometimes they would switch to other instruments, such as the calabash. "There were times when they just clapped so that the sound wouldn't carry and people couldn't find the terreiro." Regardless of what modifications were necessary to avoid detection, Baba Pecê asserted, "Orixá danced just the same."

Similarly, when we asked Mãe Pauli if Candomblé could continue with all the changes that people like her were forced to make to avoid detection by the drug traffickers, she explained that the religion is not going to die and people are not going to leave the religion. However, when asked specifically about whether Candomblé could continue without atabaques she responded, "Candomblé cannot continue in this way. Not that way, no. Without atabaque, without toque, no." A moment later, she clarified, "With clapping, you can create a song.

But without a song, it wouldn't be possible [for the religion to continue]." Similarly, Mãe Jaciara responded that

> the atabaque, the music, is what connects us to the sacred. Music is what puts us in a trance. If they remove atabaques, they are saying that you will no longer belong to Candomblé. Because everything has a story [told through music] in Candomblé. Music is fundamental, the orikis [praise poetry], the songs, the prayers.

Pai Diego, whose atabaques were seized by the police following a noise complaint in 2018, had a bleak response to this question. When we asked "What would happen if you aren't able to continue playing the drums?" Pai Diego responded, "It would all be over. Atabaques are the most important instrument to call the orixá to Earth. The *ogans* conduct the arrival of the orixá *through* the atabaque. So, unfortunately, without *akoró*, *gan*, *cherí*, the religion would die." Master drummer Ricardo Costa says:

> Without drums, our religion Candomblé cannot exist. It would die. The drum and the drummer are the mantra of our faith. Without drum, song, and dance, there is no communication with the divine, no direction for our ceremonies. The drum is part of the liturgy of Candomblé. It is absolutely necessary.

Drummer Sandro Teles added: "The drums are the basic elements of communication between us [humankind] and the orixás, nkisis, and voduns. If you eliminated that communication, it would be ... *complicado* [complicated, difficult]."

Finally, although not speaking directly about the drums, Iyá Rosiane shared chilling words that reminded us of the gravity of the impact of religious racism. She talked to us at length about the great diversity of Afro-Brazilian religious communities, stressing that there are at least 25 different categories of African heritage religions in Brazil. Therefore, she said,

> when we are talking about this genocide, this violence against the terreiros, we are not realizing how much diversity is at stake in this sense. How much of ancestral memories are exposed to this type of violence, which is a violence that really exterminates. Because when you silence a 90-year-old woman, you are destroying the memory of this family, the memory of this people, the memory of this community.

HOW CAN WE RESPOND TO RELIGIOUS INTOLERANCE/ RELIGIOUS RACISM TODAY?

In most interviews, we tried to conclude with a question about what measures could be taken to help combat religious racism in Brazil. It seems fitting to close this book with a reflection on some of those responses.

Desirée Tozi, who works for IPHAN, reminded us about the utility of cultural heritage recognition as a tool that some terreiros could use. While Desirée was careful to stress that this process does not provide blanket protection and support from the government, she explained that as soon as a terreiro has been documented in the cultural heritage process, "the state cannot say now that it does not know these people. It knows. It is aware that there are people there, producing culture, reproducing tradition. You can no longer argue ignorance." The number of terreiro communities seeking heritage recognition and building museums attests to a widespread belief or hope that these processes create some public recognition of the value of Afro-Brazilian religions and that they will, as Desirée suggests, at least prevent the government from turning a blind eye to their existence and plight.

Mãe Jaciara mentioned that she thought that it was important to engage with the media "because we don't have the media in our favor." She described the media as "perverse" and said being able to have the story of her mother (Mãe Gilda, who died of a heart attack after being defamed by one Evangelical church and having her terreiro invaded by another) "in any space that has visibility for other people to read, to understand what Candomblé is, that we don't worship the devil, that we don't kill little children, that we worship the force of nature, that we care about the environment, is very important."

A few of our interlocutors responded with specific tactics to avoid noise complaints. Perhaps the most interesting idea came from Doté Amilton, leader of Vodun Zo terreiro. He explained that he had added holes beneath the *pagodó* (platform that holds the atabaques) in order for the sound to remain mostly inside the terreiro and not spill out and bother neighbors. "It doesn't hold the sound in completely," he told us, "but it dampens or diminishes it. Even still, the drum sound travels. I have a god daughter who lives in São Cristôval (another neighborhood blocks away) and she can hear when we play."

Some other people stressed that it was the responsibility of Afro-Brazilian religious communities to be "good neighbors" and to adjust their ceremonial practices to ensure that they are not disturbing others. Mãe Jaciara's response exemplified the experiences of several of our informants:

> Candomblé people have in many cases altered the schedule of when sacred ceremonies with music happen. Back in the day, ceremonies would go all night long until morning, easy. Now I begin ceremonies at 6 or 7 pm and by midnight I'm sleeping. Sometimes to shorten the ceremony we sing three songs when seven are called for traditionally. Or twenty one *cantos* should be sung, and we do only seven. This changes our religious practice because music is so important.

Lawyer Patrícia Zappone in the Federal District described several ways in which she believes that communication with one's neighbors is central to eliminating these cases. We asked whether she was familiar with any cases of religious racism involving noise pollution complaints. She responded by explaining the laws regarding noise pollution that prohibit you from playing after 10 pm and regulate decibel levels.

Patrícia characterized these conflicts as a question of "How much can you annoy another person?" She explains that some terreiros are in the middle of the city, in a residential area. They come to her for advice on how to avoid conflicts between neighbors devolving into court cases. Patrícia says "We try conciliation, mediation, and usually create a Conduct Adjustment [an agreement like those mentioned in

Chapter 4] between the caretaker of the barracão (terreiro) and the community." She also suggested that the terreiro bring neighbors into their space to show them what it is and demystify it. In particular, Patrícia argues,

> When you go to play [the atabaques], knock on [the neighbor's] door to [let them know] "I will play for the orixá, we will have the Águas de Oxalá, we will play for Oxum, or there will be the festa do Boiadeiro, the festa da Padilha." Communicate with your neighborhood so you don't have a problem. But if you have a neighbor who happens to have animosities, we go to court.

Most people talked about broader responses. For instance, a number of different people discussed the efficacy (or impotence) of the police forces. We have already mentioned some of these comments in Chapter 5 (highlighting that victims of violence in Rio completely dismissed the idea of filing a complaint with the police) and Chapter 6 (discussing police violence against terreiro communities). Although few (if any) individuals seemed to believe that the solution lay in investing further in police forces, in several conversations, our interlocutors suggested modifications to police training that could improve interactions between officers and Afro-Brazilian religious communities. For instance, Ekedi Rose suggested that police officers (including recently developed special police forces that are designed to respond to hate crimes like race and religious discrimination) are poorly trained and are not representative of the populations they serve. She gave the example of delegations that are supposed to investigate crimes against women but do not have any women in the delegation. She suggested that likewise the officers who respond to cases involving Afro-Brazilian religions are Evangelicals or others who have no respect for or understanding of these faiths.

Others focused on different aspects of the problem of policing. Túlio Aguiar argued that there need to be more efforts to ensure that people of the terreiro understand their rights. At this time, they often don't know what constitutes a crime against them (especially with regard to crimes of intolerance) and what they can do to encourage the prosecution of such crimes. It is worth noting that, in prior, less formal conversations, other devotees and activists have raised a similar point. To this end, there are a few organizations that have begun printing pamphlets and organizing awareness campaigns that explain to Afro-Brazilian religious communities what rights they have and provide phone numbers and other information about who to contact if they experience intolerance. One such office is SEPROMI – the Secretary for the Promotion of Racial Equality of the Government of the State of Bahia.[4]

Unlike the discussion of police forces, several people made favorable comments about the few offices like SEPROMI that exist in Brazil. Most notably, Ilzver Matos argued that the solution to religious racism involved thinking about the problem more broadly than crime and focusing on investing in racial equality. He said,

> Bahia has the only statewide Office of Racial Equality. The city of Salvador has an office to promote racial equality. Maranhão has an extraordinary office for racial equality. I think the existence within state and city governments of serious organizations with resources and autonomy (power) dedicated to these issues along with strong agitation (activism) by terreiros and Black people in general can revolutionize situations as has happened in other states.

In addition to his general comments about the usefulness of offices of racial equality in addressing religious racism, Ilzver had a specific suggestion about how to combat discriminatory noise complaints. One will recall that Ilvzer is an attorney who has worked on cases of noise pollution in Sergipe. According to him, one of the challenges in the investigation of these cases was that authorities often failed to take decibel measurements before taking action against Afro-Brazilian religious communities who have been the target of noise complaints (see Chapter 4). Ilzver reported that a new organization had been created in Sergipe to rectify this problem. This organization sets requirements that must be met before a case can go forward. Among these requirements is the taking of decibel level measurements at the accused temple. Ilzver averred that more guidelines like this could prevent individual neighbors from harassing people.

Sometimes, observations about what doesn't solve the problem were just as important as suggestions for what might. In conversations with many devotees of Afro-Brazilian religions over the course of the past several years, both for this project and otherwise, they often express a desire to bring more visibility to religious racism, particularly by going to the United Nations or other international human rights forums. However, Jandira Mawusí, Ekedi of Terreiro Bogum, told us that she had participated in three different meetings with the United Nations, and she explained that "None brought a return. The UN brought nothing back." Therefore, she said, "we're tired of just talking, just pointing out, just saying, look, this is happening."

Another observation about what doesn't work came in response to when we asked several people about whether conversations with neighbors, in order to simply build better relationships or to ask permission before having a party or ceremony, would reduce the likelihood of noise complaints. While many people seemed to agree that it was important to be respectful, it is essential to remember that throughout the book, we have cited examples of people who described themselves as "good neighbors" and who were careful not to bother anyone in their communities. They limited the hour and frequency of drumming, and installed sound insulation. They purchased large properties in peripheral areas to ensure that they would be far from neighbors and unlikely to produce sounds that would travel beyond their property lines. Nevertheless, neighbors filed noise complaints against them. In some cases, religious leaders reported good relationships with these neighbors (and even performed rituals for these neighbors) prior to learning of the complaints.

In addition to these examples, Ekedi Rose provided a perspective on the relationship with neighbors that raised important points about the social implications of this approach. When asked about whether religious leaders should ask permission or notify all their neighbors before having a party or ceremony, Ekedi Rose replied, "We can't move backwards. If all religions are equal then we can't accept the idea that this is a practice that is only applied to African religions." Furthermore, she explained that if you keep asking permission then the religion turns into something "permissible" – something that can only happen with outward approval. She clarified,

> With a big event, like a march through the city, this would make sense but not for everyday ceremonies. We want protection but we don't want to be asking permission. Our ancestors fought a lot for this, for us to have our rights, so we don't have to ask permission.

Perhaps some of our most interesting responses about how to respond to religious racism came from a question that Dr. Vaughan asked in many interviews. The question was slightly different each time but was generally something like "If someone throws a rock at your roof [because stoning temples is a common form of harassing Afro-Brazilian religious communities], how would you respond?" Essentially, we wanted to know how people would react to a direct assault on themselves or their community. Would they confront the person? Yell? Fight? Call the authorities?

Mãe Baiana, a religious leader from Brasília whose terreiro was burned down (possibly by arsonists, although the authorities declared it an accident) in 2015, took a very passive approach. She said "I don't answer with the same stone, okay?" She explained, "First because I'm from terreiro. I'm from santo. I'm from orixá. I cannot respond in the same way as the people who assaulted me. I cannot attack in the same way… The orixás didn't teach me that way, right? So we always respond differently." Mãe Baiana did not describe exactly how she would approach the attacker but said that it would be "without aggression" and in a manner that shows that things can be different and shows how devotees of Afro-Brazilian religions should be treated.

Perhaps the most radical suggestions about how to combat religious racism come from Mãe Jaciara, who we have mentioned previously, and Mãe Dora, a religious leader/activist in Brasília. Mãe Jaciara described a situation that occurred one day, when she and her daughter went to buy ice cream. Mãe Jaciara was sitting in her car while her daughter approached the vendor. She recounted

> the guy sold her the ice cream, but she was wearing Candomblé clothes. Then he said, Jesus has a plan in his life, he will save her [Jaciara's daughter]. I took the ice cream and threw it in his face. I said, no. If Jesus has a plan, he doesn't have one for *your* life. You're there in plastic slippers, selling ice cream and I'm here in my car with air conditioning.

Mãe Dora is known for arguing that Black people need to be less patient and pliant in their responses. She told us that, in her opinion,

> Black people need to stop being so sweet, so understanding, soft spoken, loving, etc. because our aggressors do not understand that language; they only seem to understand the language of violence. So only when you begin to strike back at racists (*bater na cara deles*) do they understand and show any respect.

In a later part of the interview, she repeated a similar stance, "White people don't understand respect. I think we Black people are too defensive. We need to take a more proactive stance." To explain why she adopted this approach, Mãe Dora said, "I reflect a lot about how in the U.S., the Black rights movement has embraced a more aggressive tone [even though actual violent retaliation has never been a widespread effective strategy]; that this backbone, this renegade stance has given the U.S. Blacks more credibility, leverage, and traction."

Mãe Dora gave us numerous examples about how she embodies this more "aggressive" philosophy. For instance, when we asked if she has changed her religious practice in any way to avoid religious intolerance, she responded,

> No, I haven't changed anything and will not. I don't need to change because if the church next to my house does their ceremonies and celebrations and everyone respects them, I deserve the same. Every time you

> cede space, you lose. People try to paint me as crazy. But I'm not. I can't abandon what my ancestors, my orixás, my nkisis taught me.

In response to instances of physical violence, Mãe Dora explained that her approach was to respond in kind. "If they throw one rock at me, I will throw a half dozen back! Yes, I am *that* person! Because I don't accept abuse. It's absurd. I'm not going to close my door and hide. I'm going to attack back." Far from theoretical talk, Mãe Dora recounted an incident in which a pastor and a group of followers arrived at the door of her house to curse her. She explains, "I literally let the dogs out so that they would respect me."

In the spirit of the words of Mãe Jaciara and Mãe Dora, we end this book by inviting you to listen to Track 4 featuring the Vassi rhythm with a song for Ogum, orixá of war.

Please visit Fulcrum to hear this audio file.

Track 4: Vassi.

Notes

Preface

1. https://g1.globo.com/ba/bahia/noticia/2023/09/04/suspeitos-de-matar-lider-quilombola-mae-bernadete-sao-presos-na-bahia-pra-publicar-assim-suspeito-pri sao-mae-bernadete.ghtml.

2. https://agenciabrasil.ebc.com.br/en/direitos-humanos/noticia/2023-08/quilo mbo-leader-mae-bernadete-shot-dead-six-years-after-son-was-killed (last accessed August 19, 2023).

3. Facebook post by Sandro Teles, August 17, 2023 (last accessed August 20, 2023).

4. Instagram post by @juniorpakapym, August 17, 2023 (last accessed August 20, 2023).

Introduction

1. Interview with Pai Diego, February 22, 2021.
2. Boaz, *Banning Black Gods*, 141–159.
3. Boaz, *Banning Black Gods*, 166–174.
4. Boaz, *Banning Black Gods*, 115–133.
5. Boaz, *Banning Black Gods*, 72–86.
6. Boaz, *Banning Black Gods*, 19–34.
7. Boaz, *Banning Black Gods*, 120–121.
8. Boaz, *Banning Black Gods*, 174–177.
9. Castanha, *Religiões Afro-Brasileiras em Belo Horizonte*; Neto and Oliveira, "Liberdade Religiosa Ao Som Dos Atabaques"; Guimarães, "Os direitos dos povos de terreiros na encruzilhada."
10. Bortoleto, "Não viemos para fazer aliança," 55–60.
11. Da Silva, "Políticas públicas para o enfrentamento do racismo religioso," 128.
12. Castanha, *Religiões Afro-Brasileiras em Belo Horizonte*, 61.
13. Da Silva, "Políticas públicas para o enfrentamento do racismo religioso," 126.
14. Montero, "The 'Culture of Justification,'" 210.
15. Oliveira, "Religiões Afro-Brasileiras E O Racismo," 41; Mota, *Ser Com O Outro*, 52–53.
16. Da Silva, "Políticas públicas para o enfrentamento do racismo religioso," 127.

17. Castanha, *Religiões Afro-Brasileiras em Belo Horizonte*, 71.

18. Oliveira, "Religiões Afro-Brasileiras E O Racismo," 43.

19. Mota, *Ser Com O Outro*, 43–44.

20. Nascimento, "Intolerância ou racismo?," 15.

21. Da Silva, "Políticas públicas para o enfrentamento do racismo religioso," 129; Nascimento, "Intolerância ou racismo?," 15.

22. Oliveira, "Religiões Afro-Brasileiras E O Racismo," 48.

23. Da Silva, "Políticas públicas para o enfrentamento do racismo religioso," 129–130; Nascimento, "Intolerância ou racismo?," 15.

24. Oliveira, "Religiões Afro-Brasileiras E O Racismo," 45–46.

25. Mota, *Ser Com O Outro*, 52.

26. Oliveira, "Religiões Afro-Brasileiras E O Racismo," 46.

27. Mota, "Diálogos Sobre Religiões De Matrizes Africanas," 40–41.

28. Da Silva, "Políticas públicas para o enfrentamento do racismo religioso," 134.

29. Nascimento, "O fenômeno do racismo religioso," 53.

30. Miranda, "Intolerância religiosa e discriminação racial," 351.

31. Italics in original. Rodrigues, *A Luta por um Modo de Vida*, 234.

32. We did not ask about racial identity; however, some people made statements such as "as a white person..." or "obviously, I am Black, so..."

Chapter 1

1. J. Lorand Matory contends that the Yoruba diaspora consists of all the peoples who practice Yoruba-derived culture. Communities in different regions like Nigeria, Brazil, Cuba, Puerto Rico, and the U.S. share common historical and spiritual roots. Furthermore, these communities are aware of and influence each other's religious practices (Matory, *Sex and the Empire*).

2. Edwards and Mason, *Black Gods*, 3–4.

3. Nkisi and vodun are Kongo and Dahomeyan entities or divinities that are similar to orixá.

4. The blood of the animals, symbolic of *life energy*, is poured upon ritual objects, including stones that represent orixás, drums, and so on. Portions of the animals' innards and some extremities are carefully removed and situated as offerings to the ancestors and/or orixás. The meat is often then prepared and eaten by participants in the ceremony and/or by the wider religious community as part of a ritual meal. This "sacrifice" is conducted with a sense of sacred reverence, far from the gory scenes of "African devil worship" depicted in films and other distorted representations that seek to demean Africana religions.

5. Historically, many outsiders would have glossed this belief as "magic"; however, this terminology is loaded with derogatory meanings as it has often been used to "other" or differentiate between Western and non-Western religions.

6. Johnson, *Secrets, Gossip, and Gods*, 12.

7. Murrell, *Afro-Caribbean Religions*, 167.

8. Murrell, *Afro-Caribbean Religions*, 174; Voeks, "African Medicine and Magic," 63.

9. Voeks, "African Medicine and Magic," 67.

10. Johnson, *Secrets, Gossip, and Gods*, 48.

11. Hale, *Hearing the Mermaid's Song*, 3.

12. Johnson, *Secrets, Gossip, and Gods*, 52.

13. Ortiz, "Ogum and Umbandista Religion," 95; Johnson, *Secrets, Gossip, and Gods*, 53.

14. A rhythm that makes use of two or more different rhythms simultaneously. African diaspora music makes extensive use of this principle, layering rhythms on top of one another to create a complex composite whole.

15. Manuel, *Caribbean Currents*, 120.

16. Crioula/o is defined as a "Brazilian-born black" (João Reis, "Batuques," 2.). In certain contexts the term can also be a racial slur.

17. Howard, *Drums in the Americas*, 105.

18. There is some variation due to the persistence of different African traditions that survived within certain terreiros. More research is needed on this topic.

19. Interview with Brazilian master percussionist Iury Passos (July 2021).

20. Interview with Brazilian master percussionist José Mário Bezerra da Silva (Mario Pam) (October 2021).

21. A generic term for Afro-Brazilian dances accompanied by percussion and often song.

22. Interview with Brazilian Master percussionist Ricardo Costa (April 2021).

23. Interview with Brazilian Master percussionist Ricardo Costa (April 2021).

24. Queiroz, "Umbanda, Music, and Music Therapy," no page.

25. Gidal, "Musical and Spiritual Innovation," 240.

26. Queiroz, "Umbanda, Music, and Music Therapy," no page.

27. Gidal, "Musical and Spiritual Innovation," 239.

28. For more information about atabaque drumming in Candomblé, see Lühning and Encarnação da Mata, *Os cânticos que encantaram Pierre Verger*; also Kirk Brundage, *Afro-Brazilian Percussion Guide: Candomblé* (Alfred Music, 2011).

29. Interview with Brazilian Master percussionist Ricardo Costa (April 2021).

30. Harding, *Candomblé and the Alternative Space*, 213–215. Historian João José Reis agrees that "the many forms taken by slave celebration often confused those responsible for its control. Slave masters, police and religious and political authorities regularly disagreed on what to do about [batuque]." They could fear it or "they could view it as good way of placating the tensions in the slave quarters, as a healthy distraction and even as a right as long as it could be considered 'honest and innocent', to use the words of a seventeenth-century Jesuit priest." Reis, "Batuque," 202.

31. Johnson, "Profane Language, Horrid Oaths and Imprecations," 255–277.

32. Johnson, "Profane Language, Horrid Oaths and Imprecations," 266–267.

33. Johnson, "Profane Language, Horrid Oaths and Imprecations," 265.

34. Johnson, "Profane Language, Horrid Oaths and Imprecations," 271.

35. Johnson, "Profane Language, Horrid Oaths and Imprecations," 270–271.
36. Handler and Frisbie, "Aspects of Slave Life," 15.
37. Handler and Frisbie, "Aspects of Slave Life," 15.
38. Reis, "Batuque: African Drumming and Dance," 202.
39. Port, "Bahian White," no page numbers.
40. Harding, *Candomblé and the Alternative Space*, 209.
41. Reis, "Batuque," 212.
42. Conrad, *Children of God's Fire*, 264.
43. Conrad, *Children of God's Fire*, 264.
44. Conrad, *Children of God's Fire*, 261.
45. Conrad, *Children of God's Fire*, 262.
46. Johnson, "Profane Language, Horrid Oaths and Imprecations."
47. Sublette, *Cuba and Its Music*, 22–23.
48. Sublette, *Cuba and Its Music*, 22–23.
49. Barcia, *Seeds of Insurrection*, 125.
50. Johnson, "Profane Language, Horrid Oaths and Imprecations."
51. Frank, *Stono Rebellion*.
52. Frank, *Stono Rebellion*. Interestingly, this language mirrored the preamble of the Barbados law from 1688 that stated that the provisions banned musical instruments "which may call together, or give sign or notice to one another, of their wicked designs and purposes." Handler and Frisbie, "Aspects of Slave Life," 8.
53. South Carolina Slave Code of 1740, Section XXXVI, available at Excerpts From South Carolina Slave Code Of 1740 No. 670 (1740) – US History Scene (last visited October 22, 2021).
54. Reis, "Batuque," 207.
55. Conrad, *Children of God's Fire*, 404.
56. Conrad, *Children of God's Fire*, 404.
57. Conrad, *Children of God's Fire*, 255.
58. Harding, *Candomblé and the Alternative Space*, 217.
59. Reis, "Batuque," 207.
60. Reis, "Batuque," 208.
61. Hertzman, *Making Samba*, 34.
62. Hertzman, *Making Samba*, 34–36.
63. Hertzman, *Making Samba*, 31–65.
64. Borges, "Healing and Mischief," 182–183.
65. Borges, "Healing and Mischief," 183.
66. Reis, "Candomblé in Nineteenth-Century Bahia," 130.
67. Reis, "Candomblé in Nineteenth-Century Bahia," 130.
68. Reis, "Candomblé in Nineteenth-Century Bahia," 130.
69. Reis, "Candomblé in Nineteenth-Century Bahia," 130.
70. Harding, *Candomblé and the Alternative Space*, 46.
71. Reis, "Candomblé in Nineteenth-Century Bahia," 130.
72. Johnson, *Secrets, Gossip and Gods*, 74.
73. Harding, *Candomblé and the Alternative Space*, 46.

74. Johnson, "Law, Religion and 'Public Health,'" 14.

75. Harding, *Candomblé and the Alternative Space*, 212.

76. Harding, *Candomblé and the Alternative Space*, 212–213.

77. Harding, *Candomblé and the Alternative Space*, 213.

78. Conrad, *Children of God's Fire*, 256.

79. Conrad, *Children of God's Fire*, 258.

80. Parés, "A Formação do Candomblé," 139 (quoted in Gordenstein, "Planting Axé in the City," 77).

81. Johnson, *Secrets, Gossip and Gods*, 77.

82. Gordenstein, "Planting Axé in the City," 77.

83. Johnson, "Law, Religion and 'Public Health,'" 14 (Reis, "Nas malhas do poder escravista: a invasão do Candomblé," 113).

84. Harding, *Candomblé and the Alternative Space*, 218–220.

85. Harding, *Candomblé and the Alternative Space*, 123.

86. Harding, *Candomblé and the Alternative Space*, 75–76.

87. Johnson, "Law, Religion and 'Public Health,'" 20.

88. "Trans-Atlantic Slave Trade- Estimates," Slave Voyages, www.slavevoyages.org.

89. Port, "Bahian White," no page numbers.

90. Port, "Bahian White," no page numbers.

91. Port, "Bahian White," no page numbers (citing Rodrigues 1904: 257).

92. Alonso and Smith, *The Development of Yoruba Candomblé Communities*, 80.

93. Da Silva, "Políticas públicas para o enfrentamento do racismo religioso," 30.

94. Alonso and Smith, *The Development of Yoruba Candomblé Communities*, 80.

95. Port, "Bahian White," no page numbers.

96. Port, "Bahian White," no page numbers.

97. Interestingly, Dain Borges argues that there was no direct discussion of the need to control Afro-Brazilian religions during the drafting of these new penal codes and no Candomblé communities protested them. Borges, "Healing and Mischief," 184, 187.

98. Rafael and Maggie, "Sorcery Objects," 281; Johnson, "Law, Religion and 'Public Health,'" 19.

99. Rafael and Maggie, "Sorcery Objects," 282; Johnson, "Law, Religion and 'Public Health,'" 19.

100. Rafael and Maggie, "Sorcery Objects," 282; Johnson, "Law, Religion and 'Public Health,'" 19.

101. Rafael and Maggie, "Sorcery Objects," 282; Johnson, "Law, Religion and 'Public Health,'" 19.

102. Rafael and Maggie, "Sorcery Objects," 285.

103. Rafael and Maggie, "Sorcery Objects," 286; Johnson, "Law, Religion and 'Public Health,'" 25.

104. Alonso and Smith, *The Development of Yoruba Candomblé Communities*, 78.

105. Alonso and Smith, *The Development of Yoruba Candomblé Communities*, 92.

106. Gordenstein, "Planting Axé in the City," 72.

107. Lühning, "Acabe com esse santo," 200.
108. Da Silva, "Políticas públicas para o enfrentamento do racismo religioso," 31.
109. Castanha, *Religiões Afro-Brasileiras em Belo Horizonte*, 41–42.
110. Alonso and Smith, *The Development of Yoruba Candomblé Communities*, 97.
111. Alonso and Smith, *The Development of Yoruba Candomblé Communities*, 99–102; Lühning, "Acabe com esse santo," 202.
112. Da Silva, "Políticas públicas para o enfrentamento do racismo religioso," 34.
113. Matory, *Black Atlantic Religion*, 162–163.
114. Matory, *Black Atlantic Religion*, 158–160.
115. Brazil, Penal Code, available at DEL2848compiled (planalto.gov.br).
116. A term used to refer to some Afro-Brazilian religions, typically those of Bantu origin with Indigenous and Catholic influences.
117. Hayes, "Black Magic and the Academy," 292.
118. Hayes, "Black Magic and the Academy," 292.
119. Hayes, "Black Magic and the Academy," 292.
120. Gidal, "Musical and Spiritual Innovation," 237.
121. Port, "Bahian White," no page numbers.
122. Port, "Bahian White," no page numbers.
123. Matory, *Black Atlantic Religion*, 115–148.
124. Hayes, "Black Magic and the Academy," 298.
125. Borges, "Healing and Mischief."
126. Hayes, "Black Magic and the Academy," 302–305; Hayes, *Black Magic at the Margins*, 38.
127. Interview with master drummer Mario Pam from afro bloco Ilê Aiyê, July 2021.
128. Hayes, *Black Magic at the Margins*, 38.
129. Rafael and Maggie, "Sorcery Objects," 286.
130. Hayes, *Black Magic at the Margins*, 35.
131. Hayes, "Black Magic and the Academy," 284.
132. Hayes, *Black Magic at the Margins*, 35.
133. Port, "Bahian White," no page numbers.
134. Da Silva, "Políticas públicas para o enfrentamento do racismo religioso," 47; Mota, *Ser Com O Outro*, 47.

Chapter 2

1. Instituto Brasileiro de Geografia e Estatística, "Bahia," https://cidades.ibge.gov.br/brasil/ba/panorama (last visited September 10, 2023).
2. The IBGE (Instituto Brasileiro de Geografia e Estatística), the government office that is responsible for collecting and maintaining census data, uses five official categories for race or color: yellow (*amarela*), white (*branca*), Indigenous (*indígena*), brown (*parda*), and Black (*preta*). The racial breakdown was as follows: *amarela* 161,502; *branca* 3,080,929; *indígena* 56,742; *parda* 8,335,917; *preta* 2,376,441.

3. Instituto Brasileiro de Geografia e Estatística, "História & Fotos," IBGE | Cidades@ | Bahia | Salvador | História & Fotos.

4. "Trans-Atlantic Slave Trade- Estimates," Slave Voyages, www.slavevoyages.org/assessment/estimates (last visited September 10, 2023).

5. Instituto Brasileiro de Geografia e Estatística, "Salvador," https://cidades.ibge.gov.br/brasil/ba/salvador/panorama (last visited September 10, 2023).

6. Instituto Brasileiro de Geografia e Estatística, "Salvador | Pesquisa | Censo | Amostra – Religião," https://cidades.ibge.gov.br/brasil/ba/salvador/pesquisa/23/22107 (last visited September 10, 2023); 1,386,842 people (51.8%) self-identified as brown and 733,253 (27.4%) self-identified as Black.

7. Declared affiliations included: 40,295 Candomblé, 6,120 Umbanda, 47,069 Umbanda and Candomblé; 645 Other Afro-Brazilian Religions.

8. Declared affiliations included: 24,806 Candomblé, 2,855 Umbanda, 28,019 Umbanda and Candomblé, 358 Other Afro-Brazilian Religions.

9. In Salvador, of the people who self-identified as Candomblé and Umbanda, 211 were *amarela*, 2,445 *branca*, 198 *indígena*, 10,296 *parda*, and 14,869 *preta*. In Bahia, of the people who self-identified as Candomblé and Umbanda, 395 were *amarela*, 4,457 *branca*, 350 *indígena*, 19,388 *parda*, and 22,479 *preta*. They don't break down Candomblé, Umbanda, and other Afro-Brazilian religions in the online database.

10. Acarajé are fritters made of mashed black-eyed peas fried in red palm oil. The fritters themselves are a ritual food for the orixá Iansã. As street food, the fritters are cut open and stuffed with a variety of condiments including shrimp, hot pepper, and so on.

11. International Commission to Combat Religious Racism, "Religious Racism in Brazil," 42.

12. "Valongo Wharf Archaeological Site," UNESCO, https://whc.unesco.org/en/list/1548/ (last visited February 9, 2022).

13. "Trans-Atlantic Slave Trade- Estimates," Slave Voyages, www.slavevoyages.org/assessment/estimates (last visited February 9, 2022).

14. "Valongo Wharf Archaeological Site," UNESCO, https://whc.unesco.org/en/list/1548/ (last visited February 9, 2022).

15. Catherine Osborn, "Tour Rio De Janeiro's Oldest Slave Port With This New App," July 18, 2017, NPR, www.npr.org/2017/07/18/537948535/tour-rio-de-janeiros-oldest-slave-port-with-this-new-app

16. Instituto Brasileiro de Geografia e Estatística, Rio de Janeiro, https://cidades.ibge.gov.br/brasil/rj/pesquisa/23/22107?detalhes=true (accessed February 4, 2022). 6,332,408 people identified as brown and 1,937,291 as Black. There were 8,269,699 brown and Black people in total.

17. Instituto Brasileiro de Geografia e Estatística, Rio de Janeiro, https://cidades.ibge.gov.br/brasil/rj/pesquisa/23/22107?detalhes=true (last visited February 4, 2022). Declared affiliations included: 50,967 Candomblé, 89,626 Umbanda, 141,783 Umbanda and Candomblé, 1,190 Other Afro-Brazilian religions.

18. Tenda Espírita Nossa Senhora da Piedade, "Zélio Fernandino de Moraes," www.tensp.org/blank (last visited February 11, 2022).

19. Conduru, "Das casas às roças," 181–186.

20. Bahia, "O Rio de Iemanjá," 188.

21. Bahia, "O Rio de Iemanjá," 192.

22. Bahia, "O Rio de Iemanjá," 200.

23. Gabriel Luiz, "Destruído por incêndio, terreiro do DF reabre após dez meses fechado," *G1 Globo*, October 5, 2016, http://g1.globo.com/distrito-federal/noticia/2016/10/destruido-por-incendio-terreiro-do-df-reabre-apos-dez-meses-fechado.html.

24. "The Quilombo of Palmares Is Established," 90.

25. Maggie, *Medo do feitiço*, 252.

26. Rafael and Maggie, "Sorcery Objects," 292; Maggie, *Medo do feitiço*, 252.

27. It is important to recall that the term "republican" has shifted over time. At this time, the concept of "republican" was likely still tied to the people who overthrew the monarchy in 1889 and founded the Republic of the United States of Brazil, which lasted until 1930.

28. Rafael, "Muito Barulho," para 3.

29. Rafael, "Muito Barulho," para 44–48.

30. Maggie, *Medo do feitiço*, 252.

31. Rafael, "Muito Barulho," para 51.

32. Maggie, *Medo do feitiço*, 252–253.

33. Rafael, "Muito Barulho," para 56–59.

34. Rafael, "Muito Barulho," para. 64.

35. Rafael, "Muito Barulho," para 63–64.

36. Rafael and Maggie, "Sorcery Objects," 292–301.

37. Rafael, "Muito Barulho," para 65–66.

38. Fernandes, *O sincretismo religioso no Brasil*, 9.

39. Rafael, "Muito Barulho," para 74.

40. Rafael, "Muito Barulho," para 69.

41. Fernandes, *O sincretismo religioso no Brasil*, 10: "Não existe mais o 'terreiro' que hoje é uma comum sala de visitas, nem o 'pegi', desaparecido."

42. Fernandes, *O sincretismo religioso no Brasil*, 17.

43. Fernandes, *O sincretismo religioso no Brasil*, 18.

44. Gonçalves, *O sincretismo religioso no Brasil*, 11.

45. Rafael, "Muito Barulho," para 75–76.

46. Instituto Brasileiro de Geografia e Estatística, "Maranhão," https://cidades.ibge.gov.br/brasil/ma/panorama.

47. Instituto Brasileiro de Geografia e Estatística, "São Luís," https://cidades.ibge.gov.br/brasil/ma/sao-luis/panorama. Of these, 574,919 identified as *parda* and 131,589 as *preta*, for a total of 706,508 people.

48. IPHAN, "Terreiros Tombados," http://portal.iphan.gov.br/pagina/detalhes/1312/.

49. Museu AfroDigital MA, "CASA DAS MINAS," February 17, 2022, www.museuafro.ufma.br/?p=5794.

50. Interview with Pai Eusébio at Casa das Minas, July 2021.

51. Interview with Pai Eusébio at Casa das Minas, July 2021.

52. Declared affiliations included: 3,706 Umbanda, 4,369 Umbanda and Candomblé, 81 Other Afro-Brazilian religions, 582 Candomblé.

53. Declared affiliations included: 76 Candomblé, 1,025 Umbanda, 1,166 Umbanda and Candomblé, and 64 other Afro-Brazilian religions, for a total of 2,331 people.

54. Drum lesson with master drummers Renato Fera and Whalisson Crioulo at Ilê Ashé Ogum Sogbô in São Luís, July 2021.

55. Interview with Neto Azile, in São Luís, July 2021.

56. "Estátua de Iemanjá é alvo de vandalismo na praia do Olho d' Água, em São Luís; pai de santo aponta intolerância religiosa." *G1 Globo*, July 23, 2023, https://g1.globo.com/ma/maranhao/noticia/2023/07/23/estatua-de-iemanja-e-alvo-de-vandalismo-na-praia-do-olho-d-agua-em-sao-luis-pai-de-santo-aponta-intolerancia-religiosa.ghtml (last visited August 14, 2023).

57. Caminhos Language Centre, "Top 5: Main Traditional Brazilian Festivals," June 11, 2020, https://caminhoslanguages.com/blog/traditional-brazilian-festivals/ (last visited July 13, 2023).

58. Instituto Brasileiro de Geografia e Estatística, "Rio Grande do Sul," https://cidades.ibge.gov.br/brasil/rs/panorama. A little more than 1.1 million people self-identified as "brown" and a mere 587,888 claimed Black identity.

59. Instituto Brasileiro de Geografia e Estatística, "Rio Grande do Sul, | Pesquisa | Censo | Amostra – Religião," https://cidades.ibge.gov.br/brasil/rs/pesquisa/23/22107?detalhes=true. A total of 315,198 self-identified as devotees of Afro-Brazilian religions: 8,438 Candomblé, 140,315 Umbanda, 157,599 Candomblé and Umbanda, 8,846 other Afro-Brazilian religions.

60. Rio Grande do Sul, Brazil: Lei no. 11.915 (2003).

61. Oro, "The Sacrifice of Animals," 1–2.

62. Rio Grande do Sul, Brazil: Lei no. 11.915 (2003); Conte, "Umbanda," 49.

63. Rio Grande do Sul, Brazil: Lei no. 12.131 (2004); Oro, "The Sacrifice of Animals," 2.

64. Assembléia Legislativa. Estado do Rio Grande do Sul, Plenary Sessions, 3 August 2004.

65. *Exmo. Sr. Dr. Procurador-Geral de Justiça v. Assembléia Legislativa do Estado do Rio Grande Do Sul and Exmo. Sr. Governador Do Estado do Rio Grande do Sul*. Case No. 70010129690, Court of Justice in the State of Rio Grande Do Sul, April 18, 2005.

66. *Exmo. Sr. Dr. Procurador-Geral de Justiça v. Assembléia Legislativa do Estado do Rio Grande Do Sul and Exmo. Sr. Governador Do Estado do Rio Grande do Sul*. Case No. 70010129690, Court of Justice in the State of Rio Grande Do Sul, April 18, 2005.

67. "Não fala nada. Nós chamaremos a atenção porque somos brancos."

68. "Logo ouvimos galinhas cacarejando, gansos grasnando, o balir de ovelhas, os berros de cabras e gritos assustados de pássaros. E, como toque de fundo, o constante soar dos tambores."

69. "Max olha para mim, como a dizer: Agora é manter a calma."

70. "Quando entramos no grande e único cômodo do rancho, o soar rítmico dos tambores é tão forte, que tenho que colocar o algodão nos ouvidos - que havia levado junto comigo."

71. "Decapitam-nas com facões afiados. Afora o soar rítmico dos tambores, a matança é feita em silêncio."

72. "Rodeado pelos tamboreiros, que aceleram suas batidas, e excitado pelo frenético bater de palmas dos presentes, o Orixá Supremo dança no centro, enquanto o sangue do boi escorre sobre ele, tingindo sua bela vestimenta..."

73. https://ilereideagostinho.blogspot.com/2013/05/as-religioes-afro-brasileiras-e.html.

74. Assembleia Legislativa, Rio Grande do Sul, Brazil: Proposição, PL 21 2015.

75. Pozzobom, Jorge. PARECER DA COMISSÃO N° 20/2015. *Comissão de Constituição e Justiça*, May 12.

76. Assembléia Legislativa. Estado do Rio Grande do Sul, Plenary Sessions: June 2, 2015

77. Extraordinary Remedy RE 494601. 2006. Protocol Number 2006/68373, Tribunal de Justiça Estadual, Rio Grande Do Sul, May 26. www.stf.jus.br/portal/processo/verProcessoDetalhe.asp?incidente=2419108 (accessed on January 13, 2019).

78. Extraordinary Remedy RE 494601. 2006. Protocol Number 2006/68373, Tribunal de Justiça Estadual, Rio Grande Do Sul, May 26. www.stf.jus.br/portal/processo/verProcessoDetalhe.asp?incidente=2419108 (accessed on January 13, 2019).

Chapter 3

1. "Organiza a proteção do patrimônio histórico e artístico nacional," Decree No. 25, November 30, 1937, Del0025_37 (planalto.gov.br).
2. Shirey, "Transforming the Orixás," 67.
3. Stansky, *Persecution and Permanence*, 23.
4. Selka, "Cityscapes and Contact Zones," 407.
5. Dos Santos, "A Mixed-Race Nation," 123–124.
6. Selka, "Cityscapes and Contact Zones," 407.
7. Selka, "Cityscapes and Contact Zones," 407.
8. Hedegard, *Racialized Cultural Capital*, 44.
9. Alonso and Smith, *The Development of Yoruba Candomblé Communities*, 9.
10. Matory, *Black Atlantic Religion*, 169–172.
11. Shirey, "Transforming the Orixás," 68.
12. Hedegard, *Racialized Cultural Capital*, 10.
13. Stansky, *Persecution and Permanence*, 37.

14. Butler, "Ginga Baiana," 168.
15. Shirey, "Transforming the Orixás," 68.
16. Shirey, "Transforming the Orixás," 75–76.
17. Shirey, "Transforming the Orixás," 76.
18. Miranda, "Intolerância religiosa e discriminação racial," 351–352.
19. Giumbelli, "When Religion Is Culture," 405.
20. Stansky, *Persecution and Permanence*, 41.
21. Shirey, "Transforming the Orixás," 69.
22. Sergio Maggio, "Patrimônio imaterial, Praça dos Orixás é pedaço da África em Brasília," *Metrópoles*, December 15, 2018, www.metropoles.com/tipo-assim/patrimonio-imaterial-praca-dos-orixas-e-pedaco-da-africa-em-Brasília.
23. Edirley Martins Honorio, "Praça dos Orixás e Festa de Iemanjá serão Patrimônio Cultural Imaterial," Fundação Cultural Palmares, December 7, 2018, www.palmares.gov.br/?p=52644.
24. "Estátua é depredada na Praça dos Orixás," *Metrópoles*, www.metropoles.com/distrito-federal/estatua-e-depredada-na-praca-dos-orixas/amp.
25. Instituto do Patrimônio Histórico e Artístico Nacional.
26. Shirey, "Transforming the Orixás," 75–77.
27. Dourado, *Orixás do Dique do Tororó*, 88; Dos Santos, "O Reino de Deus no Legislativo Municipal," 7–8; Shirey, "Transforming the Orixás," 77.
28. Dourado, *Orixás do Dique do Tororó*, 88.
29. Shirey, "Transforming the Orixás," 75.
30. Dos Santos, "O Reino de Deus no Legislativo Municipal," 9.
31. Dos Santos, "O Reino de Deus no Legislativo Municipal," 9.
32. Maria Frô, "Pastor Candidato quer eliminar referências públicas das religiões afro-brasileiras na Bahia," *Geledes*, September 27, 2014, www.geledes.org.br/pastor-candidato-quer-eliminar-referencias-publicas-das-religioes-afro-brasileiras-na-bahia/.
33. Eduardo Dias and Hilza Cordeiro, "Vandalismo? Orixá do Dique do Tororó aparece sem o braço esquerdo," *Correio*, October 21, 2019, www.correio24horas.com.br/noticia/nid/vandalismo-orixa-do-dique-do-Tororó-aparece-sem-o-braco-esquerdo/.
34. Interview with Maria Alice da Silva, December 2020; "Salvador: Conservação da Pedra de Xangô é tema do primeiro Patrimônio É 2021," *Jornal Grande Bahia*, February 21, 2021, www.jornalgrandebahia.com.br/2021/02/salvador-conservacao-da-pedra-de-xango-e-tema-do-primeiro-patrimonio-e-2021/.
35. Interview with Maria Alice da Silva, December 2020.
36. www.centrodeculturas.ba.gov.br/2014/07/15385/centro-historico-de-salvadorrecebeu-visita-do-rei-nigeriano-de-oyo.html; https://theunknownnigeriablog.blogspot.com/2014/07/alaafin-of-oyo-in-salvador-brazil-for.html.
37. www.youtube.com/watch?v=QeP4cS8S-4U.
38. www.bahia.ba.gov.br/2014/07/noticias/cultura/preservacao-do-patrimonio-cultural-na-bahia-e-exemplo-para-a-nigeria/.

39. Yasmin Garrido, "Ministério Público vai ser chamado para intervir em agressão à Pedra de Xangô," *Correio*, December 31, 2018, www.correio24horas.com.br/noticia/nid/ministerio-publico-vai-ser-chamado-para-intervir-em-agressao-a-pedra-de-xango/.

40. www.nordesteusou.com.br/noticias/rei-da-nigeria-visita-a-bahia-para-torna-la-capital-yoruba-das-americas/; www.premiumtimesng.com/entertainment/travels/266398-ooni-of-ife-to-embark-on-10-day-historical-visit-to-brazil.html.

41. "Salvador: Conservação da Pedra de Xangô é tema do primeiro Patrimônio É 2021," *Jornal Grade Bahia*, February 21, 2021, www.jornalgrandebahia.com.br/2021/02/salvador-conservacao-da-pedra-de-xango-e-tema-do-primeiro-patrimonio-e-2021/; Yasmin Garrido, "Ministério Público vai ser chamado para intervir em agressão à Pedra de Xangô," *Correio*, December 31, 2018, www.correio24horas.com.br/noticia/nid/ministerio-publico-vai-ser-chamado-para-intervir-em-agressao-a-pedra-de-xango/. As of December 8, 2021, there are only seven sites recognized through this process. Fundação Gregório de Mattos, "Bens Tombados," http://culturafgm.salvador.ba.gov.br/index.php/patrimonio/bens-materiais/bens-tombados (last visited December 8, 2021).

42. Prefeitura do Salvador, "Prefeitura faz tombamento da Pedra de Xangô nesta quinta (04)," May 3, 2017, www.comunicacao.salvador.ba.gov.br/index.php/pautas/49914-prefeitura-faz-tombamento-da-pedra-de-xango-nesta-quinta-04.

43. See *Pedra de Xangô:um Lugar Sagrado Afro-brasileiro em Salvador* and *Normas Brasileiras da Construção*, vols. 1–3.

44. Interview with Maria Alice Pereira da Silva, December 2020.

45. *Mãe Stella de Oxossi: Perfil de Uma Lideranca Religiosa*, Vera Felicidade de Almeida Campos, 9.

46. Tailane Muniz, "Com 8,5 metros, homenagem a Mãe Stella de Oxóssi é inaugurada," *Correio*, April 9, 2019, www.correio24horas.com.br/noticia/nid/com-85-metros-homenagem-a-Mãe-stella-de-oxossi-e-inaugurada/.

47. "Em vídeo, evangélico associa estátua de Oxóssi ao diabo," *Leia Já*, April 10, 2019, www.leiaja.com/noticias/2019/04/10/em-video-evangelico-associa-estatua-de-oxossi-ao-diabo/.

48. Juliana Brito, "Monumento a Mãe Stella de Oxóssi é alvo de vandalism," *Midia 4P*, September 19, 2019, https://midia4p.cartacapital.com.br/monumento-a-Mãe-stella-de-oxossi-e-alvo-de-vandalismo/.

49. "Grupo faz ato contra a intolerância religiosa após ataque a estátua de Iemanjá," NSC Total, September 22, 2019, www.nsctotal.com.br/noticias/grupo-faz-ato-contra-a-intolerancia-religiosa-apos-ataque-a-estatua-de-iemanja.

50. "Escultura em homenagem a Mãe Stella de Oxóssi é incendiada em Salvador," *Folha de S. Paulo*, December 4, 2022, https://www1.folha.uol.com.br/cotidiano/2022/12/escultura-em-homenagem-a-mae-stella-de-oxossi-e-incendiada-em-salvador.shtml (last visited July 13, 2023).

51. Rego, "Caso Mãe Gilda."

52. Ialorixá Mãe Gilda é homenageada com busto na Lagoa do Abaeté – Jornal Correio (correio24horas.com.br), www.correio24horas.com.br/noticia/nid/ialorixa-mae-gilda-e-homenageada-com-busto-na-lagoa-do-abaete/ (accessed on March 26, 2021).

53. Rego, "Caso Mãe Gilda"; Silva 2014.

54. Congresso Nacional, Law 11.365, December 27, 2007, www.planalto.gov.br/ccivil_03/_ato2007-2010/2007/lei/l11635.htm (accessed on March 26, 2021).

55. "Busto Mãe Gilda," www.culturafgm.salvador.ba.gov.br/images/stories/SitiosHistoricos/bustos/pdf/Mãegilda.pdf.

56. "Filha Do Orixá Ogum, Nasceu Em 03 Outubro De 1935 Tornando-Se Fundadora Do Axé Abassa De Ogum. Morreu Em 21 De Janeiro De 2000, Apesar De Viver Em Um Estado Laico, Por Conta Da Intolerância Religiosa. Temos Muitos Caminhos A Trilhar Em Busca Da Liberdade E Da Igualdade, Na Diversidade. Kosi Mi Fara Owé, Nada No Mundo Que Possa Contra Mim, Aqui Estamos," Salvador, November 28, 2014.

57. Natália Blanco, "Denúncia: Pela segunda vez o Busto de Mãe Gilda de Ogum é atacado e apedrejado em Salvador, Bahia," July 15, 2020, https://kn.org.br/noticias/ataque-busto-Mãe-gilda/7616.

58. Conselho de Desenvolvimento da Comunidade Negra.

59. Secretaria de Promoção da Igualdade Racial do Estado.

60. Reinauguração do busto de Mãe Gilda reforça combate à intolerância," *Itapuã City*, Nov 28, 2016, www.itapuacity.com.br/reinauguracao-do-busto-de-mae-gilda-reforca-combate-intolerancia/.

61. "Busto de Mãe Gilda é alvo de vandalismo em Salvador; suspeito foi levado para delegacia," *G1 Globo*, July 15, 2020, https://g1.globo.com/ba/bahia/noticia/2020/07/15/busto-de-mae-gilda-e-alvo-de-vandalismo-em-salvador-suspeito-foi-levado-para-delegacia.ghtml.

62. Secretaria de Promoção da Igualdade Racial, "Sepromi acompanha caso de depredação do busto de Mãe Gilda e apoiará restauração," July 16, 2020, www.sepromi.ba.gov.br/modules/noticias/makepdf.php?storyid=2514 (accessed March 26, 2021).

63. Yasmin Aguirre, "Busto em homenagem a Mãe Gilda é atacado por criminoso," Dicas Jornalismo, July 18, 2020, https://labdicasjornalismo.com/noticia/3760/busto-em-homenagem-a-mae-gilda-e-atacado-por-criminoso.

64. IPHAN, "Terreiros Tombados," http://portal.iphan.gov.br/pagina/detalhes/1312/ (accessed on December 6, 2021).

65. www.culturatododia.salvador.ba.gov.br/vivendo-area.php?cod_area=9 (accessed December 9, 2021).

66. Castillo, *The Alaketu Temple*, 93.

67. Gordenstein, "Planting Axé in the City," 75.

68. http://casadeOxumarê.com.br/index.php/2015-07-12-20-45-13 (accessed on December 9, 2021).

69. http://terreirodogantois.com.br/index.php/o-terreiro/ (accessed on December 9, 2021).

70. Clara Souza Ferreira Rocha and Mayara Mychella Sena Araújo, "Federação," *Observatório de Bairros Salvador*, https://observatoriobairrossalvador.ufba.br/bairros/federacao (accessed on December 11, 2021).

71. https://observatoriobairrossalvador.ufba.br/bairros/federacao.

72. 8-%20REGIONALIZA%C7%C3O.pdf (salvador.ba.gov.br).

73. "Engenho Velho da Federação," *Observatório de Bairros Salvador*, https://observatoriobairrossalvador.ufba.br/bairros/engenho-velho-da-federacao (accessed on December 11, 2021).

74. Terreiro do Bate Folha, "O Terreiro," www.terreirobatefolha.com/bate-folha (last visited December 11, 2021).

75. Interview with Desirée Tozi, April 2021.

76. Interview with Baba Pecê, January 2021.

77. Júlia Vigné, "Terreiro Oxumarê, em Salvador, é alvo de intolerância religiosa," Correio, October 31, 2018, www.correio24horas.com.br/noticia/nid/terreiro-Oxumarê-em-salvador-e-alvo-de-intolerancia-religiosa/.

78. Interview with Rose Mary Jesus (Ekedi Rose), January 2021.

79. IPHAN, "Terreiro Zogbodo Male Bogun Seja Unde- Cachoeira (BA)," http://portal.iphan.gov.br/pagina/detalhes/1626/.

80. Cristina Pita "Fogo destrói árvores e plantas sagradas da Roça do Ventura," Acervo Combate Racismo Ambiental, January 30, 2013, https://acervo.racismoambiental.net.br/2013/01/10/ba-fogo-destroi-arvores-e-plantas-sagradas-da-roca-do-ventura/.

81. "Terreiro Ilê Axé Icimimó Aganjú Didè," Cachoeira Patrimônio e Memória, https://cachoeirabahia.com/?page_id=543.

82. "Ataque a comunidade do centenário Terreiro Ilê Axé Icimimó Aganjú Didê na Cidade de Cachoeira, Bahia, um reflexo do racismo religioso," SibILiNO NeGRo PeNSanTE March 13, 2019, https://sibilinonegropensante.blogspot.com/2019/03/ataque-comunidade-do-centenario.html.

83. Ministerio Público do Estado da Bahia, Recomendação Nº 01/2019, Procedimento nº 003.9.221442/2019, March 1, 2019, recomendacao-terreiro-icimimo-grupo-penha-1.pdf (mpba.mp.br) https://infomail.mpba.mp.br/wp-content/uploads/2019/03/recomendacao-terreiro-icimimo-grupo-penha-1.pdf.

84. "Integrantes de terreiro denuncia incêndio motivado por intolerância religiosa no recôncavo baiano," *G1 Globo*, November 16, 2019, https://g1.globo.com/ba/bahia/noticia/2019/11/16/integrantes-de-terreiro-denuncia-incendio-motivado-por-intolerancia-religiosa-no-reconcavo-baiano.ghtml.

85. "Terreiro Ilê Axé Icimimó Aganjú Didè recebe solidariedade na ALBA," June 14, 2020, Bahia Já www.bahiaja.com.br/politica/noticia/2020/06/14/terreiro-ile-axe-incimimo-aganju-didie-recebe-solidariedade-na-alba,126664,0.html.

86. Interview with Pai Duda, January 2021.

87. Instagram post by Incimimó devotee @nara_couto on behalf of Pai Duda, September 1, 2023 (last accessed September 8, 2023).

88. "Terreiro Ilê Axé Incimimó Aganjú Didè recebe solidariedade na ALBA," June 14, 2020, Bahia Já, www.bahiaja.com.br/politica/noticia/2020/06/14/terreiro-ile-axe-incimimo-aganju-didie-recebe-solidariedade-na-alba,126664,0.html.

89. Instituto do Patrimônio Artístico e Cultural da Bahia, "Terreiro Mokambo recebe certificado de tombamento neste domingo (23), às 14h," September 20, 2017. www.ipac.ba.gov.br/noticias/terreiro-mokambo-recebe-certificado-de-tombamento-neste-domingo-23-as-14h

90. Instituto do Patrimônio Artístico e Cultural da Bahia, "Terreiro Mokambo recebe certificado de tombamento neste domingo (23), às 14h," September 20, 2017, www.ipac.ba.gov.br/noticias/terreiro-mokambo-recebe-certificado-de-tombamento-neste-domingo-23-as-14h.

91. Interview with Pai Rychelmy, December 2020.

Chapter 4

1. Interview with Ilzver Matos, October 2021.
2. See generally Skidmore, *Black Into White.*
3. www.laurodefreitas.ba.gov.br/2021/noticias/historia-do-municipio/118.
4. www.laurodefreitas.ba.gov.br/2021/noticias/historia-do-municipio/118.
5. www.laurodefreitas.ba.gov.br/2021/noticias/perfil-do-municipio/120.
6. www.laurodefreitas.ba.gov.br/2021/noticias/perfil-do-municipio/120.
7. www.laurodefreitas.ba.gov.br/2021/noticias/lauro-de-freitas-arvores-sao-adornadas-de-branco-por-adeptos-do-candomble-com-pedido-de-paz-e-respeito/1478.
8. www.laurodefreitas.ba.gov.br/2021/noticias/historia-do-municipio/118.
9. www.laurodefreitas.ba.gov.br/2021/noticias/comunidades-do-candomble-pedem-respeito-e-tolerancia-na-alvorada-dos-ojas-em-lauro-de-freitas/814.
10. De Souza, "The Religious Persecution," 262–267.
11. Interview with Vilson Caetano de Sousa Jr., January 2021.
12. Interview with Vilson Caetano de Sousa Jr., January 2021.
13. De Souza, "The Religious Persecution," 263.
14. De Souza, "The Religious Persecution," 264.
15. De Souza, "The Religious Persecution," 264.
16. De Souza, "The Religious Persecution," 265.
17. Interview with Vilson Caetano de Sousa Jr., January 4, 2021.
18. Interview with Vilson Caetano de Sousa Jr., January 4, 2021.
19. De Souza, "The Religious Persecution," 267.
20. Case No 8016209-29.2019.8.05.0000, 2nd Criminal Court of the District of Ilhéus (2ª Vara do Sistema dos Juizados Especiais da Comarca de Ilhéus), February 7, 2019; Chapter IV, Article 42, Section III, Decree no. 3,688/41, 1941, DEL3688 (planalto.gov.br).
21. Case No 8016209-29.2019.8.05.0000, 2nd Criminal Court of the District of Ilhéus, February 7, 2019; Página 388 da Caderno 1 - Administrativo do Diário de Justiça do Estado da Bahia (DJBA) de 27 de Março de 2019, DJBA 03/27/2019 - Pg.

388 - Notebook 1 - administrative | Bahia State Justice Daily | Jusbrasil Diaries; Case No 8020203-02.2018.8.05.0000, 2nd Criminal Court of the District of Ilhéus (2ª Vara do Sistema dos Juizados Especiais da Comarca de Ilhéus), March 27, 2019.

22. Danilo Matos, "Ilhéus: Justiça Obriga Pai De Santo A Varrer Rua E Proíbe Trabalhos Em Terreiro," Ilhéus 24hrs, June 13, 2013, https://ilheus24h.com.br/ilheus-justica-obriga-pai-de-santo-a-varrer-rua-e-proibe-trabalhos-em-terreiro/.

23. Danilo Matos, "Ilhéus: Justiça Obriga Pai De Santo A Varrer Rua E Proíbe Trabalhos Em Terreiro," Ilhéus 24hrs, June 13, 2013, https://ilheus24h.com.br/ilheus-justica-obriga-pai-de-santo-a-varrer-rua-e-proibe-trabalhos-em-terreiro/.

24. Zoom interview with Pai Joselino, March 2021.

25. In our interview Pai Joselino also referred to this legislation as the Noise Law (Lei do Barulho) and the Law of Peace (Lei do Sossego).

An interesting note about the city law in Aracaju is that it expressly prohibits batuques and "other similar amusements" (*outros divertimentos congêneres*) that disturb the neighborhood unless conducted with a special permit (Article 22, Section 7). There is no authorized decibel level or hours for performance; they are simply prohibited without permit. LEI Nº 1.789, De 17 de Janeiro de 1992, PREFEITURA MUNICIPAL DE ARACAJU, www.aracaju.se.gov.br/userfiles/concursos/lei_1789-1992_meio-ambiente.pdf.

26. https://intoleranciareligiosadossie.blogspot.com/2017/09/ministerio-publico-limita-atabaques-e.html; www.otempo.com.br/cidades/barulho-op%C3%B5e-vizinhos-e-templo-1.1502368?text=o+Centro+Esp%C3%ADrita+Il%C3%AA+Ax%C3%A9+e+Sang%C3%B4+entendem+que+est%C3%A3o+se%E2%80%A6.

27. Mota, "Diálogos Sobre Religiões De Matrizes Africanas," 38.

28. Interview with Túlio Aguiar (representative of Cenarab), April 2022.

29. http://intoleranciareligiosadossie.blogspot.com/2017/09/ministerio-publico-limita-atabaques-e.html.

30. Interview with Túlio Aguiar (representative of Cenarab), April 2022.

31. "Não existe candomblé sem os três atabaques (tipo de tambor). É a mesma coisa de uma missa sem padre, uma igreja católica sem sino." www.otempo.com.br/cidades/barulho-opoe-vizinhos-e-templo-1.1502368?text=o+Centro+Esp%C3%ADrita+Il%C3%AA+Ax%C3%A9+e+Sang%C3%B4+entendem+que+est%C3%A3o+se%E2%80%A6.

32. Conselho Nacional do Ministério Público CNMP, 20th Sessões Ordinárias de 2017, October 24, 2017.

33. "O nome disso é intolerância religiosa, não há outra expressão jurídica que possa qualificar um tipo de conduta como essa."

34. These sad details are also discussed in Castanha, *Religiões Afro-Brasileiras em Belo Horizonte*, 103.

35. Grupo de Estudos Braulio Goffman, Tat'etu Josué d'Ogum, August 16, 2016, www.youtube.com/watch?v=Suvb45SQGZY&fbclid=IwAR04Q6QRAq1fNOig8mxqSwUYVau_Hqc_vm42FJbZ_HHrJgb0EUWRt00PUxQ; Rosiane Rodrígues de Almeida, "Intolerância Religiosa e Redes Sociais," Revista Lumen et Virtus, Vol

VIII, no. 18, March 2017, www.jackbran.com.br/lumen_et_virtus/numero_18/PDF/INTOLERANCIA%20RELIGIOSA%20E%20REDES%20SOCIAIS.pdf; www.facebook.com/groups/fenacabsudeste.

36. Federação Nacional de Culto Afro Brasileiro, May 7, 2019, www.facebook.com/groups/1344701018921871/search/?q=Josue.

37. https://noiseawareness.org/info-center/common-noise-levels/ (accessed on March 24, 2022).

38. Guilherme Batista, "Mãe de santo promete se acorrentar em frente ao Fórum de Londrina," Bonde, September 30, 2014, www.bonde.com.br/bondenews/londrina/mae-de-santo-promete-se-acorrentar-em-frente-ao-forum-de-londrina-343482.html (last visited March 11, 2022); Case No. 0001000-29.2013.8.16.9000, Special Civil Court of the Central Forum of the District of the Metropolitan Region of Londrina, Dec. 5, 2013).

39. https://tj-pr.jusbrasil.com.br/jurisprudencia/838557630/processo-civel-e-do-trabalho-processo-de-conhecimento-procedimento-de-conhecimento-procedimentos-especiais-procedimentos-regidos-por-outros-codigos-leis-esparsas-e-regimentos-mandado-de-seguranca-ms-10002920138169000-pr-0001000-2920138169000-acordao.

40. (7) Ato contra a Intolerância Religiosa | Facebook.

41. http://awure.jor.br/home/centro-de-umbanda-promove-protesto-contra-intolerancia-religiosa-em-londrina/ (This link is broken. Last visited September 15, 2020).

42. "Juizado Especial Criminal de Olinda condenou babalorixá a 15 dias de prisão por "toque dos tambores sagrados" em sua casa," *Geledes*, April 21, 2017, www.geledes.org.br/juizado-especial-criminal-de-olinda-condenou-babalorixa-15-dias-de-prisao-por-toque-dos-tambores-sagrados-em-sua-casa/; "Sacerdoté de umbanda é condenado por perturbação de sossego," *Diario de Pernambuco*, April 12, 2017, www.diariodepernambuco.com.br/noticia/vidaurbana/2017/04/sacerdote-de-umbanda-e-condenado-por-perturbacao-de-sossego.html (last visited March 24, 2024); Amanda Stephanie, "Racismo em condenação de babalorixá por perturbação do sossego alheio," *Todos Negros do Mundo*, April 20, 2017, http://todosnegrosdomundo.com.br/racismo-em-condenacao-de-babalorixa-por-perturbacao-do-sossego-alheio/.

43. "Sacerdoté de umbanda é condenado por perturbação de sossego," *Diario de Pernambuco*, April 12, 2017, www.diariodepernambuco.com.br/noticia/vidaurbana/2017/04/sacerdote-de-umbanda-e-condenado-por-perturbacao-de-sossego.html (last visited March 24, 2024).

44. Lei No 12,789, April 28, 2005, https://leisestaduais.com.br/pe/lei-ordinaria-n-12789-2005-pernambuco-dispoe-sobre-ruidos-urbanos-poluicao-so-no-ra-e-protecao-do-bem-estar-e-do-sossego-publico-e-da-outras-providencias.

45. "Por manifestações religiosas, bem como, sinos de igrejas e instrumentos litúrgicos utilizados no exercício de culto ou cerimônia religiosa." Lei No 14,225 of December 13, 2010, https://leisestaduais.com.br/pe/lei-ordinaria-n-14225-2010-pernambuco-modifica-a-lei-n-12789-de-28-de-abril-de-2005.

46. Conselho Nacional do Ministério Público CNMP, 20th Sessões Ordinárias de 2017, October 24, 2017.

47. Interview with Ilzver Matos, October 2021. Ilzver talked about this in the interview and has also written about such cases and how, when decided based on subjective evidence, they open the possibility for judgments that are prejudiced against devotees of Afro-Brazilian religions and contrary to the principles of religious freedom. See Neto and Oliveira, "Liberdade Religiosa Ao Som Dos Atabaques," 144–148.

48. Interview with Ilzver Matos, October 13, 2021.

49. Pelli, "Religious Intolerance in the Land of the Festivals," 48–54.

50. Pelli, "Religious Intolerance in the Land of the Festivals," 48–54.

51. Pelli, "Religious Intolerance in the Land of the Festivals," 48–54.

52. He also discusses this case in a journal article. Oliveira, "Movimentos Afrorreligiosos," 3

53. Interview with Ilzver Matos, October 2021.

54. Grupo de Estudos Braulio Goffman, Tat'etu Josué d'Ogun, August 16, 2016, www.youtube.com/watch?v=Suvb45SQGZY&fbclid=IwAR04Q6QRAq1fNOig8mxqSwUYVau_Hqc_vm42FJbZ_HHrJgb0EUWRt00PUxQ.

55. Grupo de Estudos Braulio Goffman, Tat'etu Josué d'Ogun, August 16, 2016, www.youtube.com/watch?v=Suvb45SQGZY&fbclid=IwAR04Q6QRAq1fNOig8mxqSwUYVau_Hqc_vm42FJbZ_HHrJgb0EUWRt00PUxQ.

56. https://cidadeverde.com/noticias/251417/em-1-mes-terreiros-de-umbanda-de-teresina-sofreram-quatro-ataques.

57. Interview with Ana Paula Mendes de Miranda, February 2021.

58. Onisajé, "Report of Religious Racism," 258–261.

59. Marcelo Ferrão, "A Intolerância Religiosa que mata na Bahia: 'queima satanás, liberta senhor, destrói a feitiçaria,'" *Geledes*, June 7, 2015, www.geledes.org.br/a-intolerancia-religiosa-que-mata-na-bahia-queima-satanas-liberta-senhor-destroi-A-feiticaria.

Chapter 5

1. "Polícia prende 'Bonde de Jesus.'" 2019. Polícia Prende 'Bonde de Jesus' que Atacava Terreiros de Umbanda e Candomblé (2019). Estado de Minas. August 18, www.em.com.br/app/noticia/nacional/2019/08/18/interna_nacional,1078089/policia-prende-bonde-de-jesus-que-atacava-terreiros-de-umbanda-e-can.shtml (accessed on September 28, 2020).

2. "Polícia prende 'Bonde de Jesus.'" 2019. Polícia Prende 'Bonde de Jesus' que Atacava Terreiros de Umbanda e Candomblé (2019). Estado de Minas. August 18, www.em.com.br/app/noticia/nacional/2019/08/18/interna_nacional,1078089/policia-prende-bonde-de-jesus-que-atacava-terreiros-de-umbanda-e-can.shtml (accessed on 28 September 2020).

3. "Polícia prende 'Bonde de Jesus.'" 2019. Nelson Lima Neto e Tiago Rogero, "No Rio, Traficantes Proíbem Moradores De Usar Branco Por 'remeter A Candomblé

E Umbanda," *Koinonia*, August 25, 2019, http://intoleranciareligiosadossie.blogspot.com/2019/08/no-rio-traficantes-proibem-moradores-de.html.

4. Cunha, "Da Macumba Às Campanhas De Cura E Libertação," 231.

5. Oosterbaan, *Transmitting the Spirit*, 23.

6. Favelas in Rio de Janeiro, Past and Present: The Origins of Rio's Favelas and Early Activism (this is a companion website to the 2021 third edition of James N. Green and Thomas E. Skidmore's textbook *Brazil: Five Centuries of Change*, published by Oxford University Press.)

7. Straubhaar, "A Broader Definition of Fragile State," 44.

8. Interview with Rosiane Rodrigues, February 2021.

9. Rodrigues also talks about this in a journal article: Rodrigues, "A favela é de Jesus," 150–151.

10. Reporter Mario Monken made similar claims in a 2006 news article about the traffickers. Monken, "Tráfico é Acusado de Vetar Umbanda no Rio," *Folha de Sao Paulo*. February 4, 2006, https://www1.folha.uol.com.br/fsp/cotidian/ff0402200614.htm.

11. Rodrigues, "A favela é de Jesus," 148–149.

12. Russo, *Ilha do Governador*, 89.

13. Russo, *Ilha do Governador*, 90.

14. Russo, *Ilha do Governador*, 97.

15. Jobim was a well-known Brazilian musician who helped create and popularize bossa nova.

16. Russo, *Ilha do Governador*, 95.

17. Bahia, "O Rio de Iemanjá," 195–196.

18. Bahia, "O Rio de Iemanjá," footnote 53. "Muitos pais de santo se referem à Ilha do Governador em suas memórias de infância e adolescência dos anos 1950 em diante."

19. "O crescimento das religiões afro, em especial a umbanda, pode ser visto, por exemplo, na matéria do Jornal do Brasil de 30 de dezembro de 1966, que cita cerca de 400 mil umbandistas e 18 mil tendas, que compreendem as praias da Ilha Governador, Paquetá e Sepetiba." Bahia, "O Rio de Iemanjá," 203.

20. Jon Lee Anderson, "Gangland," *The New Yorker*, October 5, 2009, www.newyorker.com/magazine/2009/10/05/gangland (accessed on September 28, 2020); "Crime e Preconceito: Mães e Filhos de Santo são Expulsos de Favelas por Traficantes Evangélicos," *Geledes*. January 19, 2015, www.geledes.org.br/crime-e-preconceito-maes-e-filhos-de-santo-sao-expulsos-de-favelas-por-traficantes-evangelicos/ (accessed on September 28, 2020); Monken, "Tráfico é Acusado de Vetar Umbanda no Rio," *Folha de Sao Paulo*, February 4, 2006, https://www1.folha.uol.com.br/fsp/cotidian/ff0402200614.htm (accessed on September 28, 2020).

21. Rodrigues, "A favela é de Jesus," 159–160.

22. Rodrigues, "A favela é de Jesus," 158–160.

23. Prefeitura Nova Iguaçu, "A Cidade," www.novaiguacu.rj.gov.br/cidade/.

24. Terreiros that have applied for IPHAN protection are: Culto Corte Real da Nação de Ijexá – Ilê Ti Osum Omi Iya Iiya Oba Ti òdô Ti Ogum Alé (Belford Roxo);

Terreiro Ilê Omulu Oxum (São João do Meriti); Tenda Espirita Vovó Maria Conga de Arruda (Estácio neighborhood, Rio de Janeiro); Terreiro Santo Antônio dos Pobres – Ilê Ogum Megegê Asé Baru Lepé (Duque de Caxias); Terreiro de Candomblé Asé Nassó Oká Ilê Osun (Nova Iguaçu).

25. Cid, de Souza, and Vieira, "Tombamento De Terreiros De Candomblé," 548–549.

26. This figure includes 3,333 devotees of Candomblé, 3,787 devotees of Umbanda, 7,302 devotees of Umbanda and Candomblé, and 182 devotees of other Afro-Brazilian religions.

27. "Sétimo Terreiro é Depredado em Nova Iguaçu nos últimos Meses," *Geledes*, September 8, 2017, www.geledes.org.br/setimo-terreiro-e-depredado-em-nova-iguacu-nos-ultimos-meses/ (accessed on September 28, 2020); United States Department of State, International Religious Freedom Report (2017), www.state.gov/wp-content/uploads/2019/01/Brazil-2.pdf (accessed on November 25, 2020).

28. Marcos Nunes, "Polícia Identifica Suspeitos de Ataques Contra Terreiros na Baixada Fluminense," *Extra Globo*, September 13, 2017, https://extra.globo.com/casos-de-policia/policia-identifica-suspeitos-de-ataques-contra-terreiros-na-baixada-fluminense-21818164.html (accessed on September 28, 2020); Luisa Bustamante, "Em nome de Jesus," Bandidos Destroem Terreiro no Rio. *Veja*, October 8, 2017, https://veja.abril.com.br/brasil/em-nome-de-jesus-bandidos-destroem-terreiro-no-rio/ (accessed on September 28, 2020).

29. "Campos está entre as Cidades do RJ Com Mais Casos de Intolerância Religiosa em 2019," *G1 Globo*, May 28, 2019, https://g1.globo.com/rj/norte-fluminense/noticia/2019/05/28/campos-esta-entre-as-cidades-do-rj-com-mais-casos-de-intolerancia-religiosa-em-2019.ghtml (accessed on September 28, 2020).

30. David Barbosa, "Terreiro de Candomblé é Invadido Pela Segunda vez por Traficantes em Nova Iguaçu," *Extra Globo*, March 28, 2019, https://extra.globo.com/casos-de-policia/terreiro-de-candomble-invadido-pela-segunda-vez-por-traficantes-em-nova-iguacu-23557091.html (accessed on September 28, 2020); Berenice Seara, "Tráfico Monta Quartel-General em Terreiro de Candomblé na Baixada Fluminense," *Extra Globo*, April 4, 2019, https://extra.globo.com/noticias/extra-extra/trafico-monta-quartel-general-em-terreiro-de-candomble-na-baixada-fluminense-23584321.html (accessed on September 28, 2020); United States Department of State, International Religious Freedom Report (2019), www.state.gov/wp-content/uploads/2020/06/BRAZIL-2019-INTERNATIONAL-RELIGIOUS-FREEDOM-REPORT.pdf (accessed on November 25, 2020).

31. "Campos está entre as Cidades do RJ Com Mais Casos de Intolerância Religiosa em 2019," *G1 Globo*, May 28, 2019, https://g1.globo.com/rj/norte-fluminense/noticia/2019/05/28/campos-esta-entre-as-cidades-do-rj-com-mais-casos-de-intolerancia-religiosa-em-2019.ghtml (accessed on September 28, 2020).

32. Devotees include 2,849 Candomblé, 4,879 Umbanda, 7,826 Umbanda and Candomblé, and 98 other Afro-Brazilian religions. IBGE, São Gonçalo, https://cidades.ibge.gov.br/brasil/rj/sao-goncalo/pesquisa/23/22107?detalhes=true (last visited January 24, 2022).

33. Samuel Lima, "Religion in Rio's Favelas," *Rio On Watch*, May 11, 2011, www.rioonwatch.org/?p=1151 (accessed on September 28, 2020).

34. Lima, "Religion in Rio's Favelas."

35. Interview with Babalorixá Alexandre Savi and Babalorixá Gilmar de Iansã, 2021.

36. International Commission to Combat Religious Racism, Religious Racism in Brazil, June 15, 2022, www.religiousracism.org/brazil.

37. "Ataque a templo de umbanda evidência intolerância religiosa," *Notícias de Terreiro*, January 28, 2019, https://noticiasdeterreiro.com.br/2019/01/28/ataque-templo-de-umbanda-evidencia-intolerancia-religiosa/ (last visited December 28, 2021).

38. Eduardo Schiavoni, "Terreiro de umbanda e alvo de bomba e praticantes sao espancados em SP," February 6, 2020, https://noticias.uol.com.br/cotidiano/ultimas-noticias/2020/02/06/terreiro-de-umbanda-e-alvo-de-bomba-e-praticantes-sao-espancados-em-sp.htm?cmpid=copiaecola (last visited December 29, 2021); "Líder de centro de umbanda se diz vítima de intolerância após ataque com bomba e agressão em SP," February 8, 2020, https://g1.globo.com/sp/ribeirao-preto-franca/noticia/2020/02/08/dona-de-centro-de-umbanda-se-diz-vitima-de-intolerancia-apos-ataque-com-bomba-e-agressao-em-sp.ghtml (last visited December 29, 2021).

39. Milena Schäfer, "Centro De Umbanda É Atacado A Tiros Por Vizinho Em Caxias Do Sul," *Pioneiro Geral*, February 10, 2020, https://gauchazh.clicrbs.com.br/pioneiro/geral/noticia/2020/02/centro-de-umbanda-e-atacado-a-tiros-por-vizinho-em-caxias-do-sul-12187878.html (accessed on January 3, 2022).

40. U.S. Department of State, International Religious Freedom Report: Brazil (2016), available online at: www.state.gov/reports/2016-report-on-international-religious-freedom/brazil/.

41. Cíntia Cruz "Placa na Baixada diz que cidade 'pertence ao Senhor Jesus' e vira alvo de críticas," *Extra Globo*, August 6, 2018, https://extra.globo.com/noticias/rio/placa-na-baixada-diz-que-cidade-pertence-ao-senhor-jesus-vira-alvo-de-criticas-22951395.html (last visited July 20, 2022).

Chapter 6

1. Interview with Doté Amilton, January 2021.

2. Interview with Doté Amilton, January 2021; www.correio24horas.com.br/noticia/nid/eles-jamais-apontariam-arma-para-um-padre-diz-lider-de-terreiro-invadido-por-pms-na-liberdade/.

3. Interview with Pai Diego, February 2021.

4. This translates to "basic basket" and refers to a package of essential foods provided to low-income families each month.

5. "Policias Militares de Santa Catarina Invadem Templo Umbandista e Acabam com Culto," *Jornal Flit Paralisante: Polícia, Política, Justiça e a Liberdade de Expressão*, July 14, 2010, https://flitparalisante.wordpress.com/2010/07/14/policiais-militares-de-santa-catarina-invadem-templo-umbandista-e-acabam-com-culto/ (accessed February 16, 2022).

6. Histórico da UCAP, Tenda de Umbanda Caboclo Pajelança Blogspot, November 3, 2012, https://tendacaboclopajelanca.blogspot.com/search/label/ABUSO%20DE%20AUTORIDADE.

7. Ana Paula Gonçalves, "Umbandistas pedirão respeito e liberdade em manifestação neste sábado," OCP News, February 23, 2018, https://ocp.news/geral/umbandistas-pedirao-respeito-e-liberdade-em-manifestacao-neste-sabado-24 (accessed March 13, 2022).

8. Instituto Brasileiro de Geografia e Estatística, "Corumbá," www.ibge.gov.br/cidades-e-estados/ms/corumba.html.

9. Marques Viegas and Oliveira Martins, "A Religiosidade Afro-Brasileira Na Fronteira," 115.

10. Moretzsohn Rocha, "Sonoridades Afro-Brasileiras Em Corumbá," 122.

11. Marques Viegas and Oliveira Martins, "A Religiosidade Afro-Brasileira Na Fronteira," 114–115.

12. João Pedro Godoy e Caio Tumelero, "Umbandistas denunciam violência policial e intolerância religiosa em terreiro de MS, mas PM nega," *G1 Globo*, November 1, 2021, https://g1.globo.com/ms/mato-grosso-do-sul/noticia/2021/11/01/umbandistas-denunciam-violencia-policial-e-intolerancia-religiosa-em-terreiro-de-ms-mas-pm-nega-video.ghtml?fbclid=IwAR0pVWq2rBxHvONjM0XP6PEpW32ay3vPwTHrMEMoM359tbR2oglVn2VLZIo.

13. https://amp-al.jusbrasil.com.br/noticias/1970945/direitos-humanos-discute-ato-de-intolerancia-religiosa?ref=serp; https://oab-al.jusbrasil.com.br/noticias/1911246/oab-e-adeptos-do-candomble-tem-encontro-com-magistrada-e-secretario-de-defesa-social?ref=serp.

14. https://amp-al.jusbrasil.com.br/noticias/1970945/direitos-humanos-discute-ato-de-intolerancia-religiosa?ref=serp; https://oab-al.jusbrasil.com.br/noticias/1911246/oab-e-adeptos-do-candomble-tem-encontro-com-magistrada-e-secretario-de-defesa-social?ref=serp.

15. Lucas Simões, "Policial lidera destruição de terreiro," O Beltrano, 2017, www.badernanoticias.com/portfolio/policial-lidera-destruicao-de-terreiro/ (last visited July 16, 2022).

16. Interview with Babazinho de Oxalá, December 2020.

17. "Terreiro de Mãe Corina sofre com perseguição religiosa e abusos da Guarda Municipal de Diadema," Olhar de um Cipó, January 31, 2017, http://olhardeumcipo.blogspot.com/2017/01/terreiro-de-mae-corina-sofre-com.html.

18. "Violação à liberdade religiosa: MP ajuíza ação de reparação de dano moral coletivo," Jornal da Cidade, September 12, 2018 (last visited July 16, 2022).

19. "'Exu corona' e terreiro queimado escancaram intolerância religiosa na pandemia," Justiça ao minuto, November 5, 2020, www.noticiasaominuto.com.br/brasil/1735894/exu-corona-e-terreiro-queimado-escancaram-intolerancia-religiosa-na-pandemia (last visited July 16, 2022).

20. ICCRR database, cases 6, 65 and 313. www.religiousracim.org/brazil.

21. Nilson Marinho e Thais Borges, "PMs invadem terreiro, atiram contra templo e prendem ogã no Subúrbio," *Correio*, January 30, 2018 (last visited July 16, 2022).

22. "Ylê Axé Odé Omí Uá," Terra Magazine, April 11, 2010, https://psicod.org/levantamento-de-casos-de-racismo-e-intolerncia-religiosa-contr.html?page=29.

23. Anna Virginia Balloussier, Daniela Arcanjo, "Universal se une a quartéis para amenizar o estresse e dar força a policiais militares," *Folha de S. Paulo*, February 9, 2020, https://www1.folha.uol.com.br/poder/2020/02/universal-se-une-a-quarteis-para-amenizar-o-estresse-e-dar-forca-a-policiais-militares.shtml.

24. See cases 52, 241, 306. www.religiousracim.org/brazil.

25. Rodrigo Pedroso and Taylor Barnes, "Fury Over Brutal Beating in Brazil Amid Pattern of 'Daily' Violence, Activists Say," CNN, November 27, 2020, www.cnn.com/2020/11/27/americas/joo-alberto-silveira-freitas-brazil-intl/index.html; "Killing of Black Man by Guards at Brazil Supermarket Sparks Protests," BBC News, November 20, 2020, www.bbc.com/news/world-latin-america-55020915; Terrence McCoy, "Black Man's Death After Savage Beating by Security Guards Outrages Brazil," *Washington Post*, November 20, 2020, www.washingtonpost.com/world/brazil-black-man-beaten-to-death/2020/11/20/87acdc24-2b3a-11eb-9c21-3cc501d0981f_story.html.

26. Andrew Fishman, "Deadliest Police Raid in Rio de Janeiro History Kills at Least 28," *The Intercept*, May 8, 2021, https://theintercept.com/2021/05/08/brazil-police-massacre-rio-jacarezinho/,

27. Terrence McCoy, "Rio Police Were Ordered to Limit Favela Raids During the Pandemic. They're Still Killing Hundreds of People," *Washington Post*, May 20, 2021.

28. "Brazil: Investigate Rio Police Command for Deadly Raid," *Rio on Watch*, May 31, 2021, www.hrw.org/news/2021/05/31/brazil-investigate-rio-police-command-deadly-raid.

29. "Brazil: Investigate Rio Police Command for Deadly Raid," *Rio on Watch*.

30. McCoy, "Rio Police Were Ordered."

31. Indu Pandey, "Vigils on Two Continents: A Comparative Analysis of Police Brutality in Brazil and the United States," *Harvard International Review*, June 5, 2020, https://hir.harvard.edu/vigils-on-two-continents/.

32. Lívia Peres Milani, "Triggering Police Violence in Brazil," NACLA, April 10, 2019.

33. Andrea Zellhuber, "Police Brutality in Brazil," À Propos, April 2021, www.swisspeace.ch/apropos/police-brutality-in-brazil/.

34. "Good Cops Are Afraid: The Toll of Unchecked Police Violence in Rio de Janeiro," Human Rights Watch, 2016, 1.

35. "Good Cops Are Afraid," 20–25.

36. "Good Cops Are Afraid," 26–30.

37. Working Group, *People of African Descent*, para 67.

38. Report of the Special Rapporteur on Minority Issues, 10–11.

39. "Good Cops Are Afraid," 41.

40. "Good Cops Are Afraid," 38–39.

41. "Good Cops Are Afraid," 84.

42. Working Group, *People of African Descent*, para 77.

43. Pandey, "Vigils on Two Continents."
44. "Good Cops Are Afraid," 5.
45. "Good Cops Are Afraid," 16–17.
46. Pandey, "Vigils on Two Continents"; Report of the Special Rapporteur on Minority Issues, 11.
47. Working Group, *People of African Descent*, para 69.
48. Pandey, "Vigils on Two Continents."
49. Report of the Special Rapporteur on Minority Issues, para. 85 (2015).
50. www.cnn.com/2018/06/25/us/permit-patty-san-francisco-trnd/index.html.
51. McNamarah, "White Callar Crime"; Fields, "Weaponized Racial Fear"; Mann, "What's Your Emergency?"

Chapter 7

1. Interview with Mãe Jaciara, January 2021.
2. Interview with Pai Carlos, December 2020.
3. "Black State Rep. Thanks God for Slavery," *The Grio*, March 4, 2018, https://thegrio.com/2018/03/04/black-state-rep-thanks-god-slavery/.
4. Secretaria de Promoção da Igualdade Racial do Governo do Estado da Bahia.

Bibliography

Interviews

Ana Paula Méndes De Miranda, scholar and professor, February 2021

Baba Alan Crave, leader of Casa das Águas (Nova Iguaçu, Rio de Janeiro), January 2021

Baba Alexandre Savi, religious leader from São Gonçalo (Rio de Janeiro), March 2021

Baba Pecê, leader of Casa de Oxumarê (Salvador, Bahia), January 2021

Babazinho de Oxalá, religious leader from the Federal District, December 2020

Desirée Tozi, Director of the Department of Cooperation and Development at IPHAN, April 2021

Doté Amilton, leader of Terreiro Vodun Zo (Salvador, Bahia), January 2021

Ilzver Matos, an attorney and scholar from Acaraju, Sergipe, October 2021

Iury Passos, Brazilian master percussionist, July 2021

Iyá Rosiane Rodrígues de Almeida, a religious leader and scholar from Rio de Janeiro, February 2021

Jandira Mawusi, Ekedi of Terreiro Bogum (Salvador, Bahia), February 2021

José Mário Bezerra da Silva (Mario Pam), master percussionist from afro bloco Ilê Aiyê, July 2021 and October 2021

Maria Alice Pereira da Silva, attorney, activist, and author of two books about the Pedra de Xangô, December 2020

Mãe Baiana, a religious leader from Brasília, December 2020

Mãe Dora, a religious leader/activist in Brasília, December 2020

Mãe Jaciara de Oxum (Jaciara Ribeiro), leader of Ilê Axé Abassá de Ogum (Itapuã, Salvador, Bahia), January 2021

Mãe Pauli de Oxumarê, a Candomblé priestess from Ilha do Governador (Rio de Janeiro), March 2021

Neto Azile, director of the Casa do Tambor de Crioula museum and cultural center (São Luís), July 2021

Pai Anderson de Oxalá, leader of Ilê Axé Alá Obatalandê (Lauro de Freitas, Bahia), February 2021

Pai Carlos Brottas, religious leader from Cajazeiras, Bahia, December 2020

Pai Diego, religious leader from Iturama, Minas Gerais, February 2021

Pai Duda, leader of Terreiro Ilê Axé Icimimó Aganjú Didè (Cachoeira, Bahia), January 2021

Pai Gilmar de Iansã (Gilmar Hughes), a babalorixá and undersecretary of the Coordination for the Defense of Diffuse Rights and Combating Religious Intolerance (Codir) of the City of Niterói (Rio de Janeiro), March 2021

Pai Eusébio, leader of Casa das Minas (São Luís), July 2021

Pai Joselino, religious leader from Sergipe, March 2021

Pai Rychelmy, leader of Casa do Mensageiro (Barra de Pojuca, Bahia), December 2020

Patrícia Zappone, a lawyer-practitioner who lives in Brasília, December 2021

Ricardo Costa, Brazilian master percussionist, April 2021

Rose Mary Jesus (Ekedi Rose de Ogum), Ekedi of Casa de Oxumarê (Salvador, Bahia), January 2021

Túlio Aguiar, representative of Cenarab (Minas Gerais), April 2022

Vilson Caetano de Sousa Jr., professor at the Federal University of Bahia and babalorixá of Ilê Obá L'Okê (Lauro de Freitas, Bahia), January 2021

Secondary Sources

Almeida, Rosiane Rodrígues de. "A Favela É De Jesus": O Fechamento Dos Terreiros No Rio De Janeiro," *AVÁ* 38 (2021): 143–166.

Almeida, Rosiane Rodrígues de. *A luta por um modo de vida: enfrentamento ao racismo religioso no Brasil.* Eduff, 2022.

Alonso, Miguel, & Norman K. Smith. *The Development of Yoruba Candomblé Communities in Salvador, Bahia, 1835–1986.* Palgrave Macmillan, 2014.

Bahia, Joana. "O Rio de Iemanjá: uma cidade e seus rituais," *Revista Brasileira de História das Religiões* 10, no. 30 (2018): 177–215.

Barcia, Manuel. *Seeds of Insurrection: Domination and Resistance on Western Cuban Plantations, 1808–1848.* Louisiana State University Press, 2008.

Bascom, William. *The Yoruba of Southwestern Nigeria.* Waveland Press, 1984.

Boaz, Danielle. *Banning Black Gods: Law and Religions of the African Diaspora.* Pennsylvania State University Press, 2021.

Boaz, Danielle. "Exoticizing Terrorism: Religious Bias and the Unchecked Threat of Evangelical Extremism in Brazil," *Journal of Religion & Society* 23 (2021): 1–20.

Boaz, Danielle. "Obeah, Vagrancy, and the Boundaries of Religious Freedom: Analyzing the Proscription of 'Pretending to Possess Supernatural Powers' in the Anglophone Caribbean," *Journal of Law and Religion* 32, no. 3 (2017): 423–448.

Boaz, Danielle. "'Spiritual Warfare' or 'Crimes against Humanity'?: Evangelized Drug Traffickers and Violence Against Afro-Brazilian Religions in Rio de Janeiro," *Religions: Special Issue on Religion and Violence* 11, no. 12 (2020): 640–657.

Borges, Dain. "Healing and Mischief: Witchcraft in Brazilian Law and Literature, 1890–1922," in Ricardo D. Salvatore et al. (Eds.), *Crime and Punishment in Latin America: Law and Society Since Late Colonial Times* (pp. 181–210). Duke University Press, 2001.

Bortoleto, Milton. "'Não viemos para fazer aliança': Faces do conflito entre adeptos das religiões pentecostais e afro-brasileiras." MA thesis, Universidade De São Paulo, 2014.

Burnham, Thorald M. "Makandal, François," in Colin A. Palmer (Ed.), *Encyclopedia of African-American Culture and History* (2nd ed., vol. 4; pp. 1362–1363). Macmillan Reference USA, 2006.

Butler, Kim D. "Ginga Baiana – The Politics of Race, Class, Culture, and Power in Salvador, Bahia," in Hendrik Kraay (Ed.), *Afro-Brazilian Culture and Politics: Bahia, 1790s to 1990s* (pp. 158–175). M.E. Sharpe, 1998.

Castanha, Taísa Domiciano. *Religiões Afro-Brasileiras em Belo Horizonte e Região Metropolitana: Conflitos, Violência, e Legitimação.* Ph.D. dissertation, Universidade Federal de Minas Gerais, 2018.

Cid, Gabriel da Silva Vidal, Luciane Barbosa de Souza, & Sandra Regina Fabiano do Rosario Vieira. "Tombamento De Terreiros De Candomblé: Algumas Questões Iniciais Sobre O Caso Do Estado Do Rio De Janeiro," *Anais do IX Seminário Internacional de Políticas Culturais,* Fundação Casa de Rui Barbosa, 2019.

Conduru, Roberto. "Das casas às roças: comunidades de candomblé no Rio de Janeiro desde o fim do século XIX1," *Topoi* 11, no. 21 (July–December 2010): 178–203.

Conrad, Robert Edgar. *Children of God's Fire: A Documentary History of Black Slavery in Brazil.* Princeton University Press, 1984.

Conte, Andreza. "Umbanda: Apontamentos Sobre A Interferência Da Religião No Estado E O Estudo Da Lei." Bachelor's thesis, University of Santa Cruz do Sul, 2016.

Cunha, Christina Vital Da. "Da Macumba Às Campanhas De Cura E Libertação: A Fé Dos Traficantes De Drogas Em Favelas No Rio De Janeiro," *Revista TOMO* 14 (2009): 229–265.

De Sousa Jr., Vilson Caetano. "The Religious Persecution of Casa do Rei e Senhor das Alturas," *Journal of Africana Religions: Roundtable on Religious Racism in Brazil* 9, no. 2 (2021): 262–267.

Dos Santos, Adriana Martins. "O Reino de Deus no Legislativo Municipal: Bolinhos de Jesus, Orixás do Tororó e Outras Historias," Sociabilidades Religioas: Mitos, Ritos, Identidades, *XI Simpósio Nacional Da Associação Brasileira de História Das Religiões.* www.abhr.org.br/wp-content/uploads/2013/01/art_SANTOS_legislativo_municipal.pdf.

Dourado, Cláudia Marques. "Orixás do Dique do Tororó: Simbologia e problemática cultural da população afrodescendente baiana." Post-graduate dissertation, Ethnic and African Studies, Universidade Federal Da Bahia, 2009.

Edwards, Gary, & John Mason. *Black Gods: Orisa Studies in the New World.* Yoruba Theological Archministry, 1985.

Epstein, Dena. *Sinful Tunes and Spirituals: Black Folk Music to the Civil War.* University of Illinois Press, 2003.

Fields, Shawn. "Weaponized Racial Fear," *Tulane Law Review* 93, no. 4 (2019): 931–1003. http://doi.org/10.2139/ssrn.3355891.

Frank, Andrew. "Stono Rebellion," in Junius P. Rodriguez (Ed.), *Encyclopedia of Emancipation and Abolition in the Transatlantic World.* Routledge, 2007.

Gidal, Marc Meistrich. "Musical and Spiritual Innovation, Participation and Control in Brazil's Umbanda and Quimbanda Religions." *Ethnomusicology Forum* 22, no. 2 (2013): 232–253.

Giumbelli, Emerson. "Presença Na Recusa: A África Dos Pioneiros Umbandistas," *Revista Esboços* 17, no. 23 (2010): 107–117.

Giumbelli, Emerson. "When Religion Is Culture: Observations About State Policies Aimed at Afro-Brazilian Religions and Other Afro-Heritage," *Sociologia & Antropologia* 8, no. 2 (2018): 401–426.

Gonçalves Fernandes, Albino. *O sincretismo religioso no Brasil*. Editora Guaíra limitada, 1941.

Gordenstein, Samuel Lira. "Planting Axé in the City: Urban Terreiros and the Growth of Candomblé in Late Nineteenth-Century Salvador, Bahia, Brazil," *Journal of African Diaspora Archaeology and Heritage* 5, no. 2 (2016): 71–101. https://doi.org/10.1080/21619441.2016.1204791.

Guimarães, Andréa Letícia Carvalho. "Os direitos dos povos de terreiros na encruzilhada: o uso do atabaque e o meio ambiente," *Revista Científica de Direitos Humanos* 1, no. 1 (2018): 179–196.

Hale, Lindsay. *Hearing the Mermaid's Song: The Umbanda Religion in Rio de Janeiro*. University of New Mexico Press, 2009.

Handler, Jerome, & Charlotte J. Frisbie. "Aspects of Slave Life in Barbados: Music and Its Cultural Context," *Caribbean Studies* 11, no. 4 (January 1972): 5–46.

Harding, Rachel Elizabeth. "Candomblé and the Alternative Space of Black Being in Nineteenth Century Bahia, Brazil: A Study of Historical Context and Religious Meaning." ProQuest Dissertations Publishing, 1997.

Hayes, Kelly. "Black Magic and the Academy: Macumba and Afro-Brazilian 'Orthodoxies,'" *History of Religions* 46, no. 4 (May 2007): 283–315.

Hayes, Kelly. *Black Magic at the Margins: Macumba in Rio de Janeiro*. Ph.D. dissertation, University of Chicago, 2004.

Hedegard, Danielle. *Racialized Cultural Capital and Inequality: A Comparative Study of Blackness in Brazil's Tourism Market*. Ph.D. dissertation, University of Arizona, 2011.

Hertzman, Marc A. *Making Samba: A New History of Race and Music in Brazil*. Duke University Press, 2013.

Howard, Joseph. *Drums in the Americas: The History and Development of Drums in the New World From the Pre-Columbian Era to Modern Times*. OAK Publications, 1967.

International Commission to Combat Religious Racism. "Religious Racism in Brazil," August 22, 2022. www.religiousracism.org/brazil.

Johnson, Daniel. "Profane Language, Horrid Oaths and Imprecations: Order and the Colonial Soundscape in the American mid-Atlantic, 1650–1750," *Social History* 46, no. 3 (2021): 255–277.

Johnson, Paul Christopher. *Secrets, Gossip, and Gods: The Transformation of Brazilian Candomblé*. Oxford University Press, 2005.

Johnson, Paul Christopher. "Law, Religion and 'Public Health' in the Republic of Brazil," *Law and Social Inquiry* 26 (2001): 9–33.

Lesser, Jeff. *Immigration, Ethnicity, and National Identity in Brazil, 1808 to the Present*. Cambridge University Press, 2013.

Lühning, Angela. "'Acabe com esse santo, Pedrito vem aí.' – Mito e realidade da perseguição policial ao candomblé baiano entre 1920 e 1942," *Revista USP*, 28 (1996): 194–220. https://doi.org/10.11606/issn.2316-9036.v0i28p194-220.

Lühning, Angela Elisabeth, & Sivanilton Encarnação da Mata. *Os cânticos que encantaram Pierre Verger*. Editorial Arole Cultural, 2021.

Maggie, Yvonne. *Medo do feitiço: Relações Entre Magia e Poder no Brasil*. Arquivo Nacional, 1992.

Mann, Justin Louis. "What's Your Emergency?: White Women and the Policing of Public Space," *Feminist Studies* 44, no. 3 (2018): 766–775.

Manuel, Peter. *Caribbean Currents: Caribbean Music from Rhumba to Reggae* (3rd ed.). Temple University Press, 2016.

Marques Viegas, Ana Claudia, & Sergio Ricardo Oliveira Martins. "A Religiosidade Afro-Brasileira Na Fronteira: Terreiros de Umbanda em Corumbá- MS," *Revista de historia* 6, no. 12 (July–December 2014): 106–122.

Mason, John. *Orin Orisa: Songs for Selected Heads*. Yoruba Theological Archministry, 1992.

Matory, J. Lorand. *Black Atlantic Religion: Tradition, Transnationalism, and Matriarchy in the Afro-Brazilian Candomblé*. Princeton University Press, 2005.

Matory, J. Lorand. *Sex and the Empire That Is No More: Gender and the Politics of Metaphor in Oyo Yoruba Religion*. University of Minnesota Press, 1994.

McNamarah, Chan T. "White Caller Crime: Racialized Police Communication and Existing While Black," *Michigan Journal of Race and Law* 24 (2019): 335–415. https://repository.law.umich.edu/mjrl/vol24/iss2/5.

Miranda, Ana Paula Mendes de. "Intolerância religiosa e discriminação racial: duas faces de um mesmo problema público?" In Antonio Carlos de Souza Lima et al. (Eds.), *A antropologia e a esfera pública no Brasil: Perspectivas e Prospectivas sobre a Associação Brasileira de Antropologia no seu 60o Aniversário* (pp. 329–363). Associação Brasileira de Antropologia, 2018.

Montero, Paula. "The 'Culture of Justification' in the Production of Public Religiosities in Brazil," in Jose Mapril et al. (Eds.), *Secularisms in a Postsecular Age? Religiosities and Subjectivities in Comparative Perspective* (pp. 207–229). Palgrave Macmillan, 2017.

Moretzsohn, Rocha, & Carmem Silvia. "Sonoridades Afro-Brasileiras Em Corumbá: Um Estudo Sobre Representações Musicais Em Rituais De Umbanda," *Iluminuras, Porto Alegre* 13, no. 31 (July–December 2012): 118–143.

Mota, Emília Guimarães. "Diálogos Sobre Religiões De Matrizes Africanas: Racismo Religioso E História," *Revista Calundu* 2, no. 1 (2018): 23–48.

Mota, Emília Guimarães. *Ser com o outro, conviver e cuidar: Enfrentamentos Cotidianos Ao Racismo Religioso*. Ph.D. dissertation, Universidade Federal De Goiás, 2019.

Murrell, Nathaniel Samuel. *Afro-Caribbean Religions: An Introduction to Their Historical, Cultural, and Sacred Traditions*. Temple University Press, 2010.

Nascimento, Wanderson Flor do. "Intolerância ou racismo?" *Hora Grande* 167 (2016): 15.

Nascimento, Wanderson Flor do. "O fenômeno do racismo religioso: desafios para os povos tradicionais de matrizes africanas," *Revista Eixo, Brasília-DF* 6, no. 2 (Special Edition) (2017): 51–56.

Neto, Pedro Meneses Feitosa, & Ilzver de Matos Oliveira. "Liberdade Religiosa Ao Som Dos Atabaques e Sua Relativização discricionária pelo poder judiciário," *Conference Paper: XVII Congresso Nacional Do Conpedi Porto Alegre, Rio Grande do Sul*, 2018.

Oliveira, Ariadne Moreira Basilio de. "Religiões Afro-Brasileiras E O Racismo: Contribuição Para a categorização Do Racismo Religioso." MA thesis, Universidade de Brasília, 2017.

Oliveira, Ilzver de Matos. "Movimentos Afrorreligiosos E Suas Estratégias Jurídicas Contra Casos De Racismo Religioso Em Sergipe," *Revista de Movimentos Sociais e Conflitos* 3, no. 2 (2017): 1–20.

Onisajé. "Report of Religious Racism against O Ilê Axé Oyá L'adê Inan," *Journal of Africana Religions: Roundtable on Religious Racism in Brazil* 9, no. 2 (2021): 258–261.

Oosterbaan, Martijn. *Transmitting the Spirit: Religious Conversion, Media, and Urban Violence in Brazil*. Pennsylvania State University Press, 2017.

Oro, Ari Pedro. "The Sacrifice of Animals in Afro-Brazilian Religions: Analysis of a Recent Controversy in the Brazilian State of Rio Grande Do Sul." *Religião e Sociedad* 1 (2006): 995–1014.

Ortiz, Fernando. *Africanía de la música folklórica de Cuba*. Editorial Letras Cubanas, 1993 [1951].

Ortiz, Renato. "Ogum and Umbandista Religion," in Sandra Barnes (Ed.), Africa's Ogun: Old World and New (pp. 90–102). Indiana University Press, 1989.

Paton, Diana. *The Cultural Politics of Obeah: Religion, Colonialism and Modernity in the Caribbean World*. Cambridge University Press, 2015.

Paton, Diana. "Witchcraft, Poison, Law and Atlantic Slavery," *William and Mary Quarterly* 69, no. 2 (2012): 235–264.

Pelli, Ronaldo. "Religious Intolerance in the Land of the Festivals," *Index on Censorship* 42, no. 4 (December 2013): 48–54.

Port, Mattijs van de. "Bahian White: The Dispersion of Candomblé Imagery in the Public Sphere of Bahia," *Material Religion* 3, no. 2 (2007): 242–274.

Queiroz, Gregorio Jose Pereira de. "Umbanda Music and Music Therapy," *Voices* 15, no. 1 (2015). https://doi.org/10.15845/voices.v1i1.780.

"The Quilombo of Palmares Is Established," in Jennifer Stock (Ed.), *Global Events: Milestone Events Throughout History* (vol. 3; pp. 89–91). Gale, 2014.

Rafael, Ulisses N. "Muito barulho por nada ou o 'xangô rezado baixo': uma etnografia do 'Quebra de 1912' em Alagoas, Brasil," *Etnográfica* 14, no. 2 (2010): 289–310.

Rafael, Ulisses N., & Yvonne Maggie. "Sorcery Objects Under Institutional Tutelage: Magic and Power in Ethnographic Collections," *Vibrant* 10, no. 1 (2013): 276–342.

Ramsey, Kate. *The Spirits and the Law: Vodou and Power in Haiti*. University of Chicago Press, 2011.

Rego, Jussara. "Caso Mãe Gilda," *Koinonia* 3, no. 13 (2008). www.koinonia.org.br/tpdigital/detalhes.asp?cod_artigo=256&cod_boletim=14&tipo=Artigo.

Reis, João José. "Batuque: African Drumming and Dance Between Repression and Concession, Bahia, 1808–1855." *Bulletin of Latin American Research* 24, no. 2 (2005): 201–214. https://doi.org/10.1111/j.0261-3050.2005.00132.x.

Reis, João José. "Candomblé in Nineteenth-Century Bahia: Priests, Followers, Clients," *Slavery & Abolition* 22, no. 1 (2001): 91–115. https://doi.org/10.1080/714005177.

Roman, Reinaldo. *Governing Spirits: Religion, Miracles and Spectacles in Cuba and Puerto Rico, 1898–1956*. University of North Carolina Press, 2007.

Russo, Paulo Roberto. "Ilha Do Governador: Considerações Acerca de Seu Processo de Ocupação." *Geo UERJ: Revista Do Departamento de Geografia*, no. 2, (2016): 89–100.

Santos, Jocelio Teles dos. "A Mixed-Race Nation: Afro-Brazilians and Cultural Policy in Bahia, 1970–1990," in Hendrik Kraay (Ed.), *Afro-Brazilian Culture and Politics: Bahia, 1790s to 1990s* (pp. 117–133). M.E. Sharpe, Inc., 1998.

Schweitzer, Kenneth. *The Artistry of Afro-Cuban Batá Drumming: Aesthetics, Transmission, Bonding, and Creativity*. University of Mississippi Press, 2013.

Selka, Stephen. "Cityscapes and Contact Zones: Christianity, Candomblé, and African Heritage Tourism in Brazil," *Religion* 43, no. 3 (2013): 403–420. https://doi.org/10.1080/0048721X.2013.798163.

Shirey, Heather. "Transforming the Orixás: Candomblé in Sacred and Secular Spaces in Salvador da Bahia, Brazil," *African Arts* (Winter 2009): 62–79.

Silva, Caio Isidoro da. "Políticas públicas para o enfrentamento do racismo religioso (2003–2006)." M.A. thesis, Universidade Estadual Paulista "Júlio de Mesquita Filho", 2020.

Skidmore, Thomas E. *Black Into White: Race and Nationality in Brazilian Thought*. Duke University Press, 1993. https://doi.org/10.1515/9780822381761.

Stansky, Victoria. "Persecution and Permanence: Re-Negotiating Brazil's Identity, Religious Intolerance, and Consuming Candomblé." MA thesis, University of California, Santa Barbara, 2012.

Straubhaar, Rolf. "A Broader Definition of Fragile State: The Communities and Schools of Brazil's Favelas," *Current Issues in Comparative Education* 15, no. 1 (2012): 41–51.

Sublette, Ned. *Cuba and Its Music: From the First Drums to the Mambo*. Chicago Review Press, 2007.

Vaughan, Umi, & Carlos Aldama. *Carlos Aldama's Life in Batá: Cuba, Diaspora, and the Drum*. Indiana University Press, 2012.

Vélez, María Teresa. *Drumming for the Gods: The Life and Times of Felipe García Villamil, Palero, Santero, and Abakuá*. Temple University Press, 2000.

Voeks, Robert. "African Medicine and Magic in the Americas," *Geographical Review* 83, no. 1 (1993): 66–78.